The Elizabethan Conquest of Ireland:
A Pattern Established 1565-76

The Elizabethan Conquest of Ireland:

A Pattern Established 1565–76

NICHOLAS P. CANNY

Department of History,
University College, Galway, Ireland

BOOKS
10 East 53d St. New York 10022
(a division of Harper & Row Publishers, Inc.)

BARNES & NOBLE BOOKS

First published in the USA 1976 by
HARPER & ROW PUBLISHERS, INC.
BARNES AND NOBLE IMPORT DIVISION
10 East 53rd Street, New York 10022

Barnes and Noble Books
ISBN 0-06-490954-9
Library of Congress Catalog Card No: 75-10019

Set by Input Typesetting Ltd., London
and printed in Great Britain by
Redwood Burn Limited,
Trowbridge, Wiltshire

Contents

Preface   ix
1 Irish society at the accession of Queen Elizabeth I   1
2 An unwelcome inheritance: the English presence
   in Ireland at the accession of Queen Elizabeth   29
3 The new departure: a programme for the
   conquest of Ireland   45
4 The programme in action – colonization   66
5 The programme in action – provincial presidencies   93
6 The breakdown: Elizabethan attitudes towards the Irish   117
7 The breakdown: Irish reactions to the Elizabethan conquest   137
8 Conclusion: a pattern established, 1565-76   154
   Notes   164
   Bibliography   186
   Index   199

Do mo mhuintir
agus
Do Morwena is Solenn

Preface

The Elizabethan conquest of Ireland is a subject which has been more remarked upon than studied. Most writing on the subject has been limited to a narrative of the various military engagements with little understanding of the circumstances and motives behind the conflict. The obvious exception to this generalization is Professor D. B. Quinn of Liverpool who has shown that there was both purpose and method behind the Elizabethan intervention in Ireland. Quinn, for example, was the first to suggest 1565 as a turning point in Irish history, and to this extent the book is an outgrowth of his scholarship. I am by no means certain, however, that he will concur with my findings.

When I first undertook my task I was confident that the Elizabethan conquest was of crucial importance in Irish history. As the work progressed I became convinced that it was equally important for English history, both in forming Elizabethan attitudes and in providing an outlet for younger sons. Besides this, I have pursued the trail set by D. B. Quinn in arguing that subsequent English colonization in Virginia was a logical continuation of the Elizabethan conquest of Ireland.

The book is based on an exhaustive study of all relevant sources, and I am painfully aware that my interpretation may be too personal as I strove to draw some coherence from an amorphous pile of documents. Some critics have suggested that the subsequent pattern of conquest deviated from the plan laid down in 1565, and they have pointed to Bingham's rule in Connacht and Fitzwilliam's settlement in Monaghan to support their view. It is, of course, true that one cannot construct a model of a coherent, integrated, completely consistent policy, logically pursued and valid as an explanation for every action of government. Nevertheless, I still hold that the settlement which resulted from the conquest and the methods employed in bringing it about were remarkably consonant with the programme outlined in the years 1565-76. It is my sincere hope that my interpretation of events will provoke other scholars to compel me to modify my views. In the short term I will be more than satisfied if my critics judge me to have answered Professor Sir John Neale who once challenged me 'to make sixteenth-century Ireland interesting'.

It remains for me to enumerate my debts. I am greatly indebted to the Graduate School of Arts and Sciences, and to the Department of History at the University of Pennsylvania for a four year fellowship which enabled me to work towards the Ph.D. dissertation on which this book is based. *An Bord Scoláireachtaí Cómalairte,* Dublin also lightened the financial burden with a travel grant. The editor of the *William & Mary Quarterly* kindly permitted me to include material that first appeared in article form in that journal.

The librarians and staff of the various institutions in which I worked were invariably courteous and co-operative. I would like especially to register my appreciation to the staffs of the Public Record Office, London, the British Museum, the Bodleian Library, the National Library of Ireland, the Essex County Record Office, the Library of Trinity College, Dublin, the Public Record Office, Dublin, the University of Pennsylvania Library, and the Library of University College, Galway.

Mr Brian Trainor of the Public Record Office, Belfast, was more than helpful in lending me his typescript of the 'Fitzwilliam Papers' of which he is preparing an edition for the Irish Manuscripts Commission. His was only one of the many kindnesses that convinced me of the existence of an international community of scholars, of which only a few names can be mentioned. David B. Quinn was always ready with stimulating and constructive criticism when commenting on different drafts, and Miss Katherine Simms of the Dublin Institute for Advanced Studies gave me of her time and knowledge when criticizing the first chapter. Professor Joel Hurstfield of London and those who attended his seminar at the Institute of Historical Research during the session 1969-70 were tolerant of my efforts to divert their attention to Ireland, while their intimate knowledge of the English scene shaped my understanding of the period. Fr. Brendan Bradshaw of St John's College, Cambridge was at all times encouraging, and I regret that his book on the dissolution of the Irish monastic orders appeared too late for me to derive full benefit from it. I am grateful to the staff and graduate students at Pennsylvania for sustaining an atmosphere conducive to writing and reflection, and to my colleagues and students at Galway for helpful comments, and for their forbearance while the final draft was being composed. Throughout the whole undertaking my friend and teacher Professor Richard S. Dunn of the University of Pennsylvania fortified me with his unique blend of warm encouragement and penetrating criticism. My greatest debt is registered in the dedication. I wish to thank Mrs Deana Dryden, Mrs Bernie McCarthy, and Mrs Angela McNamara who typed the manuscript at different stages of development, and Miss Philomena Byrne who devoted much time to detecting verbal infelicities.

In quotations I have adhered to the form of the source used except for the expansion of some abbreviations which might obscure the meaning, and in dating I have used the modern system throughout. The contractions used in footnotes are as recommended by Professor T. W. Moody in his *Rules for Contributors to Irish Historical Studies* (revised edition, supplement I, January 1968, to *Irish Historical Studies*).

Nicholas P. Canny

1

Irish Society at the Accession of Queen Elizabeth I

Sixteenth-century Ireland bore little resemblance, either in its social, economic or political aspects, to the country as it is today. The first striking difference was that the habitable area of the country was then much smaller, with up to half the island covered by undrained bog or scrubby forest. Communication by land was almost non-existent, and an administrator in Dublin would have much preferred to journey to London than to attempt to penetrate the extremities of Kerry. Even more formidable would have been a commission to travel to Ulster, of which province the Dublin government had little information. As late as 1609 Sir John Davies admitted that Ulster was 'heretofore as unknown to the English here as the most inland part of Virginia as yet unknown to our English colony there'.[1]

Apart altogether from the physical obstacles to travel, there was the danger of attack from some lord or chieftain. Merchants, for example, found it necessary to negotiate protections from local lords. Outlying lords seldom ventured to Dublin when summoned by the government, and one of their principal excuses was fear of passing through a neighbour's territory. The earl of Desmond, for example, when summoned to London in the 1560s chose to embark from Waterford rather than traverse the lands of his enemy, the earl of Ormond, whose territory blocked his way to Dublin. Lords considered themselves unsafe, even within their own territories, and seldom travelled abroad without a large retinue. This, in part, explains the strong opposition to the various attempts by the government to abolish private armies. The lord deputy, according to Sir Edmund Butler, would have him 'ride up and down the country like a priest', thus implying that only members of the privileged learned class, such as clergy, poets or brehons, might pass unmolested.[2] Again it was the unruly nature of the country which dictated that every chieftain who submitted to the government under the policy of surrender and regrant received a farm of land in the pale, thus enabling him to maintain his retinue while attending to official business in Dublin.

The result of this was that travel in Ireland was relatively rare. The journey that Turlough Luineach O'Neill made from Benburb to Lough Swilly, where he wanted to sample the wares of a Spanish wine merchant, was considered a formidable undertaking. Neither was anybody surprised when, suitably imbibed on his return journey, he was swept from his horse when crossing a river, thus contacting pneumonia. Calough O'Donnell was less adventurous and when summoned to Carrickfergus he chose to travel by sea in a curragh rather than risk a land journey through O'Neill territory.[3]

Not even the government officials were able to overcome the difficulties of travel in Ireland. Before 1558, few lord deputies had made extensive tours through the country, and the geography of the island remained an obstacle to the English army in Ireland throughout Queen Elizabeth's reign. The earl of Sussex, and after him Sir Henry Sidney, toured extensively through the provinces but always accompanied by troops, and even then they travelled by boat whenever suitable craft were available. Connacht was reasonably accessible to the government because, after the Leix-Offaly plantation, officials could proceed without hindrance to Athlone and were able to hire small boats to convey them across the Shannon to the plains of Connacht. In their expeditions to Munster, the two lord deputies tended to march through the earldom of Ormond to Waterford, and from there local merchants conveyed them by boat to Youghal, Cork and Kinsale. There appears to have been a passage way from Cork to Kilmallock, and from thence they proceeded through Limerick to Galway and Athenry and back to Dublin by Athlone. Ulster was the most inaccessible province since the inhabitants were hostile, there were no roads or bridges, and boats were not available for hire. No lord deputy, in the sixteenth century, visited the province without the full backing of the army, and even then they were vulnerable to cold and rain, as well as attacks from the Irish chieftains who were able to select suitable sites for ambush and then disappear into the woods and bogs.[4]

As a result of this limited travel, Ireland remained much more localized than other western-European countries. While it is true that the majority of the population everywhere remained close to their place of origin, in Ireland the same held true for the ruling element. In sixteenth-century England, for example, the gentry travelled regularly to London to attend at parliament, and many of the nobility spent most of their time at the centre of power. Again, in France and Spain the courts or educational centres served as meeting places for members of the political nation, but Ireland lacked such a focal point. The Irish house of commons was composed principally of townsmen and landowners from the Pale, while only the nobility in the Pale, the ecclesiastical lords from the eastern sees, and the earl of Ormond, could be counted on to attend either the upper house of parliament or great councils in Ireland. There was no major educational centre in Ireland and few, besides Palesmen or clients of the earl of Ormond, sought an education in England. What little education the majority of rulers acquired was at the local level, and they were trained to seek power within their lordships rather than to participate in central administration. It is evident, therefore, that Ireland was a geographic expression. Instead of a centralized state, there existed a congeries of small states, some ruled after the Gaelic manner, others under feudal control, but all jealous of their independence from a central government or superior authority.

Most of the great lords were, therefore, cut off from Dublin as a metropolis because they rarely ventured outside their areas of jurisdiction. Looked at from the other point of view, the extent of a lord's territory could be measured by the distance for which his safe-conduct was valid. If a chieftain feared a lord's vengeance sufficiently to pay him black rent and obey his proclamations then, to all intents and purposes, he was his subject. In other words every Irish overlord, whether Gaelic or Anglo-Irish, held sway over people rather than territory. We find at the mid-fifteenth century that Mac Murrough was lord of the various Gaelic septs of Leinster but was, in turn, a vassal of the White Earl of Ormond. When, later in the century, the Great Earl of Kildare came to prominence, Mac Murrough responded to the swing in power by switching his allegiance from Ormond to Kildare who was now the more powerful overlord.[5] All of this suggests that when the history of late medieval Ireland comes to be written it must be done in terms of lordships rather than of a centralized unit; a task, I understand, that Kenneth Nicholls has well under way.

No records exist to give us even an idea of the population of the country. Everything suggests that it was thinly populated, and the number of inhabitants cannot have exceeded one million.[6] Towns were mostly confined to the coast, and the only settlements considered of consequence by English observers were Waterford, Dublin, Cork, Limerick, Galway and Drogheda. There were many small towns in the Pale, and on the south coast Youghal and Kinsale were of some commercial importance. The only inland towns of significance were those, such as Kilmallock and Athenry, which served as as distribution points for their parent towns, in those instances, Limerick and Galway. Kilkenny was exceptional in that it did not depend on a single port town, and New Ross combined the advantages of the ports and the inland towns.

Again we lack figures for the population of the towns, but all contemporary descriptions suggest they were small. The various portrayals of Irish towns appearing on maps show them to have been small settlements, certainly by contemporary English standards, but verbal accounts are sometimes at variance with this evidence. Drogheda which appears small in Googe's pen-and-ink drawing was, by all accounts, a relatively large settlement by Irish standards, and Moryson described it as 'a faire and well inhabited towne'. Dublin was primarily an administrative centre and its commerce was hindered by a bad harbour.[7] The chief imports of Dublin were manufactured goods, notably cloth, luxury items for the government officials, and large quantities of coal. The principal exports from Dublin were the usual Irish produce, such as animal skins, tallow and yarn. Contemporaries considered Drogheda to be a more important trading centre than Dublin and, while this cannot be borne out by statistics, Drogheda exported large quantities of Irish raw materials in exchange for English manufactured goods, and wine from the Continent.[8] Both Drogheda and Dundalk were strategically located to serve the needs of Gaelic Ulster as well as the Pale, and the merchants sent 'their owne servants and factors called graye merchantes throughe owt all the Irishe contrees where they can procure particular ffrendshipp to bye upp theare the yrish wares, and brynge and utter theirs unto the Irishmens owne houses not sparing also ... to furnisshe them of armor, weapon and munytyon covertlye weare yt warre or peace'.[9]

This witness was obviously opposed to the activities of the grey merchants, and they were the subject of frequent legislation in the Irish parliament. Their activities were objected to because their monopoly of trade with the Irish was prejudicial to the inland towns of the Pale, such as Trim, Ardee, Navan, Athboy, Kells and Mullingar, which had once thrived on trade with Gaelic areas but which were, by the 1560s, 'sore decayed and in maner desolate'. Many Palesmen, no less than English officials, objected to these roving merchants and called for legislation declaring 'that noo merchannt, neither his servannt, shall goe out of the cittys and townes wherein they dwell to the intent to buy or sell any manner of wares; and that they which dwell in Dublin and Drogheda shall bargain wares with theme which dwell in the borrough towns in the country'. [10] Another objection was the recognition that grey merchants were part of a system of pre-emption whereby lords oppressed their own tenants. The acts of 33 Henry VIII and 11 Elizabeth dealing with grey merchants deemed them to be forestallers, and thereby associated them with the practice of fore-stalling that was mentioned repeatedly along with other methods of profiteering, such as purveyance and granting monopolies, by which Gaelic and feudal lords alike increased their revenues. Opportunities for this sort of manoeuvring were particularly rife in Ulster where merchants needed a safe-conduct from an overlord before venturing forth. Instances of safe-conducts to merchants being issued by overlords are in evidence from the mid-fifteenth century. Archbishop John Bole of Armagh, who concerned himself particularly with trade, in 1458 made O'Neill of the Fews swear to protect any merchants who might come in the archbishop's train to Armagh. O'Neill received an annual pension for his protection and similar considerations were granted to all who issued protections. [11]

It is likely that McCarthy Mór, then earl of Clancar, received payment from the English merchant, John Corbine, when in June 1568 he assured him 'that anny manne maie passe' in his name. This last example shows that English traders, no less than Palesmen, were willing to negotiate protections, and this is by no means an isolated case. John Denton, a merchant-tailor of London, asserted that when he suffered adversity in his English business he came to Ireland 'with certaine wares crediting and delivering the same to dyvers capetens'. This business was not without risk, however, and we learn that in the attack made on Athlone by the O'Moores and O'Connors in 1573 'they killed iii merchants that came from Galwaye where of two Englishmen and one Frenchman'. [12]

This evidence shows that merchants were able to traverse the boundaries of Irish lordships and thus, to an extent, break down local isolation. What has been said, however, indicates that merchants were allowed to trade in an area only when it was to the advantage of the ruling lord. Lords, both feudal and Gaelic, also exercised control over the towns in their localities, and this is one of the factors that hindered the development of commercial life in Ireland. The earls of Desmond had terrorized the coastal towns of Munster for centuries, and in the sixteenth century we know that the earl levied a tax on every cart and beast that was brought to the markets at Kilmallock and Rathkeale. [13] The earl of Ormond, in like manner, claimed praisage on the wines imported through Youghal and Kinsale, and he exercised powerful control over the small settlements at Clonmel, Cashel and Fethard. The Clanricard Burkes strove constantly to control the town of Athenry, and the earl petitioned the queen for the customs of Galway. The earl of Thomond, likewise, sought the 'custom of the havens in his territory'. [14] Not even the towns of the Pale were exempt from control by overlords. Dundalk had been liable to pay black rent to the Great O'Neill since 1430, when it was first extorted from the townsmen by Eoghan Mac Néill Oig. The merchants of Dundalk were naturally resentful of this claim, but they were compelled to pay it sporadically down to the mid-sixteenth century. Shane O'Neill, for example, knew how to force the townsmen to bend to his wishes, and they claimed they were 'almost undun' when Shane denied them 'comers with the people of his country'. It is in the light of this information that we can appreciate Shane's demand to have 'the town of Dundalk unto him as the townes of the west be to the arle of Desmond'. [15]

It would appear, therefore, that only Dublin and Waterford were free from the control of an overlord. Contemporary observers reported that Waterford was a more flourishing commercial centre than Dublin and dominated the surrounding country-side. The absence of any great landowner in its vicinity accounted for this, and the contact that Waterford maintained with English towns, notably Bristol, ensured that there was a regular infusion of English population into an area which had originally been heavily settled by the Normans. Sir Henry Sidney, in 1567, found the people there 'verie civill' and the area 'full of industrie'. Edmund Tremayne found Ireland generally short of 'artificers' except 'Waterford and the country about that be verie dilligent working of their milles'. It is obvious that he was referring to weaving in the area, but there is evidence that boat builders found ready employment there. The Waterford merchants were also shipowners and Edmund Campion found 'Waterford full of traffique with England, France and Spaine by means of their excellent good haven'. [16]

The work done by Miss Ada Longfield cites concrete evidence to support these impressionistic views. That writer noted a flourishing trade between the Munster towns and those of Wales and south-west England, with wool, hides, fur, fish and timber as the principal exports, and salt, wine and silk as the chief imports. The smaller towns of Munster, notably Cork, Youghal and Kinsale, as well as the two western ports, Galway and Limerick, also conducted trade with Spanish and French merchants, who exchanged large quantities of wine, salt and weapons for Irish raw materials.[17] All of these towns, unlike Waterford, had to come to an arrangement with the local lords to ensure their safety, and not even this guaranteed them uninterrupted trade. The Spanish fishermen who came annually to fish off the Munster coast had, by the 1560s, extended their activities to include trade. There is evidence that local landowners allowed the Spaniards to land and construct tents, when they were drying and salting their catch, in return for a certain tax, and furthermore permitted them to purchase fish from the local fishermen. English critics asserted that the Spanish intruders supplied the Munster lords with arms, and Sidney noted that the Spaniards landing at the havens were 'growen into such an acquayntannce with the people as not onelie they doe yerelie take from thence an incredible quantitie of fish . . . but also eche things ells of anny price which your countrie here breadeth as hide, tallowe, fell, wooll and flaxe, fleashe and yarne all which were wonte to be solde to the forenamed townes'. This trade was, by all accounts, considerable, and one observer claimed that two hundred sail fished in those waters and carried away '2,000 byffs and hyds and tallow'. The trade was certainly encouraged by the local lords who thus forestalled the merchants of the Munster towns, and were probably handsomely rewarded by the Spaniards.[18]

None of the Gaelic parts of the country boasted any major urban settlement, but this does not mean that there was no commercial life in Gaelic Ireland. In Ulster it appears that there were minor settlements at Carrickfergus, Ardglass, Derry, Downpatrick, Armagh, Cavan and Donegal, and in the Gaelic west both Sligo and Dingle were trading centres. Furthermore there is evidence that merchants, English as well as Continental, landed cargoes in the remote harbours of the north and west. Wine from the Continent was frequently conveyed to Dingle and Sligo, but there are references to ships unloading on Lough Swilly. It appears that merchants from Bristol ventured as far as Asseroe in O'Donnell country in 1573 and furnished the lord 'aswell with victuell as with municon'. This does not appear to have been as isolated incident, since an Englishman, John Smyth, who travelled extensively in Ulster in 1569 asserted that Dominick Chester and other merchants of Bristol 'do yearely travell thyther and haunt that waye and receave the commodytye of those partes, both in salmons and other greate commodyties as hides, yarne, tallowe, and suche other necessaryes'. It is likely that these Bristol and Westchester

merchants paid the local chieftains for protection, since Smyth saw
no source of danger to them with 'Cnockefergus and thile of man to
freend and all allonng the coaste of Ireland so that no man is to hurt
them but the Scotts onlye'. [19]

The grey merchants, as was mentioned, conducted trade
throughout the Gaelic areas, and there are also references to annual
fairs in certain locations. Cavan was traditionally one such centre 'to
the which the Irish trade from the remoter parts was wonted to come
and there to trafikke with theis porte townes'. Sir Henry Sidney
described Cavan as 'a greate towne and castell in Oreylies countrye',
but the same witness claimed that the annual fair had, by 1566, been
'longe tyme discontynued' because of unsettled conditions. The
town did, however, remain as a meeting place of the Pale with Gaelic
Ulster down to the Ulster Plantation. Sidney emphasized that Cavan
was 'distant from Kelles but 20 myles of open and playne land', thus
suggesting that there were no obstacles to contact between the two
centres. When, in 1606, Sir John Davies held an inquisition at
Cavan, he encountered there 'not only the natives of the county of
Cavan, but also inhabitants of Westmeath and other parts of the
Pale bordering upon this country whereof some pretended title to
land'. Davies upheld their claim and included on the jury some who
'were foreign inhabitants of the Pale, and yet freeholders of this
county'. [20]

Everything suggests that the O'Reilly lordship of Cavan was a
relatively peaceful region, and the fair was in all probability held
under the aegis of the ruling chieftain. It is likely that the O'Neills of
Ulster preferred to grant franchises to roving merchants rather than
to sponsor fairs such as that held at Cavan, but it is probable that
small fairs and markets were held periodically throughout the
province. Thus the great number of licences to hold fairs and
markets granted by the Dublin government at the beginning of the
seventeenth century was probably an attempt to formalize the
existing situation. The English governors at Carrickfergus attracted
trade to their outpost, 'where not onely all kyndes of things of that
country breede was to be sould, but out of the English Pale, the Ile of
Man, and Scotland, came moch merchandize, victualls, and other
comodities, and out of France in one sommer three barkes of fourtie
tonnes apiece discharged their loading of excellent Gascoigne wyne,
the which they sould for nineteen cowe skynnes the hoggeshed'. [21]
There was a quickening interest in the trading possibilities of Ulster
from the middle of the fifteenth century onwards, if we are to judge
from the competing claims of James Dokray, mayor of Drogheda,
and Richard Heron, merchant of the staple of Calais, to be constable

of the castle of Carrickfergus, not in itself a paying proposition.[22] The merchants of Bristol and Chester maintained an interest in the region, and there was also the trade conducted by the Gaelic Irish themselves. There is evidence that a trade in timber between the Irish and the Scots was particularly active in the sixteenth century, and there were complaints that the Scots invaders of Ulster were provided with boards for the making of their galleys from the woods of Ulster. Any such felling and processing of timber could have been accomplished only with the sanction of a ruling chieftain.[23]

Fairs and markets, such as those at Cavan and Carrickfergus, were not confined to Ulster. It appears that a fair was held at Tralee whenever the earl of Desmond went there to collect his rents, and the duties paid by visiting merchants were another source of income to the earl. Enniscorthy was a trading centre for the Gaelic areas of Leinster, where a fair by 'farre the greatest of any in Ireland', was 'held yearely, and usually at a day certayne'. There came to this fair, 'besides a multitude of country people, the most of the merchannts of the good town of Washford [Wexford], either in their owne persons, their wiefs, or their servants . . . whither . . . they came by water'.[24] A trade in timber between the Wicklow men and Dubliners was already established in the fourteenth century and continued into the sixteenth. This trade was also in a sense connected with the problem of safe-conducts, since the woods were the preserve of the Gaelic Irish, and it was neither easy nor safe for the Palesmen to go out and help themselves. In 1303-5 it was necessary to take a hostage from Gilpatrick Mac Mahon, lord of Farney, to ensure 'that the Kings men of Adtherde [Ardee, Co. Louth] may henceforth go securely to the woods in those parts and cut timber and other necessaries in the woods and carry them away, without impediment of Gilpatrick on his men'.[25] The Gaelic Irish did not leave all the trade to the Palesmen, and there is evidence that the Wicklow Irish were particularly enterprising. In 1471 there were attempts to curb the trade in corn between Dublin and Wicklow, but seemingly to little avail since Sidney reported that the Wicklow Irish 'were wont to buy their bread in Dublin, or barter for the same by giving fire-wood, they were then able to sell corn not only in Dublin, but by boats to send it to Carrickfergus, and other parts of the north of Ireland where corn was deer'. There was also a coastal trade in 'great wood or boords' which were in much demand because of 'thearle of Argyles diligence in making of galleys'. There are references also to the lords of west Connacht supplying Galway with firewood, and Limerick appears to have been considerably dependant on the Gaelic Irish of Thomond to supply them with corn. Thus it appears that there was commercial activity throughout the entire country, and the fact that limited amounts of English money and some Spanish coin were in circulation in the remote areas bears further testimony to this.[26] It has been noted throughout, however, that trade was almost everywhere under the control of the local lord who benefited greatly from the collection of duties and the granting of monopolies and safe-conducts.

The merchants, while they were the only ones who had consistent contact with foreigners and who circulated with relative ease through the country, were nevertheless a small element of the population. The vast majority of the people were peasants who tilled the soil and tended cattle for the landowners. All descriptions that are available agree that the lot of the Irish peasant was extremely hard by contemporary European standards. It appears that they dwelt in small huts or cabins constructed of either wattles or mud and covered with thatch. Most of these appear to have been one-roomed structures without any chimney or window and each, presumably, housed a family. These were generally clustered together in hamlets and, in the Anglo-Irish areas, even villages. There seems to be nothing to support the general belief that the peasants in the more Anglicized areas were treated more favourably than their counterparts under Gaelic control. Housing conditions seem to have been quite similar. Luke Gernon described the cottages in County Limerick as 'built of underwood, called wattle, and covered some with thatch and some with green sedge, of a round forme and without chimneys, and to my imaginacon resemble so many hives of bees'. This description would certainly fit the representations of Ulster houses that appear on maps of the late sixteenth century. Fynes Moryson looked with disdain on the dwelling of the Ulster peasant, which he described as 'a cabin made of boughes of trees, and covered with turffe', but this could have been little worse than the habitat of the peasant in the Pale of which we have no clear evidence.[27]

It appears also that the degree of exploitation of the peasant by his lord was no less severe in the Anglo-Irish areas than under Gaelic rule. One observer claimed that the peasants were everywhere tenants at will, 'and as thei be this badlie used in dedes, so do thei not terme them by any other name then chorles, being by this order . . . a moste miserable kind of people as is to be found in any place, and this is no better in thenglish Pale than in other partes of the realme, saving that by thassistance of the armie thei mai tille theire grownd more safelie, and are not so often destroyed nor burned'. The lords were held totally responsible for this condition, because 'every superior ruleth over such as be undre hym at his wil and pleasure . . . suffering no tenant to have assurance underneth hym but until another wil give hym more'. Many of the original inhabitants of English descent were squeezed out by such unfavourable treatment, and some did 'slippe away into England and els where' and were replaced by native Irish who proved themselves more amenable tenants.[28] When we take this into consideration we can see that it would be ridiculous to suppose that the life style of tenants in the Pale was essentially different from elsewhere in the country.

Since this is an aspect of sixteenth-century Irish life that has, hitherto, escaped the notice of historians it will bear with some substantiation. Lord-Lieutenant Sussex stated categorically that 'many people within the English Pale set their lands to tenants of Irish birth and blood to enhance their rents, whereby the English people decay and the Irish increase'. The landowners of the Pale, according to Sir Henry Sidney, 'take so mutch of the tennant as they have in effect worn out all the Inglyshry and placed Irish churles', a fact that is borne out by Lord Chancellor Gerrard who noted 'a generall increase of people in the Pale of Yrish in birthe who laboure the soyle termed cottyers of noe habilyte in substance'. Another observer went further and stated categorically that 'the most part of the undertenants' were 'not of the birthe of the Inglish Pale but such of the Irishe as will yeild more service and rent'.[29]

The major changeover from tenants of English descent to Irish betaghs[30] seems to have been particularly noticeable in the inland parts of the Pale, more especially in Counties Kildare and Westmeath, on the lands owned by the earl of Kildare, Viscount Baltinglass and Baron Delvin. Those English who criticized the Gaelicization of the Pale alleged that the traditional occupants had fled rather than endure the high exactions demanded of them by their overlords, while the landed proprietors attributed the social disruption to the fact that their tenants were compelled to contribute to the support of the standing army. On balance, it appears that the combination of exactions, added to their rents, proved too much for the traditional tenants, and the lords, who refused to abandon their private armies, welcomed peasants from the surrounding Gaelic areas to come and settle on their lands thus ensuring that their economic position would not be undermined for lack of tenants. The cultivators in Counties Dublin and Meath do not seem to have suffered quite so much from extortion, since the lords there did not maintain private armies on a regular basis, and the peasants there may have even enjoyed an agricultural surplus in years of good harvest. It appears, nevertheless, that they too lived in a more depressed condition than did their English counterparts, because in addition to paying rent to their lords they had, simultaneously, to provide for the government's army either in the form of purveyance or direct billeting and had to bear the brunt of the 'rising out' when their lords were called upon to supplement the military resources of the governor.[31]

The principal concern of sixteenth-century landowners seems to have been to extract the maximum rent from their tenants. We know little of the conditions of lease, but it does seem that the peasants had extremely limited rights and could be summarily dismissed from the lands they cultivated. It is evident, from what has been said, that landlords in the inner Pale saw nothing wrong with displacing tenants of English origin to make room for Irish betaghs. There were also several instances where 'the land lords suffer the tenements to decaie of purpose leaving the land which was tilled to pasture', thus escaping the tax that was imposed on tilled land in the Pale for the maintenance of government troops.[32] The power of the landlord in the Pale was thus much greater than that enjoyed by his English counterpart although probably not as excessive as that wielded by the lords in the feudal and Gaelic parts of the country. This explains why the attention of the English administrators was drawn to the power of the lords which they regarded as tyrannical, barbarous and typically Irish.

Despite such strictures, it seems to be possible to overestimate the misery of the Irish tenant. If those in the Gaelic areas lived in cabins made of boughs of trees and covered with turf 'such', according to Fynes Moryson, 'are the dwellings of the very lords among them'. If they were tallaged at will by their overlord so were the upper classes in time of war, and cuddy [*cuid oiche*] and choshery [*coisir*] were primarily exactions from substantial landowners, though their effects were no doubt eventually passed down to the cultivators. The position of the peasants was undoubtedly strengthened by the fact that a scarcity of tenants prevailed throughout the country. This left the tenant with the option of transferring from one landlord to another, and there are frequent references to tenants driving herds from the lands of one lord to another to evade justice. We learn in the sixteenth century of lands within the Pale being 'barelie furnished of tennants', and cottiers were able to flee from an excessively avaricious lord. It was a cause of great concern when, in the early 1560s, many husbandmen 'went owt of thenglisshe Pale to dwell and manure' in Shane O'Neill's country. Tenants throughout the country seem to have similarly asserted this economic power, and lords were particularly concerned to prohibit their departure. In the sixteenth century Shane O'Neill forbade 'that enie in his cuntree shall come into the Englishe Pale upon paine of deth' and Hugh O'Neill sought to have 'his native followers' restored to him 'without the which he shall be long unable to plant and reinhabit his country'.[33] Both references suggest that the lords in question had suffered deprivation of tenants, and some lords had to resort to kidnapping their former husbandmen from neighbouring chieftains. An early example of kidnapping tenants comes in the register of Archbishop John Prene, 1458, when Toirdelbach Ruadh, a rowdy younger son of Henry Mac Eoghain O'Neill, with an accomplice kidnapped Angelicus and his sons, tenants of the Erenagh of Errigalkeerogue, and detained them 'cum eis in rure'. Forceful tactics continued down to the end of the Gaelic world, when we find Rory O'Donnell compelled to dwell in the Pale because Niall Garbh O'Donnell had deprived him of his tenants and herds of cattle.[34]

What has been said suggests that the only restraint on the lords' power was that tenants everywhere were in short supply, and landowners jealously guarded their control over them. It seems that the majority of peasants were employed in cultivating corn, mostly oats, and, where geography dictated, in the tending of flocks. Much of the land within the Pale was suited to tillage, and wheat was the principal crop. Most of this wheat went to feeding the population of the Pale itself and to the provisioning of the standing army. In times of prosperity there was a surplus available for export, and wheat was frequently sold to the inhabitants of the surrounding Gaelic areas including Ulster, a practice that was outlawed by the government. Tillage appears to have been practised widely throughout the feudal lordships even in the western parts of the earldom of Desmond. When McCarthy Mór invaded the territory of Lord Roche in 1568 he stole 'xv hundreth Kyne, a hundreth capels [horses] and burned vii thowssand shepe and swyne with all the corne of the countrey which was gathered in churche yeards and upon the fields'.[35]

It is commonly held that little tillage was pursued in the Gaelic areas of the country. This belief is based on the frequent assertions of writers from the Pale who, in their efforts to ingratiate themselves with the English government, fostered the notion that the native Irish were a semi-nomadic people opposed to all civility. Their allegations, however, are refuted by the casual observations of the Englishmen who penetrated the Gaelic areas during the military campaigns of the sixteenth century. Sidney discovered corn in the vicinity of Clogher, 'above 24 myles in compas' and the area 'so well inhabited as wee thinck no Irish countrie in this realm like it'. Lord

Deputy Burgh, in 1597, found on the lands of the earl of Tyrone an 'increase of corn and cattle as plentifully as in any part of England'. Walter, earl of Essex, destroyed corn in Tyrone 'not less by estimacon then to the value of £5,000', which he found 'in great plenty and in great reekes'. Essex was well aware that he was systematically wrecking a settled economy with the result that 'the people of Tyrone are dryven into great extremytie. For their corne beinge dystroyed . . . they have in effect byn utterly without bred or horsemeat so as they have lyved and doe lyve alltogether upon fleshe'.[36]

The northern extreme of Ulster was equally prosperous, and when Sir Henry Docwra raided O'Cahan's country in 1601 he spoiled and burned 'such a quantity of corne and number of houses as I should hardly have believed so small a circuit of ground could have afforded if I had not seene it'. There are also frequent references to intensive cultivation in Connacht, particularly in the more fertile southern part. Sidney described the lands of Sir Roger O'Shaughnessy as 'riche, plentifull and well ordered', and we learn from another source that O'Shaughnessy employed 'at one time, fourteen score of reapers in harvest cutting'. The Gaelic areas of Leinster, were able to produce much corn, and Lord Chancellor Gerrard in his journey through Leinster, 1577, found in Byrne's country 'the best platt of tilled grounde for so muche togeather, the best stored of cattell where pasture was of any parte I traveled in all the journey'. It was Sidney who reported on the Wicklowmen exporting corn to other areas, and he was of the opinion that 'all these Irish people . . . were ritch, and everything plentiful in their country no waste land but . . . it bare corne or horn'.[37]

All of this suggests that every piece of land that was suitable for tillage was, in fact, under cultivation in Gaelic Ireland, unless the area was particularly open to attack from a neighbouring lord. It is true, however, that, of the land under Gaelic control in the sixteenth century much was mountainous and boggy and useful only for grazing cattle and sheep. It is this factor of geography, rather than any native characteristic, which explains the extent of pastoral farming in Gaelic Ireland. Even in those areas where it predominated the people lived in settled communities. These would have been smaller than the settlements on the plains, and some may have lived in isolated homesteads, but the same held true of the upland regions in the north of England and throughout Continental Europe. During the summer months many of these peasants abandoned their homesteads and lived in temporary huts while following their herds to the rough summer pastures in the woods and mountains. Many English observers took this practice of transhumance as evidence that the Irish were nomads, but we know that they were mistaken since there is evidence that the movement was regular and controlled. The settled communities remained the centre of the social system, and even in the mountainous regions where the plough could not be used oats was sown with the spade in ridges.[38]

Little information on life in the peasant communities has come down to us. Considerable domestic industry must have been carried on, and it is not unlikely that some craftsmen, such as those who made the large galleys used by the O'Malleys in Connacht, were employed full time at their trades. It is likely that tradesmen flourished in the more sheltered and peaceful areas of the country and hired themselves out when called upon by nearby lords. Fermanagh was certainly a relatively prosperous and cultured area in the north and apparently produced the best craftsmen, for it was carpenters brought from there who constructed crossbows for the siege of Mac Dermot's Rock in 1478.[39] The Gaelic Irish were adept at working with timber as can be seen from the trade with the Scots already alluded to. Even the officials in the Dublin government acknowledged their proficiency when they purchased boards for the making of Athlone Bridge from 'certaine Irishe men'. The English were also ready to employ Irishmen as boat builders, and Dominick Lynch, a Galway merchant, was paid, in 1570, £257 11s 'for newe making and buildinge a lardge pynance of the moulde of an olde shippe and furnishinge of the same with mastes, ankers, cabulles, tacklinge and all other neccies for the expellinge of the pyrotts of that coaste'.

This establishes the fact that there were tradesmen in Galway capable of constructing a large craft, and it appears that the Irish towns were generally a haven for tradesmen who were willing to work in the surrounding region. In 1569 the government made payment of £7 9s 4d to Richard and William Rany, masons, 'for their paines beinge taken oute of Galway for the overthrowinge of diverse castelles in Connaghte'. Again when the government wished to reconstruct the town of Athenry, which had been destroyed by the sons of the earl of Clanricard, they were compelled to hire town masons, among them one Gregory Bodkin who was paid £20 for his work. It appears that masons were generally in short supply throughout the country, and the lords of Ulster were forced to employ Scotsmen to aid them in building their castles, as is suggested by the Scottish features on many of the castles of Gaelic Ulster.[40]

It is probable that women were employed in domestic industries, such as butter making, spinning, and weaving. There is plentiful evidence that linen and woollen goods were manufactured throughout the country. Fynes Moryson stated that the Irish 'abounde in flocks of sheepe, which they sheare twise in the yeere'; which suggests that sheep were reared for wool rather than meat. The wool, according to Moryson, was coarse and useful for 'working it into cloth, namely rugs (whereof the best are made at Waterford) and mantles generally worne by men and women and exported in great quantity'. Rowland White provides further confirmation that the making of freize was a major source of employment in many places in as much as 'it is one of the chefest occupacions of the lande both for outward traffique and inward nede'. The same writer complained that linen weaving was in a weak position because of the annual export of '200 thousand weights' of yarn. This testifies to the prevalence of linen spinning, and linen weaving for domestic consumptions was certainly widespread. Linen shirts made of 'xv or xvi yardes a pece' were commonly worn by men, and women wore 'kercheives of 30 yardes longe, safron smocke and mantles accordinglye superfluous'. The figures may be exaggerated, but it appears that linen weaving was still widespread, and English observers considered it to have great potential. This explains the legislation, enacted in the 1569-71 parliament, to prohibit the export of linen yarn from Ireland, which according to one enthusiastic observer provided such a boost to the weaving industry that 'both in the yrish Pale and chiefly in thenglish Pale nombers have been set on wourk and grete plenty of lardge bredthes and sondry makings were made and devyses never afore in use in this realme both of playne and striped canvas.'[41]

Fishing must also have been widespread and, as was noted, it was organized on a commercial basis in Munster. Days of fast and abstinence were probably observed, and eating meat would have been prohibited by the Church throughout Lent. There must, therefore, have been a considerable demand for fresh or dried fish, particularly during Lent. The salmon and the brown trout were esteemed as a delicacy, and netting of salmon was widespread throughout the country, while the richer salmon rivers, such as the Bann, attracted fishermen from abroad. All other fish would have been eaten for penance, but there exists an ode to a herring, probably not earlier than the seventeenth century, in which the 'honest pure bodied gentleman' is hailed as a friend of the clergy and a wholesome penance during the Lenten season – more noble, if only the lords of Ireland would appreciate it, than either the salmon or the pike.

Dá bhféachdois uaisle Banbha
Cia is mó tarbha don triur-sa
Iasg is uaisle ná an sgadán
Idir bradán is liúsa.[42]

What has been said above shows that, at the lower level at least, there was a well-organized society and economy in Ireland. It is obvious also that there was little difference between the lot of the peasants in the Anglo-Irish and Gaelic parts of the country. The little we know of the Pale suggests that a considerable number of the peasants were of native Irish origin, and, as was noted, there is evidence of some migration of peasants between the Pale and Gaelic Ulster. One early sixteenth-century commentator stated categorically that 'all the common folks' in the Pale 'for the more part are of Irish birth, of Irish habit, and of Irish language'. Contemporaries were also in agreement that peasants everywhere were exploited by their lords, and 'in the very Englishe Pale shall you not finde any other lawe betwixt lord and tennte but the verie will and pleasure of the lord'.[43] English observers commented on the almost absolute authority of the lords, thus indicating that in Ireland there was a rigid division between the cultivators and the owners of the soil. Even the Pale lacked a yeoman element, such as existed in England, and the feudal lordships did not have a vigorous gentry who might act as a counter-weight to the great lords. Outside of the Pale, every lord maintained a private army which was billeted on the husbandmen, and these soldiers, according to one observer, were 'in maner the whole substance of every contrey saving such as travell [travail] and toyle for them'.[44] There is evidence that private troops were maintained by some of the outlying lords of the Pale, and the government forces were generally billeted on the husbandmen of the Pale, thus causing great hardship there.

The peasants were forced to accept their situation because they had no recourse to higher authority. The law courts in Dublin excercised only very limited jurisdiction outside the Pale, and within the Pale their civil function seems to have been confined to disputes between landowners, rather than between lord and tenant. The Dublin administration hardly touched the provinces, as is borne out by their failure to appoint sheriffs with any regularity in counties other than those of the Pale and Counties Kilkenny, Wexford and Waterford. Even where sheriffs were appointed their function seems to have been to uphold the position of the landowners rather than right the wrongs of the husbandmen. A sheriff would always have been a landowner himself, and his principal duties were, to keep the peace in his shire (to which end he had power of martial law), to collect revenue for the Exchequer, and to organize purveyance for the troops.[45]

The sheriff was certainly the most active agent of the government in the counties of the Pale. Justices of the peace were unknown outside the Pale, and, by the mid-sixteenth century, the office seems to have become defunct even within the Pale. The more prominent landholders of the Pale were appointed commissioners of the peace for both the years 1562 and 1563 with power of martial law, but the terms of appointment made no reference to conducting quarter sessions after the English model. Their function appears to have been that of preserving the Pale from raids by the neighbouring Irish while the lord-lieutenant was absent with the army in Ulster. There is plentiful evidence that sheriffs' courts and quarter sessions, sessions of assize and, in fact, the whole structure of English local government had fallen into abeyance within the Pale. There was, according to Edmund Tremayne, 'smal use of thoffice of justice of peax in the most civile partes, no quarter sessions, few or no court barones, no lites, no inquyrie of means faultes by verdict of xii men onles it be at Dublyn or other speciall sessions when the deputie must eveyn dryve them for they wil never desire it themselves'. The landowners of the Pale seem, therefore, to have allowed the local courts, where the husbandmen might have voiced their grievances, to lapse. For disputes among themselves they found it more convenient to resort instead to the central courts in Dublin, 'for matters some times not of the value of x^s'. It is only when we recognize this that we can understand criticism such as that made by Tremayne, that within the Pale 'every superior ruleth over such as be undre hym at his wil and pleasure, though not by his caprice with quonie [coyne] and livery as it is among the mere Irish, yet as neare as he can do it, suffering no tenant to have assurance underneth hym but until another wil give hym more'.[46]

It is evident from what has been said that the condition of the peasantry in the Pale was miserable, and at that probably better than elsewhere in the country. The almost total lack of any rights rendered the Irish peasant more vulnerable than his English and western-European counterpart. In its more superficial aspects, however, society in the Pale resembled that in an English shire, with the land owned by a nobility and gentry and cultivated by a peasantry who rendered rents and services. The greatest landholder and the most influential person within the Pale was the earl of Kildare, and next in prominence were the lesser nobility, Viscounts Gormanston and Trimleston and Barons Louth, Howth, Delvin,

Slane and Baltinglass. Next in importance among the landowners were the proud gentry families, some of them representing cadet branches of the nobility, while others were Dublin merchants who had invested their profits in land. The most prominent, if not the most numerous, element among the gentry, was office holders, or their descendants, who had been rewarded with land for their services in the Dublin administration. We find here a confident, well-educated and sophisticated element of society, knowledgeable in the ways of self-preservation and grasping at every opportunity for social mobility. Many of the sons of these families attended at the Inns of Court in London, thus maintaining a life line with their cultural home, England, and at the same time equipping themselves to administer their lands and fill vacancies as they occurred in the Dublin administration. There were, in 1558, thirty-eight officers employed in the central courts and it appears that many of these, even judges of the court of Kings Bench, aspired to have their relatives succeed them in office. Some families, such as the Cusacks, Dillons and Plunketts, maintained prominent posts over several generations; this despite the fact that few of them had ever become barristers. Tremayne complained that nobody of Irish birth could have 'the ground of learning as is requisite for a judge. For thei cotnew studdie no time, thei come home pleaders that were never utter baristeres' and acquired offices 'as the country giveth and not as the place requireth'.[47]

Another behavioural pattern in which these gentry families equalled, and even surpassed, their English counterparts was a high degree of intermarriage. The outcome of this was that most members of the Dublin administration were related not only to each other but to the majority of prominent landowners within the Pale. This latter was, understandably, a feature of life that did not escape the criticisms of English commentators:

> their parcialitie must nedes be great [said Tremayne] where judges and jorors be not only of one shire in effect (for al thenglish Pale excedeth not the bignes of some two shieres in England) but also very straitly joyned to gether by parentaig and alyannce, so as if it be good law in England that none be justaces of assize in his contry it is there more dangerous that they should trye the causes of the whole realme.[48]

What has been said suggests that in terms of social organization the Pale bore a close resemblance to an English shire. The main differences were that a yeoman element appears to have been generally absent and that the landowners had unrestricted control over their tenants. The landowners of the Pale would also have differed from their English counterparts in being bilingual, and there is evidence that Irish was spoken even in Dublin. This knowledge was necessary for dealing with their tenants and retainers, and it was also of benefit to administrators, such as Lord Chancellor Thomas Cusack, who were able to deal directly with Gaelic chieftains without the use of an interpreter. This was for convenience rather than from inclination, and everything suggests that the landowners of the Pale were proud of their English origins, dressed after the English fashion, built houses modelled on those of the gentry in England, and succeeded to property under the laws of primogeniture. The inhabitants of the Pale were also reasonably under the control of London, through the administration in Dublin, and they ultimately depended upon London for protection from the Gaelic Irish of Wicklow, Ulster and the midlands.

A considerable part of Leinster, outside the Pale, most of the province of Munster, and Counties Clare and Galway were the territories ruled by the great feudal lords. These, with the exception of the earl of Thomond, were the descendants of the original Norman conquerors who had succeeded in preserving their positions against the Irish enemy by establishing power bases, thus placing themselves largely beyond the control of the government. The rulers of this extensive area all bore English titles and held their lands by feudal tenure, but they also held jurisdiction over pockets of Gaelic septs in the boggy and mountainous areas and were, therefore, both feudal lords and Gaelic captains of English lineage. Within these enclaves Gaelic customs and law flourished, and the inhabitants were not disturbed by their feudal overlord so long as they gave him 'good assurance' to pay rent, and 'did not fortify upon the same otherwyse' than their overlord should 'appoint'.[49]

The principal landholders of the rich lowlands were frequently cadet branches of the ruling family and generally of English origin. While there is evidence that provision was sometimes made for younger sons, succession to property was usually by the system of primogeniture. The majority of tenants throughout feudal Ireland were, like many of their counterparts in the Pale, Gaelic Irish and would have dressed after the Irish manner. Again like the Pale, there would have been a real difference between areas heavily settled after the Norman invasion and still speaking a kind of English in the sixteenth century (e.g., the neighbourhood of Waterford and Kilkenny) and the rest of the country-side. Even in those areas the population would have been bilingual, and the city of Waterford, in

1492, was forced to deny its inhabitants the right to plead their cases through Irish.[50]

At the accession of Queen Elizabeth all the Irish feudal lords professed loyalty to the crown, and even the outlying earl of Desmond was, on occasion, willing to support the government militarily. Each feudal lord maintained a host of armed retainers, as their English counterparts had done in the fifteenth century, and maintained in addition a force of *galloglaigh,* the descendants of thirteenth-century Scots mercenary soldiers who had obtained land in Ireland and had become a permanent feature of Irish warfare. The original purpose of these armies had been to preserve the lords against attack from the Gaelic Irish, but, by the sixteenth century, the maintenance of troops was largely a matter of prestige, and lords used them to pursue feuds against their neighbours.

The lot of the husbandmen in the feudal areas appears to have been more miserable than that of their counterparts in the Pale, and one writer has asserted categorically that in the 'Anglo-Norman areas . . . the lords' powers seem to have been much greater than in the Gaelic'.[51] This last impression may arise because Irish sources usually list rights due to the chief while Anglo-Irish sources are often complaints of abuses presented by local juries. In the absence of statistical data it would be impossible to uphold such a strong statement, but everything suggests that there were few curbs on the power of the feudal lords. The inquisitions taken prior to the Munster Plantation show that the earl of Desmond collected exorbitantly high rents, both in money and produce, from his tenants. Added to this was the cost of maintaining his army which he billeted on the householders, according to the much maligned practice of coyne and livery. Another exaction was that known as cuddy [*cuid oidche*], which provided for the entertainment of the earl and his entourage on his frequent excursions through his territory. As a result of these various exactions the husbandmen appear never to have been able to improve themselves beyond bare subsistence. Again because of incessant warfare and turmoil many areas, such as those bordering the earldoms of Ormond and Desmond, were completely desolate. Only a few of the exactions have been mentioned, but all contemporaries were agreed that the most burdensome was that of coyne and livery. Edmund Tremayne referred to the Irish kern as 'those idle loyterors that are the catterpillars of the comon welth', and Sir John Davies protested that coyne and livery 'made the lord an absolute tyrant and the tenant a very slave and villain, and in one respect more miserable than bond-slaves. For commonly the bond-salve is fed by his lord, but here the lord was fed by his bond-slave'.[52]

The feudal lords could exercise such unrestricted control because there was virtually no government interference in their localities. Both the earls of Ormond and Desmond enjoyed palatinate jurisdiction over their territories, and it is likely that the system of law – mostly Gaelic in nature – maintained in Thomond and Clanricard was under the control of the ruling families. Private franchises had originally been granted to feudal lords in the hope that common law practice would thus be maintained in the areas beyond the reach of the central government. Some of the forms of common law had certainly been preserved in the palatinates of Kerry and Tipperary, but elements of Gaelic law and custom were also in evidence. Furthermore, the earls had the right of appointing officers to their courts thus ensuring that it was they rather than the king who were the ultimate arbiters.

Thus the exploited tenants and merchants had no recourse other than to submit to the will of the lord. This ensured that social divisions were more rigid in feudal Ireland than within the Pale, where the gentry at least were able to preserve their positions. The lords for the most part concentrated their energies on maintaining themselves within their lordships and extending their power outwards. The earls of Desmond had since 1468, when the then earl was executed by the lord deputy at Drogheda, only sporadic contact with Dublin and ruled as almost independent princes over Counties Kerry, Limerick, Waterford and north Cork. Much of the Desmonian power had been lost by the mid-sixteenth century, but Earl Gerald still held courts at Tralee and Any, had almost absolute control of north Kerry and Limerick, and, as late as 1568, denied the queen's sheriff the right to arrest any member of the Fitzgerald family since 'he taketh that he ought to be ther judg'.[53]

The earl of Desmond represented the independence of the feudal lords in its most aggressive form, but others were striving for a similar position. Ormond clung tenaciously to his palatinate court of Tipperary and lost no opportunity of extending power over neigh-bouring Irish lords. He enjoyed 'bonought[*buannacht*] and such Irish tributes of dyverse of the west contrie, as certeyne of the Burgs, McBryen Arrye and Odwyre', and he wished to extend his power likewise over the Irish of Wicklow when he sought from the government to be appointed 'captain of Leynster, that is to say of the Kavanaghes, Twoles, and Brynnes, for the most part rebelles and disobedient'. The earl of Ormond also claimed title to land in Connacht which was more extravagant than Desmond's aspiration to rule over Waterford.[54]

The two earls west of the Shannon, Thomond and Clanricard, were new creations and did not have jurisdictions as extensive as Desmond and Ormond, but they were, nevertheless, ambitious. Clanricard sought 'the captainship and leading of all Connaght', while Thomond, pointing to the palatinates of Kerry and Tipperary 'lookith for like libertyes in Toomond'. It is interesting to note also that Ormond sought to build up an alliance with the two western earls in his effort to outbalance the two Fitzgerald earls, Desmond and Kildare. The earl of Kildare was no longer a power to be reckoned with, since the palatinate of County Kildare and Fitzgerald control of the Gaelic midlands had been swept away in 1536 and had not been returned when Queen Mary restored Gerald, the eleventh earl, to his ancestral lands. Kildare, however, was well connected in the Pale, and he never lost hope of regaining his ancestors' greatness. Furthermore, he was bitterly opposed to the Butlers of Ormond whom he considered responsible for the Fitzgerald rebellion in 1534 that had resulted in the downfall of his house.[55]

What has been said shows that the feudal lords ruled as little kings and brooked no interference from outside. They owed theoretical allegiance to the crown in England, but they considered themselves to be the real representatives of the English interest in Ireland and rendered military assistance to the government in Dublin merely when it suited their purpose. Within their lordships they were extremely powerful, and they exploited their tenants and subordinates for the sake of military power and prestige. The towns retained some semblance of autonomy, but in reality they could thrive only as long as their business contributed to the enrichment of the lords.

The remainder of the country – almost all of Ulster and north Connacht, south-west Munster, and the wooded region of Wicklow and north Wexford – was under Gaelic control. The rulers of these areas did not recognize the authority of the crown, had a legal system of their own which was frequently at variance with common law, and preferred partible inheritance over primogeniture. On the superficial level, therefore, Gaelic society was totally different from its English counterpart. The fundamental difference between them was that land in Gaelic Ireland was owned by the sept, while under the feudal system ownership of the soil was theoretically in the hands of the lord, who distributed it among his followers in return for rents and services.

Gaelic society was therefore, in the words of Kenneth Nicholls, one of clans or lineages – known to contemporary English observers and recent historians as septs.[56] Each of these corporate units occupied a particular territory but was sometimes subject to the chieftain of a more powerful sept. Most of the lands of present day Counties Armagh and Tyrone were, for example, owned by a multitude of septs – Quinns, Hagans, Mellans, Donnellys, Devlins, Conroys, Clanemulkrevies, Clanegis, McCanns, Clanbrassells, O'Gormleys, McGilcohans, MacDonnells, to mention the more important – but each of these septs was subject to the ruling sept of O'Neill.[57] The O'Neills themselves owned some land within this large area, but their power stemmed from the fact that they could claim rents and services from such a large number of septs. Underneath these septs was the vast majority of the population who tilled the soil and tended the cattle of their superiors. It is likely that the lot of the husbandmen was extremely harsh since the only buffer between themselves and the superior lord were the lesser septs. These septs persisted as a recognizable stratum until the final overthrow of Gaelic society at the beginning of the seventeenth century, but there is plentiful evidence that powerful chieftains attempted to squeeze them out in favour of their own families.

The position of these septs was somehow preserved from the incursions of superior chieftains by the moral authority of the Gaelic lawyers who were upholders of the *status quo*. Another factor in their favour was that it was these septs who elected an overlord from among the eligible members of the ruling sept, and it was they too who were the horse-soldiers or 'rising-out' in the army of the ruling chieftain. If the lord overstepped his authority they could switch their allegiance to another member of the ruling sept, thus emasculating the elected lord. When, in the sixteenth century, Turlough Luineach O'Neill imported a large number of Scots mercenaries and billeted them on the subservient septs the latter retaliated in the only way open to them: they withdrew their support from Turlough and offered their support instead to Hugh O'Neill who eventually supplanted Turlough as captain of Tyrone. Their action, however, won them only temporary relief, since Hugh proved to be as hard a master as Turlough had been. The fact of the matter was that the free septs prospered in those areas which were less militarized, but in time of war there were few restrictions on the power of the overlord. Davies speaking of Maguire's traditional rights probably came close to the truth when he stated that 'in right he had no more and in time of peace he did exact no more; marry in time of war he made himself owner of all, cutting what he listed, and imposing as many bonaughts or hired soldiers upon them as he had occasion to use'. When we consider that Fermanagh was a relatively peaceful area in Ulster, we can gather from this statement what conditions must have been like in the O'Neill lordship which was on a war footing throughout the second half of the sixteenth century. Those who surveyed the lands of Tyrone in 1609 were hardly able to establish who had held title to land there under the Gaelic system, 'because the names and quantities of divers "balliboes" or town lands had been altered by the late earl, and so made uncertain'. [58]

Since Gaelic Ireland was on a war footing throughout most of the later sixteenth century, it is true to say that a Gaelic chieftain was no less powerful than a feudal lord. At all times the prominent Gaelic rulers were striving to extend their overlordship after the manner of the pre-invasion kings of Ireland by claiming tribute from his neighbouring lords. The O'Neills of Ulster had produced a long succession of ambitious rulers, and this explains the wide jurisdiction they held in the sixteenth century. The ruling O'Neill was not only lord of all the septs within Tyrone but claimed authority over several *ur-righthe* [sub-Kings] who were overlords in their own right – O'Cahan, McGuire, McMahon and O'Reilly. Shane O'Neill, who was the pre-eminent figure in Ulster at the accession of Queen Elizabeth, was even more ambitious than his predecessors. He sought to force O'Donnell to become subservient to him by claiming rent from the septs living under O'Donnell's jurisdiction in *Tír-Conaill,* and Shane invaded Connacht 'to requyre the trybute du in ould tyme to them that were Kings in this realm, and would have had the same yerly payde to hym self'. The impression that one gets from the sources is that every added claim to overlordship increased the burden of payments due from an area without the under-chief abating his claims. [59]

Thus it appears that the will of the lord was of no less consequence in the Gaelic parts of the country – certainly in Gaelic Ulster – than in the feudal areas. The extent to which the common people were exploited in both areas was determined by the extent to which mercenary troops were retained, since they were the real oppressors. Indeed it was probably the relief from coyne and livery and its Gaelic equivalent, which made so many church tenants, like the *nativi* of Armagh and the *puri homines* of Cloyne, content to tolerate a legal state of pure serfdom, in some cases until the seventeenth century. Not that this legal exemption was always observed by the Gaelic chieftains. The medieval archbishops of Armagh frequently complained of the unjust taxation of their tenants by the O'Neills, and they mentioned specifically the extortion of food and lodging, the upkeep of horses and hounds, and various other illicit exactions. A thirteenth-century document speaks of services of ploughing, reaping, carting and thatching imposed on the residents on church lands within the Irish areas under O'Neill, McMahon and McGuire, and mentions the captains of mercenaries enforcing the services of shoemakers, smiths and other tradesmen residing on the same church lands. Such illegal exactions probably increased during the sixteenth century as Ulster became more militarized. Shane O'Neill, for example, encroached at will upon church lands when 'at the beginning of his rebellion, [he] compelled the tenants of the said termons and herenaghs to give him uncertain rents and customs which were extorted wrongfully'. If tenants on church lands were thus exploited what must have been the condition of those who were liable to pay tax? [60]

It is evident, therefore, that the plight of the common people was hardly any different under Gaelic rule than under feudal control. Peasants in both regions were disturbed by the raids and counter raids that resulted from the efforts of overlords – Gaelic and feudal alike – to force their neighbours to subjection. The peasants in the Gaelic areas were further distressed by the internecine struggles among members of the ruling sept which resulted from the Gaelic succession system, but their counterparts in the feudal areas suffered equally since the areas were heavily militarized at all times. The outstanding feature of Irish social life at the accession of Queen Elizabeth was, therefore, the power of the overlords, and this common factor more than offset any institutional differences between the Gaelic and feudal parts of the country. Any intermediate strata between lord and peasant survived with difficulty.

The social history of sixteenth-century Ireland has been approached traditionally in terms of the Statutes of Kilkenny (1366) which stressed the cultural and ethnic differences between the various elements of Irish society. It appears that these distinctions might hold true of the outlook of the ruling element whose attitude towards the government was largely determined by their origins, but not even the most loyal feudal lord brooked any interference from a central authority. When approached from a social standpoint, therefore, it appears that the distinctions drawn in 1366 were exaggerated and are certainly not valid for the sixteenth century. There is nothing to suggest that the majority of the population fared any better under Anglo-Irish than under Gaelic rule, and there is plentiful evidence that peasants everywhere spoke Irish, dressed after the Gaelic manner, and lived in similar style cottages. Again it is evident that territorial divisions were determined by the power of an overlord rather than by the ethnic origins of the population. Even at the upper level, division by ethnic origin was far from clear because of the high degree of intermarriage between Gaelic and Anglo-Norman families over the centuries. Furthermore, Gaelic laws and customs were adopted in supposedly feudal areas, and there was some penetration of Gaelic customs even among landowners of the Pale. The Flemings of Meath were, for example, confidants of Shane O'Neill, and one of them, Thomas Fleming, 'a gent of thenglish Pale', was a foster brother to Turlough Luineach O'Neill.[61]

This suggests that even the line of the Pale was an artificial divide. The allegiance of many County Louth families must have been far from clear during the later medieval period, when they were forced to pay black rent to the Ulster chieftains and were at the same time tax-paying inhabitants of the Pale. On the other hand, there is evidence that the more southerly parts of Ulster, notably County Cavan, were considerably influenced by contact with the Pale. The market at Cavan was one point of contact, but, as was noted earlier, many from the Pale, including Baron Delvin, owned land in County Cavan. At the inquisition held at Cavan in 1610, the local landowners had their case put by 'a lawyer of the Pale retained by them'. It was also revealed that the 'inhabitants' of Cavan had through intercourse with their 'many acquaintances and alliances' in the Pale 'learned to talk of a freehold and of estates of inheritance which the poor natives of Fermanagh and Tyrconnell could not speak of'.[62]

There were, in fact, no sharp divisions in Irish society, as the inhabitants of border areas found themselves in dispute between neighbouring lords. What divisions there were, were determined by the power of the overlord rather than by any ethnic or linguistic factors. Many within the Pale were Gaelic in origin, while the Whites and Savages of north-east Ulster were of English extraction. The only ones unsure of their loyalty were those in the border areas; the others were recognized subjects to their overlord. The only inhabitants who were exempt from this general rule were the landowners within the immediate vicinity of Dublin who were subject to the government and owed services to it rather than to an overlord.

The reality of Irish society was, therefore, that it was divided into lordships rather than into ethnic or linguistic regions. The feudal lords owed theoretical allegiance to the crown, but they were jealous of their independence, and their subjection to the government was a polite fiction. In reality, therefore, they were little different from the Gaelic lords who acknowledged no authority to the crown and were independent kings in their localities. All of this suggests that Ireland at the accession of Queen Elizabeth was remarkably different from elsewhere in western Europe where the great lordships had been forced to concede considerable ground to the emergent monarchies. The power of the central government in Dublin was, obviously, extremely ineffectual, and English officials came to recognize that they could extend their influence in Ireland only at the expense of the outlying lords who, obviously, were reluctant to relinquish their power. As government representatives became more intimately acquainted with the country they grew increasingly intolerant of conditions there, most especially because local autonomy had, by the sixteenth century, come to be regarded as anachronistic, and in Ireland was seen to pose a threat both to the English interest in the country, and to the security of the English monarchy itself. Furthermore the tyranny exercised by the Irish lords over their tenants allowed the English officials to represent themselves as promoters of the commonwealth, and champions of civility. The more enterprising realized also that Ireland was by western European standards, both sparsely populated and economically under-developed, and they saw prospects there for their own enrichment and social advancement. There were, therefore, many reasons for Englishmen to involve themselves in Ireland during the second half of the sixteenth century.

2

An unwelcome inheritance:

The English presence in Ireland at the accession of Queen Elizabeth

It is evident from what has been said that the power of the Dublin government, at the middle of the sixteenth century, was extremely ineffectual. There was a court system in Dublin modelled on that of England, but its authority was recognized only in the immediate vicinity of the city. The Gaelic chieftains did not recognize the Dublin courts, and the feudal lords seldom resorted to Dublin for adjudication of their disputes. The officers of the palatinate courts settled most dissensions within the liberties of Kerry and Tipperary, and it appears that, by the sixteenth century, they had extended their jurisdiction over most of the lands ruled by Desmond and Ormond. Whatever disputes happened between feudal lords were settled by force of arms, and the government could do little to compel the contenders to resort to the courts in Dublin.

The ineptitude of the Dublin administration is best illustrated by the dispute between Thomas Butler, tenth earl of Ormond, and Gerald Fitzgerald, sixteenth earl of Desmond, that raged throughout the 1560s and 1570s. The earls were pursuing a centuries-old rivalry between the two families, but this particular outburst was occasioned by a disagreement over the terms of the marriage settlement between Ormond's widowed mother and the earl of Desmond. The latter claimed the rent from three manors in County Tipperary as his wife's dowry, but Ormond denied him this. Whenever Desmond tried to make good his claim by force Ormond retaliated by invading Desmond's lands. Desmond responded by denying Ormond passage through his lands to collect prisage on wines imported through Youghal and Kinsale.[1]

Recourse to law would have been the practical means of settling the dispute, but the perplexed Dublin government had not the means to enforce its will. Various commissions were sent to Munster to arrange a settlement, but their solution could be safely ignored after the commissioners' return to Dublin. The two earls were eventually called to London in May 1562, and the submissions made and recognizances taken there restored peace to Munster for a time. Desmond was still dissatisfied, however, because he considered that Ormond's relationship with the queen had prejudiced the settlement. In any event, the feud erupted with renewed vigour in February 1565, when the armies of the two earls engaged in a fully fledged feudal battle on the borders between Kilkenny and Waterford. The outcome was the capture of Desmond by Ormond, a lengthy government investigation, and the detention of Desmond in England from 1567 to 1573 – an extreme measure that still failed in its purpose of pacifying the province.[2]

A prolonged dispute of this nature would have been unthinkable in mid-sixteenth-century England, but the London government was hardly aware of the situation in Munster until armed conflict broke out. The episode shows up the casual way in which the London government approached its responsibilities in Ireland, as well as the ineffectiveness of the Dublin administration in controlling even those who professed loyalty to the crown. In reality, the queen's title to the crown of Ireland was an unwelcome inheritance, and little attention was devoted to that country. The government recognized that it would be enormously costly to extend effective control throughout the island and preferred half-measures aimed at containing the situation. It was considered equally inadvisable to withdraw completely and leave the country to its own devices lest Ireland should come under the control of a foreign power. This dilemma was well capsulated in 1560 by the earl of Sussex who was then lord-lieutenant of Ireland:

> I am forced by duty to give advice . . . not so much for the care I have of Ireland, which I have often wished to be sunk in the sea, as for that if the French should set foot therein, they should not only have such an entry into Scotland as her majesty could not resist, but also by the commodity of the havens here and Calais now in their possession, they should take utterly from England all kind of peaceable traffic by sea, whereby would ensue such a ruin to England as I am feared to think on.[3]

This was the attitude that had prevailed throughout the first half of the sixteenth century, with the result that the English pursued no consistent policy in Ireland. Despite a lack of policy, there was a fixed objective in the minds of successive governments: that of maintaining a secure foothold in Ireland without any cost to the crown.

The first two Tudors employed the method of aristocratic delegation, by which one of Ireland's feudal lords was appointed as lord deputy and put his private army at the Government's disposal. There were many objections to this method of managing the country, the chief one being that it was contrary to the Tudor policy of centralization, but its virtue of cheapness far outweighed its shortcomings. Henry VIII had many reasons to suspect the reliability of the earls of Kildare who served as deputies in Ireland, and he did try to curb their power, but he ignored all advice that the method of aristocratic delegation should be abandoned. The king's hand was forced, however, by the revolt in 1534 of Silken Thomas, son and heir of the ninth earl of Kildare who was then governor of Ireland. The resulting military campaign achieved the overthrow of the Fitzgerald house of Kildare and ended the phase of aristocratic delegation: Englishmen served as governors in Ireland for the remainder of the sixteenth century.

The transfer from one system to another was extremely complex. Since the English lord deputies had no private armies, it became necessary for London to provide an army of one thousand men to enable the lord deputy to maintain his position and defend the Pale from attack. This was rendered the more difficult because, with the overthrow of the Kildares, the Pale was deprived of its bulwark to the west. The Gaelic Irish of the midlands, who had hitherto been subjects of the Kildares, were now able to make direct raids on the rich lands of the Pale.

The removal of the Kildares from office was also unpopular with the former clients of the Fitzgeralds within the Pale, but even those who remained loyal to the government during the rebellion of Thomas Fitzgerald thought their position to be less secure under an English lord deputy. This latter group feared lest they should lose the virtual monopoly of office in the Dublin administration which they had hitherto enjoyed, and some were afraid that they would no longer have any part to play in formulating government policy. That there was some substance to their fears became evident when a substantial amount of the spoils accruing from the Henrician church reformation in Ireland, episcopal appointments as well as monastic property, went to Englishmen, many of them clients of Thomas Cromwell, rather than exclusively to those who had ratified the necessary legislation in the Dublin parliament.[4]

All Palesmen greatly resented the army of one thousand men over whom they had no control. The soldiers were recruited and paid for in England, but they were partially maintained by the Palesmen who paid a subsidy of 13s 4d on the ploughland towards the upkeep of the army, and who were compelled to provide food at a fixed price according to the system of purveyance that had been approved in the Irish parliament. In the outlying areas of the Pale, soldiers were billeted on the country-side and frequently refused to pay for their lodgings, thus impoverishing the tenants of the Pale. This alone was a source of resentment, but the Palesmen complained also of the misbehaviour of troops, their exemption from answering at the law courts, and the failure of captains to punish misdemeanours by martial law. The most frequent complaint was, however, that the officers enriched themselves at the expense of the Palesmen. When soldiers were not paid, it was argued, they were forced to steal from the tenants of the Pale, and the captains also profited from purveyance by reselling on the open market goods that had been purchased at the fixed price, often selling 'the hide . . . for more than was paid for the befe'.[5]

In the aftermath of rebellion, it was to be expected that a military solution for governing Ireland would appeal to the English crown, but it soon became clear that this left the Dublin government even more isolated than usual, since the army was resented even by those whom it was purporting to defend. Nobody in England would contemplate abandoning Ireland to its own devices, but a return to the old method of aristocratic delegation was more unacceptable than ever after the revolt of Thomas Fitzgerald. Yet it was becoming increasingly obvious that the existing policy was not only unpopular with the crown's most loyal subjects in Ireland, but was also a significant drain on the royal purse. One contemporary observer estimated that the English crown had spent £1,300,000 on the defence of Ireland between 1534 and 1572.[6] While this figure may be somewhat excessive, all in England were worried at the enormous and increasing expense and experimented with different policies in the hope that these would reduce the cost of Ireland to the English crown.

The more articulate of the community in the Pale recognized that the English government would be receptive to new ideas, and presented a policy for the government of Ireland which, since it promised to remove the need of a standing army in Dublin, they hoped would prove attractive to the crown. The policy had special appeal for themselves because it promised to give them a new political role in Ireland, and to guarantee their interpretation of their constitutional position under the English monarchy. The Palesmen first advanced their policy in the parliament of 1541-3 when they elevated Henry VIII from being Lord of Ireland, as his predecessors had been, to become King of Ireland, which title implied that all the inhabitants of the country, and not merely those in the vicinity of Dublin, were subjects of the English crown. By thrusting this title on Henry VIII the members of the Dublin parliament effectively committed the government of England to extending its authority to all parts of Ireland, and, as Fr. Brendan Bradshaw has shown, the means favoured by them was one of conciliation aimed at persuading the Gaelic lords to abandon their traditional ways in favour of English law and standards of civility. The policy, which has since became known to historians as surrender and re-grant, was, therefore, advanced by the Palesmen, as a sequel to their declaring Henry VIII to be King of Ireland, in the belief that their assistance would be indispensable to convince the Gaelic lords that they should embrace English civility. If they proved successful in persuading their erstwhile adversaries, the Gaelic lords, to abandon their ways, they could be confident that a standing army was no longer necessary for the defence of the Pale, and they expected that their assistance would be necessary to educate in their homes the heirs-apparent to Gaelic lordships, and to administer English law over an extended area.[7]

The king was none too enthusiastic about his new commitment in Ireland, but was persuaded by his deputy Sir Anthony St Leger, who had presided over the parliamentary proceedings in Dublin, to give the policy a fair trial. The essence of the scheme was that the ruling chieftains should surrender the lands of their lordships to the king and receive them back as a fief from the crown, the fief to pass on to the eldest son under the law of primogeniture. It was, in other words, intended to substitute the English for the Gaelic method of land tenure in the hope that the chieftains, recognizing that they held their lands from the king, would pay him due obedience, or at least desist from causing disturbances. The policy was pursued vigorously during the 1540s when Sir Anthony St Leger served as lord-lieutenant. Most of the Gaelic chieftains of Leinster surrendered, as did the principal Gaelic lords of the outlying provinces who received elevated titles from the crown. The arrangements were only paper ones, however, and, if anything, they caused further turmoil in the Gaelic areas, as those of the ruling septs who had been excluded from succession sought to overthrow the chieftains who had surrendered. The most dramatic struggle occurred in Ulster where Shane O'Neill refused to recognize the arrangement whereby his older brother, Matthew, was entitled by the law of primogeniture, to succeed their father, Con Bacagh O'Neill. Shane argued that Matthew was illegitimate and hence not eligible to succeed under English law, but in any event Shane wished to rule as a Gaelic chieftain rather than an English earl. When the government attempted to intervene on Matthew's behalf Shane retaliated by attacking the Pale. Thus the policy that was designed to secure the safety of the Pale succeeded in making its position even more precarious, and necessitated a further build up of troops to protect the Pale from attack. The O'Neill instance was quite typical, and the policy of surrender and re-grant met with limited success only in Clanricard and Thomond.

This policy, having failed in its objective of reducing the cost of Ireland to the crown, was abandoned in favour of the more restricted one of preserving the English influence in the Pale by sealing off that area from the remainder of the country. The method that most readily came to mind was that of surrounding the region with a chain of garrisons, as had been done in the vicinity of Calais to preserve the English Pale there from French attack. The inhibiting factor again was that the construction of forts and the maintenance of garrisons would be extremely costly. The danger of France intervening in Ireland and using it as a base from which to attack England was very real during the reigns of Edward VI and Mary, and there was consequently a greater willingness to spend money on Ireland's defence. Furthermore, Sir Edward Bellingham, Somerset's deputy in Ireland, argued that the garrisons would be self-financing if the soldiers were granted lands in the vicinity of the forts instead of wages. It was to procure such lands that Bellingham launched a succession of attacks upon the Gaelic areas of Leinster as a prelude to the construction of forts.[8]

After the Gaelic septs had been suitably cowed by Bellingham's show of force, the Wicklow area was divided into three administrative zones corresponding with the areas of habitation of the three septs, Byrnes, O'Tooles, and Kavanaghs. The chieftain of each of these septs was dismissed, and an English captain backed by a band of soldiers was appointed as seneschal to rule in his place. The seneschal was appointed to a fort from which to operate, was authorized to collect and finance himself from the rents and dues that had formerly appertained to the Gaelic chieftain, and he was granted power of martial law to enable him to keep order in each area. There was no attempt made to uproot the inhabitants, but what were considered the more dangerous and disruptive traits of the Irish way of life were outlawed. The government was particularly concerned that each person should have a master answerable for his conduct, and to this end the practice of 'booking' was introduced. The masterless men for whom nobody would take responsibility were driven out or executed by the seneschal. [9]

The arrangement for the Gaelic areas of the midlands was an elaboration on the seneschal scheme. Two large forts were erected by Bellingham, one at Philipstown (now Daingean) in the present County Offaly and the other at Maryborough (now Portlaoise) in the present County Laois. These were designed as the military headquarters for the subjugation of the midland areas as far as the River Shannon. The intentions were a) to confiscate the lands in the immediate vicinity of these forts and populate it with soldiers, thus rendering the forts self-financing; b) to drive the indigenous cultivators towards the River Shannon; and c) to organize the remaining Gaelic areas between the proposed plantation and the River Shannon after the seneschal model. The success of all this would have left the Pale surrounded by a secure belt of soldier-cultivators, and all Gaelic areas within striking distance of Dublin would have been under constant surveillance. It was expected that, apart from the initial building cost of the garrisons, the scheme would be self-financing, and London would thus enjoy a secure foothold in Ireland with little cost. [10]

This is a general outline of the scheme devised by the active and forward-looking deputies of King Edward and Queen Mary. It received its most comprehensive formulation from Sir Edward Bellingham in 1547, was continued reluctantly by Sir Anthony St Leger, more willingly by Sir James Croft, and enthusiastically by Sir Thomas Radcliffe, Lord Fitzwalter (and later earl of Sussex), who was lord deputy at the accession of Queen Elizabeth. Sussex inherited the plan but he adopted it as his own, and he more than anybody else expended great energy in seeking to implement it. To that end Sussex brought his immediate relatives and supporters to Ireland. Sir Henry Sidney, to whose sister Sussex was married, was vice-treasurer and treasurer at war in Ireland at the outset of Elizabeth's reign and it was considered that he would succeed Sussex as lord deputy. Sir Henry Radcliffe, a brother of Sussex, was a captain in the army in Ireland and had command of the two garrisons in Leix-Offaly, and was therefore in charge of the plantation effort. Another brother-in-law, Sir William Fitzwilliam (also married to a sister of Sidney), was in charge of the garrison of Athlone and was seneschal of the Irish areas of County Westmeath; while a loyal supporter, Sir George Stanley, marshal of the army, was seneschal of Dalton country and adjoining Gaelic areas. Control of the Wicklow mountain area was in the hands of two other captains, Sir Jacques Wingfield and Captain Nicholas Heron; Wingfield was seneschal of both the septs of Byrnes and O'Tooles and of the marches of Dublin, while Heron, based at Leighlin Castle, controlled the Kavanaghs and McMurroughs. In this way the Gaelic areas of Leinster were brought under government control, and the more important and frequently lucrative posts were in the hands of avowed supporters of Sussex.[11]

It soon became evident that the Palesmen were not in full accord with this scheme for their defence. The Leix-Offaly plantation was authorized in the parliament of 1560 on the understanding that the earl of Kildare – who had been restored to his ancestral lands by Queen Mary – should direct the project. Thus it was expected that the Fitzgeralds would regain control of the midland region, and many Palesmen hoped that they would be called upon to settle on the confiscated land. Their hopes were shattered when Sussex delegated his brother, Sir Henry Radcliffe, to organize the plantation. By 1563 the spoils had been distributed among eighty-eight individuals half of whom were military men. Twenty-nine of the grantees were native Irish and only fifteen Palesmen benefited from the plantation.[12]

The Leix-Offaly plantation was thus another source of discontent to the Palesmen, and they were equally unhappy with the seneschal system which disrupted the trade that had been pursued between the Gaelic areas of Leinster and the merchants of the Pale. Even more alarming for the Palesmen were the efforts by the followers of Sussex to gain control of local government in the obedient shires. When Nicholas Heron, captain of the fort at Leighlin Bridge and seneschal of part of Wicklow, was appointed sheriff of County Carlow it was a source of great resentment. The resentment turned to hatred when Heron was, contrary to normal practice, continued in office from 1559 to 1566. Heron was accused of embezzlement and extortion, but the attack on him was only the most extreme of many, and illustrates the bitterness that had grown up between the Palesmen and the followers of Sussex. Cries of peculation became more numerous, and one anonymous plaintiff charged that all the revenue from Ireland had gone into 'the bagges of some as the arle of Sussex, Sir Harry Radcliffe his brother, Stanley the marshal, Sir William Fitzwilliam, Wingfield, Cowlie, Stafford, Cosby, and an infinite number of such cormorants that gaping for private gayne have from naked persons enriched themselves to great wealthe and substance'.[13]

Sussex realized that he and his followers were becoming extremely isolated in Dublin, but this caused him little concern. The lord-lieutenant was conscious that the revenue from Ireland, which averaged £3,926 per year during the 1560s, was a paltry sum compared with the £18,975 provided by the English government.[14] His concern was, therefore, to pursue his policy forcefully and thus win credit for himself in England. It was all to the good if, on the way, he enriched his dependants, thus leaving the welfare of the Palesmen as a rather low priority. What Sussex did not recognize, however, was the growing concern of the government in England with his progress. The plan of sealing off the pale from attack had been launched in 1547, but it was not until 1563 that the land was distributed to the garrisons. Large sums of money had already been spent on the construction of the forts, and there was as yet no indication that the scheme would ever become self-financing. It was, in fact, generally accepted in England that the scheme had been a failure and had added to rather than subtracted from the queen's expenses. In the words of one English contemporary: 'the conquest of Leyx and Offally . . . I am assured hath cost the queene and thys cuntre more than would purchase so mutch rent ten tymes told in Ingland'.[15]

To add to the difficulties of the lord-lieutenant in Ireland, Shane O'Neill persisted in his attacks on the Pale and thus rendered meaningless whatever had been accomplished by Sussex. The only way for Sussex to salvage anything from his work was to seek to overthrow Shane O'Neill, but this would have required more troops than were then available to him. Sussex was also aware that the defeat, or even the death, of Shane was no solution to the Ulster problem since another would be elected in his place. What he wanted to accomplish, therefore, was, after the overthrow of Shane, to subdivide the province among the various members of the O'Neill sept and the lesser chieftains of Ulster, each to hold a compact area directly from the queen. Thus Sussex hoped to end the O'Neill overlordship in Ulster, and he hoped further to exclude Scots intruders from the province by establishing a soldier colony in the vicinity of the military outpost at Carrickfergus. It was his intention also to insulate the Pale against attack from Ulster by establishing a garrison at Newry.[16]

The position of the Dublin administration was, therefore, extremely precarious at the accession of Queen Elizabeth. The actions of successive English governors had alienated the landowners of the Pale from the government, and some of them yearned for the old days when Kildare had held office and furthered their interests with his own. The feudal lords were likewise resentful of change and wished for a return to the old order with one of themselves in office as deputy. Parliament was seldom called, and then only when it suited the governor's purpose. Great councils were, likewise, convened infrequently and, as a rule, only when the governor required supplementary forces for a military expedition or for dealing with some other emergency.

The mainstay of Lord-Lieutenant Sussex was, therefore, the government in London, and it was already becoming evident in the early 1560s that the queen and Privy Council were not altogether satisfied with his progress. They might have been willing to suffer silently his scheme of defending the Pale, even if it was a drain on royal finances, but his call for further backing to defeat Shane O'Neill was something they were not prepared to countenance. The queen understood the situation and stated emphatically that she could not go along with the suggestions of Sussex. It was her earnest desire, she said, to have Ireland 'in perfect obedience which seemeth cannot otherwise but with extending of force uppon some stubborne sort and with peopling [colonizing] of some partes there and specially the north possessed with Scottes'. Circumstances, however, did not favour the queen's desire, and she recommended Sussex to pursue a policy of pacification and compromise which involved recognizing Shane O'Neill as his father's legitimate heir and granting Sorley Boy Mac Donnell, the captain of the Scots in Ulster, the opportunity 'to become our trew liege man'. [17]

The queen's message was, in brief, that while the Irish, and more particularly the Ulster, situation was far from desirable it was not sufficiently urgent to warrant the expenditure necessary to bring it to order. The lord-lieutenant remonstrated vociferously against this and argued against its final acceptance by stressing: a) the use to which the Scots presence in Ulster might be put by France; b) the increasing tyranny of Shane O'Neill; and c) the facility with which both problems could be solved were the queen only willing to give him support. His argument was weakened considerably by the signing of the Treaty of Cateau-Cambrésis in 1559 which, for the moment, lessened the strategic importance of Ireland. Equally important was the counter argument formulated by the leaders in the Pale which confirmed the queen in her views and thus undermined Sussex's position. [18]

The principal spokesman for the Pale was the earl of Kildare who had a particular grievance over the Leix-Offaly plantation, and who watched his opportunity in London to proclaim in 'open speche that ther Kyngdom was kept from them by force and by such as be stranges in bloodd to them'. Kildare argued that Sussex was milking the Pale of its wealth to provide for his subordinates and was, at the same time, cheating the queen. The garrison policy, claimed Kildare, had served merely to antagonize the native Irish without providing adequate protection for the Pale. According to this argument, it would be far better to adopt a conciliatory policy towards the Gaelic Irish and leave the forts in Leix-Offaly 'to the government of suche as nede no ayde nor imposicons of the countrey', meaning Kildare and his supporters in the Pale. Thus, it was claimed, the queen would be 'disburdened of her superfluous garrisons' and the Irish revenue would be increased. It was argued also that the crown could rely upon the feudal lords to preserve order in the outlying regions if the queen would only place some trust in them. Sir Thomas Cusack, a leading light in the Pale and lord chancellor of Ireland during Queen Mary's reign, proposed that three of the Anglo-Irish lords should be appointed as presidents of the three provinces of Ulster, Munster and Connacht where they might use their private armies, in the name of the crown, to preserve peace and order.[19]

Thus two policies, which were diametrically opposed, were presented to the queen for her consideration. Both acknowledged that the Pale could not be insulated from attack unless some steps were taken to deal with its enemies outside. They differed, however, in the means by which the queen might extend her authority outside the Pale. The Palesmen favoured power being delegated to the Anglo-Irish feudal lords who could contain the Gaelic areas by a mixture of force and persuasion. Sussex, however, was opposed to any such delegation of authority, and called for a build up of military strength in Ireland so that he could launch an onslaught on Shane O'Neill and thus bring a lasting settlement to Ireland.

The queen was, obviously, not attracted to the prospect of spending more money in Ireland and yet did not want openly to abandon her representative in Ireland by supporting Kildare and the Palesmen. The years 1558 to 1565 were, therefore, years of uncertainty because the queen did not come down decisively on either side. Sussex in Ireland did what he could to bring O'Neill to heel, but his two Ulster campaigns (August 1561 and summer 1563) met with the predictable result because of the insufficiency of troops and supplies. On each occasion, Shane retreated to his fastnesses, and Sussex did not have sufficient resources either to pursue him or starve him out by prolonging the campaign into the winter. All that was accomplished by Sussex's military incursions was the burning of some corn.

The lord-lieutenant himself cannot have been surprised at the outcome, but his situation was hopeless. Shane's attacks on the Pale demanded retaliatory action, and if Sussex had failed to respond he would have left himself open to the charge of not defending the Pale. On the other hand, the queen was unwilling to supply him with the supplementary help that Sussex considered essential for a successful campaign. The reverses that he suffered, however, provided his Irish critics with an opportunity to discredit his actions in the eyes of the queen. Each aggressive phase was, therefore, followed by a phase when the queen flirted with the counter policy of the Palesmen. In the autumn of 1561, for example, Kildare returned from England with instructions to negotiate with Shane O'Neill and persuade him to visit the queen in England. Sussex was outraged at this affront and proclaimed that 'iff Shane be overthrown all is setteled, iff Shane settell all is overthrowen'. His remonstrations were in vain, and Shane was conducted to the court of Queen Elizabeth (November 1561 to May 1562) where he was accepted to mercy and was given a vague assurance that he would be created earl of Tyrone. He, in return, promised to aid the government in excluding the Scots from north-east Ulster and promised to draw his country more closely to the English way of life.[20]

Had Shane O'Neill adhered to his promises and desisted from attacking the Pale, it is likely that the queen and Privy Council would have thought nothing further of Ireland. Shane, however, was infatuated with the notion that he had been granted authority by the queen to rule all of Ulster, and he ravaged the lands of the O'Donnells of *Tír Conaill* as well as those of the Mac Donnells of Antrim. The Dublin administration was greatly alarmed at this new show of strength, but when they reprimanded him and advised him that his actions were contrary to the queen's wishes he turned his forces against the Pale. Thus the policy of the Palesmen was shown to be deficient, and the queen's emissary to Ireland reported that unless Shane was subdued Ireland would 'growe to more charges, and more perill too, then ever yt hath doon sithence the begynninge of her Majesties most royall fatheris raigne'. Not even Kildare could dispute this judgement, and London was again converted to the idea of using force 'to subvert and expell him [Shane] and not to reforme him'.[21] It was a lukewarm conversion, however. While Sussex was permitted to conduct a military campaign against Shane O'Neill, the government again refused to supplement him further, and so the campaign of 1563 met with the same fate as that of two years earlier. The lord-lieutenant was now weary of his task in Ireland and asked the queen to accept his resignation. This she did reluctantly in April 1563 but, still unwilling to take her responsibility in Ireland seriously, the queen reverted to the policy suggested by the Palesmen.

The decision arrived at in London was that Sussex should not be replaced, but instead a lord justice should be appointed in Dublin, thus downgrading the office of governor and elevating the position of the queen's loyal subjects in Ireland. The man selected for this post was Sir Nicholas Arnold who had previously been sent on some minor missions to Ireland, but who was relatively unimportant in English political circles.[22] Arnold served as lord justice until October 1565, and his purpose was to preserve the Pale free from attack and turn a blind eye to whatever was happening elsewhere in the country. Thus Shane O'Neill was allowed to exert his influence in Ulster without any check from the government. The lord justice was well aware of what was happening but argued that Ulster was beyond his jurisdiction and should, therefore, not concern him. In his report to Secretary Cecil he emphasized this viewpoint graphically:

> I am with all the wilde Irishe at the same poynet I am with beares and banddogges when I se theim fight, so that they fight earnestly indede and tugge eche other well I care not who have the woorsse.[23]

This attitude was sensible so long as Shane confined his attentions to Ulster. When, however, strengthened by his conquests in Ulster, he turned his attention to the Pale, the short-sightedness of the Arnold experiment became apparent. The army in the Pale was disgruntled by the treatment accorded to Sussex and did little to stop Shane. The Irish of the midlands detected this weakness and availed themselves of the opportunity to attempt an overthrow of the Leix-Offaly settlement. To add to Arnold's difficulty, the war between Desmond and Ormond was waged with renewed vigour on both sides. In less than a year, everything that Sussex had achieved was lost, and in 1565 it appeared that England would lose her last foothold in Ireland unless some drastic action was taken.

It is evident from what has been said that the English Privy Council in the early years of Queen Elizabeth's reign devoted even less attention to Ireland than did its counterpart during the reigns of Edward VI and Queen Mary. The reasons for this were the parsimoniousness of the queen and the fact that the threat from France, and therefore the strategic importance of Ireland, was less real after the Treaty of Cateau-Cambrésis in April 1559. Equally important was the fact that England was then going through a period of political instability, and councillors were far more concerned with jockeying for positions at court than in worrying themselves about Irish affairs.[24] One important achievement was, however, that, in spite of their indifference, most of the members of the Privy Council had, by 1565, become reasonably well informed on Irish affairs.

Most of this information was borne in upon the privy councillors as a result of the antagonism between Sussex and the earl of Leicester. Sussex was a man of considerable standing in English political life of the time, in that he was a member of the vast Howard network and a nephew of the duke of Norfolk who was leader of that faction. This grouping resented the rise to power of Lord Robert Dudley (afterwards, 1564, earl of Leicester), and one of the purposes of Sussex in Ireland was to gain control of the army there, and thus establish a power base that would be of consequence in the event of a civil war in England. Sussex was quite successful in this objective, and he came to be recognized by Leicester as the most forceful of the Howard faction. Leicester, therefore, set his mind to undermining the position of Sussex in Ireland and, if possible, using the criticism of his administration of that country as a means to disgrace him in the eyes of the queen. The conflict in Ireland between Sussex and the Palesmen became merely an extension of the power struggle at court. Leicester encouraged the earl of Kildare and the Palesmen, and ensured that their criticism of Sussex would be heard at the Privy Council, and thus receive a prominence that it would not otherwise have done.[25]

It was Leicester, for example, who won the queen over to the idea of bringing Shane O'Neill to court in 1561-2, and he himself entertained Shane during his prolonged visit. There were, then, many discussions at council level about the situation in Ulster, and the members of council thus gained much information on social and political life in Gaelic Ireland. They were informed likewise of the independence that was enjoyed by the Anglo-Irish feudal lords as a result of the various debates on the Ormond–Desmond struggle. In that instance Ormond, as a descendant of the Boleyns, was able to rely on the support of the Howard faction, thus ensuring that Leicester favoured the earl of Desmond. The net result again was that councillors, who had little interest in Irish affairs, were forced to devote some attention to the debate which they were called upon to resolve. All were thus made aware of the local nature of political life in Ireland, and, irrespective of faction, the councillors were agreed that no further authority should be granted to the Irish feudal lords.

Most attention was given to the accusations of the Palesmen, especially those charging Sussex with embezzlement. Delegations from the Pale were patronized by Leicester, and thus received audiences from the Privy Council. The queen ignored their criticism of Sussex, initially, but her suspicions had been aroused, and commissions were dispatched to Ireland in July 1562 and October 1563 to investigate the payment of troops and the financial administration of Ireland. No evidence was found against Sussex himself, but many of his captains were found guilty of fraud in the payment of troops and duly dismissed; thus Sussex's power base in Ireland was smashed.[26]

Leicester was quite pleased with this, but the real benefit of the investigations was that councillors were made aware of the chaotic state of Irish finances and the drain that Ireland was on the crown. The English attorney-general, Gilbert Gerrard was dispatched to Ireland to report on the state of finances. Gerrard admitted that all was in chaos and made it clear to the privy councillors that Ireland had escaped the administrative revolutions that had taken place in England during the reign of Henry VII and again, in the 1530s, under the guidance of Thomas Cromwell. The attorney-general devised an elaborate system of cross auditing to ensure that the returns from the crown lands in Ireland found their way to the Exchequer.[27] It was by now obvious to all that this would do nothing to alleviate the real problem which was that troops paid for in England were required to defend England's foothold in Ireland. The feelings of the Privy Council were best summed up by the secretary, Sir William Cecil. He looked to the control that Spain had over Naples and the Netherlands and argued that by comparison England's hold of Ireland was 'a strange example, and such as is not to be found againe in any place'. It seemed anomalous to Cecil that a subject kingdom should be a financial liability to the ruling monarch where:

> all other princes having any dominions distant from their owne residence, though the same be sundry tymes invaded in respect of titles or otherwayes, yet they have sufficient revenues of the same contreys to governe and defend the same, yelding some tymes a great surplus.[28]

By 1565, as a result of the numerous debates, commissioners' reports and investigations to which they had been exposed, most of the privy councillors were acutely aware of the financial loss that England was suffering in Ireland and were ready to take some action to remedy it. It was evident to them also that unless the action was drastic England would lose its foothold in Ireland. The experience of Sussex had shown that the garrison scheme of defending the Pale was not the solution required. The Arnold experiment, as well as the Ormond-Desmond feud, made it clear that entrusting further powers to already independent lords was not the answer. It was obvious that some new policy was required that would extend the English area of influence, and thus increase the crown's revenue from Ireland. Sussex had come up with such a proposal in 1562 but this had then been opposed by the Leicester faction. By 1565, however, with the Sussex power base broken, Leicester had no reason to oppose any initiative. Furthermore, Sussex was appointed a member of the English Privy Council when he returned to England, and he would have shown himself to be inconsistent if he did not press for a new policy for Ireland. Thus the council was informed and united in its call for action in Ireland. What was required was somebody who would come forward with an imaginative policy that would not entail much further expenditure in the short term, and that would hold out the prospect of Ireland, like Naples, eventually paying 'a great surplus' to the mother country. The scheme devised by the president of Wales, Sir Henry Sidney, seemed to be the solution to the conundrum, and he was duly appointed as lord deputy of Ireland in October 1565.

3

The new departure:

A programme for the conquest of Ireland

The lord deputyship of Ireland was, to office seekers in England, a relatively new post, and no consistency in selecting candidates had as yet emerged. Some of the nominees of King Henry VIII were military men, but the appointment of Sir Anthony St Leger, a close friend and sage adviser to the king, is an indication that Henry considered it to be an eminent post. St Leger continued to hold office under King Edward, but his anxiety for recall, and the fact that his less distinguished successors included one commoner among them, is proof that service in Ireland was not held in the same high esteem by office seekers as by monarchs.[1] All realized that absence in Ireland could be fatal to a career in times of quickly shifting power. Memory of Richard II's critical absence in Ireland was still alive, and the fortunes of successive governors did nothing to dispel 'that infamous observacon, noted by manie, that Ireland yeldith none other frutes to her governors, than disgrace at home'.[2]

Service in Ireland, however, held attractions for younger courtiers who wished to win recognition in the service of the crown. Queen Mary displayed considerable imagination when she chose Thomas Radcliffe, the heir apparent to the earldom of Sussex, as governor of Ireland, and he was glad of the opportunity to gain credit in English political circles. Furthermore, Sussex proved that service in Ireland could be financially rewarding. As well as his annual stipend of £1,500, Sussex was able to place his relatives and supporters in rewarding positions in Ireland. It was, as was noted, Sussex's success in Ireland that alarmed Leicester, who resented the rise to prominence of one of his rivals.[3] The ensuing acrimonious debate reduced the question of governing Ireland to the level of court intrigue, and it was recognized by the queen and Privy Council that somebody acceptable to both the Howard and Dudley factions must be found to succeed Sussex in Ireland. The lord president of Wales, Sir Henry Sidney, seemed eminently suitable, since he was a brother-in-law of both the earls of Leicester and Sussex and might be allowed to pursue a consistent policy in Ireland without enduring constant criticism from England. Sidney also saw the position as a means towards political prominence, and was forthcoming with a programme for governing the country.

Henry Sidney, born in 1529, was the eldest son of Sir William Sidney, an officer in the household of King Edward VI, and was a constant companion of the boy king. He obviously looked forward to preferment from the king, and his marriage to Mary Dudley, daughter of Northumberland, was a further assurance of favour. Advancement duly came in 1550 when he was knighted and appointed ambassador to France. The ladder on which Sidney was ascending so rapidly was snatched from under him, however, when Northumberland was disgraced. Lucky to escape imprisonment himself, he was pleased to accompany Sussex to Ireland in 1556 and served, in relative obscurity, as treasurer there; 'neither liking or liked as I had been', he wrote, 'I fancied to live in Ireland and serve as treasurer'.[4]

Sussex was married to Frances Sidney, a sister to Henry, and in those years of Sidney's greatest need he found a firm supporter in his brother-in-law. It was mutually accepted that Sidney would succeed Sussex as governor, and, as early as 1557, Sidney was laying down the conditions under which he would accept appointment. The term spent by Sussex in Ireland was, however, longer than expected, and thus Sidney's hopes of gaining prominence were quashed. With the accession of Queen Elizabeth, however, and more especially with the rise of Robert Dudley in the queen's favour, Sidney saw a renewed prospect of advancement in England and resigned his post in Ireland.[5]

It was to his wife's brother that Sidney now turned for support, and he assured Leicester that he 'cared for no one' who was the earl's enemy and that he wished to be a feather in his cap. From this time forward Sidney identified himself as a supporter of Leicester even to the extent of quartering Leicester's arms, the ragged staff, with his own and attiring his servants in Leicester's livery. As early as 1566, he consciously allowed his own personality to be subsumed under that of Leicester as can be seen from his advice to his eldest son Philip: 'remember my sonne, the noble house you are descended of by your mother's side; and thinke that only by vertuous lyf and good action you may be an ornament to that illustre familye'. When it became evident that Philip Sidney would succeed to Leicester's title and lands, there was all the more reason for the Sidney family to identify themselves as Dudley supporters.[6]

The earl of Sussex was obviously displeased at this switch of allegiance, but there was, in 1565, no personal animosity between Sussex and Sidney, and the former lord-lieutenant of Ireland had no reason to object to Sidney's appointment. Furthermore, Sidney's previous experience in Ireland made him eminently suitable for the post, as did his service, since 1560, as lord president of Wales. The fact that he had departed from Ireland before the graft of Sussex's followers had become particularly objectionable to the Palesmen meant that Sidney would be acceptable to the Irish critics of Sussex. It came as no surprise, therefore, when in 1563, on the recall of Sussex, Sidney was nominated by the queen and Privy Council to succeed him. The appointment was never finalized, however, probably because of the government's unwillingness to meet Sidney's terms, and London resorted instead to the Arnold experiment. Sidney however was frequently consulted by the Privy Council on Irish affairs, and when Arnold's period of rule proved disastrous Sidney was the obvious candidate for the lord deputyship of Ireland.[7]

Sidney, in 1565, was clear on his terms and purpose before he conceded to accept office. His conditions of acceptance were: that he should retain the presidency of Wales, that his term in Ireland would not exceed three years, and that he would have a steady supply of money, a larger army and the unqualified support of the Privy Council. Finally, he indicated that he would expect a suitable reward of land and title when he returned to England. He was satisfied that he had the solution to the government of Ireland and was confident that the appropriate machinery would be in operation within three years.[8]

The scheme outlined by Sidney was, in many ways, an elaboration upon the proposals for the government of Ireland put forward, in 1562, by Sussex. In that document, Sussex suggested that efforts to preserve the Pale from attack were futile unless some attempt was made to prevent disturbances in the remainder of the country. The lord-lieutenant recommended the establishment of provincial presidencies to control the outlying provinces of Ulster, Munster and Connacht. The presidencies envisaged by him bore little resemblance to the provincial councils in Wales and the north of England. The latter institutions were concerned primarily with the administration of justice on the local level while the presidencies as envisaged by Sussex for Ireland were to concentrate on preventing armed conflict in the provinces. The presidents were to be military men, and, like the seneschals operating in the Gaelic parts of Leinster, they were to have the support of government troops. Sussex estimated that it would cost £5,623 11s a year to maintain a presidency in Ulster and £1,124 each for the presidencies of Munster and Connacht, but he expected that the additional expense would be absorbed by the principal landowners in the provinces. In this respect also his presidency scheme was an extension of the seneschal arrangement in Leinster.[9] The similarity was all too evident to the English Privy Council who recognized that while the seneschals were reasonably successful in preserving the semblance of order, they had done nothing to change the structure of society and thus guarantee permanent peace. Furthermore, the London officials were not convinced that the provincial landowners would concede taxes for the maintenance of presidencies. These reasons contributed to the reluctance of the London government to take any decisive action in 1562, and thus Sussex's proposals were ignored

Circumstances were more favourable in 1565 when Sidney put forward his scheme. The chief factor in his favour was that the Privy Council was united behind Sidney and was then seeking a final solution to the endemic disturbance in provincial Ireland. Cecil, for example, acknowledged that the condition of Ireland was 'to be much pitied and lamented and yet not to be neglected but with all diligence and care . . . to be recovered'.[10] In the second place the scheme outlined by Sidney appeared realistic and promised to open the way for the extension of English common law over a wider area, and eventually through the entire country. While many of his ideas were based upon the suggestions of Sussex, his plan was essentially different in purpose and broke away from the limited objective of defending the Pale.

Sidney's policy was a three-pronged one aimed at dealing with the Gaelic areas of Leinster, the feudal lordships, and the outlying Gaelic regions of Ulster and south-west Munster. For the moment, Sidney accepted the continuation of the seneschal scheme for the Gaelic parts of Leinster, but he recommended it as a means by which those areas could eventually become shire ground. In this he differed from Sussex who thought only in terms of maintaining a semblance of order in that region, thus securing the Pale from attack. The seneschals were to continue enforcing order by martial means, but Sidney expected them to lead the Irish gradually towards an acceptance of common law. The chieftains were to be compelled to acknowledge the sovereignty of the queen, and the heads of the lesser septs under the Gaelic disposition were likewise to submit themselves and receive assurance in their lands from the crown. By this means it was anticipated that the overlordship of the Irish chieftains would be eroded, and that the heads of the lesser septs, secure in their lands, would be dutiful and grateful subjects of the queen. Sir William Cecil agreed with this reasoning and accepted Sidney's general 'principall that into the more estates those captenries and lands be distributed, the better it will prove for the government of the same'. Sidney favoured the continuation of the Leix-Offaly garrisons, but he redefined their role and saw the period of military rule as a transitional stage between Gaelic and English forms of government. What was envisaged, therefore, was the gradual elimination of Gaelic rule in Leinster and the absorption of the former Gaelic areas into the Pale, thus removing the necessity of a military presence in Leinster. [11]

The programme of reform for the feudal lordships, as outlined by Sidney, was based on the principle of provincial councils. This idea had certainly originated with Sussex, but the new proposals did not end with the maintenance of order. The source of disturbance, according to Sidney, was the excessive power of the feudal lords, and he regarded the primary task of the presidents to be that of undermining the power bases of the great magnates. Furthermore, he recognized that there was little possibility, in the short term, of forcing the outlying Gaelic areas to accept rule of English law. The jurisdiction of the presidents was, therefore, to be confined to those areas where English law had formerly prevailed, and to the regions that had been drawn more closely to the English way of life under the policy of surrender and regrant. There were, according to the new scheme, to be two provincial presidents; one as president of Munster, to govern the lordships of Desmond and Ormond, and the other as president of Connacht, to rule over the earldoms of Clanricard and Thomond. Each president was to have military backing, and it was proposed that the president of Munster, having the widest area of government, should have charge of one hundred horse and two hundred foot.

Most attention was devoted to the proposed presidency of Munster, and while it was acknowledged that only a military man could be an effective president at the outset, his principal function was defined as being an administrator of justice. This, for Munster, was truly revolutionary in that it implied infringing upon the palatinate rights of the earls of Desmond and Ormond. Such was the intention of Sidney, who showed by his activities, both as president of Wales and lord deputy of Ireland, that he was opposed to private jurisdictions and, in fact, to all forms of feudal excess. With the intention of eliminating these traits in Ireland, he directed that the presidents should seek to destroy any overlordship that the feudal lords enjoyed and attempt to secure the lesser nobility and gentry in their lands holding them directly from the crown. This ambition is best exemplified in his recommendation for the earldom of Thomond, which he suggested should be divided 'in to many men's hands than in one'. The Privy Council, accepting this as a valid criticism of the earlier policy of surrender and regrant, directed that for the future it should be held 'for a general and good rule that it is better for those contreys of the wild Irish to be distributed into competent government of divers than to remain at the commandment of one or few'. What was good for the converted lordships was, in Sidney's view, even more valid for the long established earldoms of Desmond and Ormond which extended over such wide areas.[12]

It is clear, therefore, that the end purpose of provincial presidencies was to undermine the power of the feudal lords by depriving them of their palatinate jurisdictions, by prohibiting the maintenance of private armies, and by truncating their power. The beneficiaries of this would have been the lesser nobility and the smaller landowners who, it was hoped, would favour the government and, like the gentry in England, act as a counter-weight to the great lords. These lesser landowners, it was expected, would then be available for local offices, such as sheriff and justices of the peace, and would also act as jurors. By this means, Sidney hoped to open the way for the extension of English common law, and to this purpose two justices were to accompany the president of Munster. Sidney, again following the example of Sussex, proposed that the presidencies should be paid for by the local landowners and tenants rather than the crown. This was to be achieved, he argued, by diverting to the president whatever rents had formerly been paid for the military support of the feudal lord. Thus power would be shifted from the earls to the representative of the crown after the proposition that:

> yf you will give the people justice, and minister lawe emongs them, and exercyse the sworde of the soveraign, and put away the sworde of the subjecte . . . thereby shall you drive the now man of warre to become the husband man.[13]

Where Ulster was concerned Sidney, like Sussex, favoured a military campaign aimed at the overthrow of Shane O'Neill and the elimination of the Scots settlers from north-east Ulster. It was to this end that he required a larger army. He recognized also that unsupported ventures, such as had been launched by Sussex, would never succeed in pinning down O'Neill. Instead, he wanted to plant garrisons on the borders of Ulster which would gradually wear down O'Neill's power. Once Shane had been defeated, it was his intention to divide most of the land of Ulster among the various members of the O'Neill family and the heads of the subservient septs within the province. The remainder of the land was to be reserved for the support of military garrisons and colonies of Englishmen which he considered necessary for the maintenance of order in the province. The reasoning behind this was that the inhabitants of Ulster were so removed from civility that planning for the introduction of common law was unrealistic, until the native population had first become inured to the English way of life, by contact with English colonists and soldiers. This aspect of the policy was not revealed in 1565, since it was decided to 'keep secrete, even from some of [the Privy Council] the intention of habitation of ynglysh men in the northe of yreland, untyll sotche tyme as Shane Onele shalbe subdued', in the hope that the Palesmen and the Gaelic enemies of Shane would be persuaded to assist the government.[14]

It is evident from what has been said in the first chapter that Sidney was correct in his diagnosis of the cause of local disturbances in Irish society. His solution was certainly original to Ireland but was influenced greatly by the experience of the early presidents of Wales, whose task had been that of placing shackles on the great marcher lords as a preliminary to administering justice in that region. Furthermore, it appeared that the scheme had a good chance of success if the queen provided the initial financial support needed for instituting the provincial presidencies, and for waging war on Shane O'Neill. Once the presidents had been established, it was anticipated that they would find support in their provinces, and Sidney was later to reveal a means by which colonies might be established in Ireland without any cost to the crown. Thus it was hoped that the queen would be won over to the idea of undertaking the conquest of Ireland, which was the final purpose of the policy outlined by Sidney.

The Privy Council were clearly confident that Sidney's proposals were realistic and would provide a solution to the endemic unrest in Ireland. Its confidence and virtual unanimity is indicated by the fact that Sir William Cecil was entrusted with working out the details with Sidney. Cecil was receptive to the reform programme, and the instructions drawn up by him for the direction of the deputy were merely an elaboration of Sidney's own suggestions. Cecil accepted that all Leinster, including the Gaelic areas, would quickly be brought under the common law, while the proposed presidencies would draw Munster and south Connacht to civility. In anticipation of this great resurgence of law and justice, Cecil called upon judges to be more active and threatened to appoint Englishmen to future vacancies on the Irish bench if the existing judges did not reform their ways. The secretary recognized that the spread of common law and the reconstruction of local administration would make possible the revamping of financial administration that had been proposed by Gilbert Gerrard after his inspection of the Irish Exchequer. This, in part, explains the enthusiasm of Cecil for the new proposals, and the best indications of his optimism were his commissioning a printed calendar of the Irish statutes for the guidance of the lord deputy, and his instructing Sidney to call a parliament in Dublin for the endorsement of the reform programme. [15]

Sidney was pleased with this relatively uncritical acceptance of his scheme. The suggestion that Englishmen be placed on the bench in Ireland met with his particular approval, and he recommended that a precedent be established when filling the vacant position of master of the rolls. Furthermore, Sidney nominated his friend and neighbour in Kent, Warham St Leger, for the presidency in Munster, and requested that he, Sir Nicholas Bagenall and the proposed master of the rolls, together with the archbishop of Armagh, the bishop of Meath and the earl of Desmond be added to the existing council in Dublin. In this way Sidney hoped to broaden the base of the Dublin council as well as to establish a faction committed to him and his programme of reform. [16]

These suggestions were accepted and integrated by the Privy Council into the final draft of the instructions. Sidney was formally appointed governor of Ireland with the title lord deputy and was granted £1,500 as a stipend. His nominees, along with the earls of Thomond and Clanricard, were added to the existing council in Dublin. The deputy and council were entrusted with the task of bringing rebellious Ulster to subjection and extending the common law throughout the realm – an undertaking that would hitherto have been unthinkable. [17]

Thus in the late autumn of 1565, Sidney set forth for Ireland with a clearly outlined programme and the firm commitment of the English Privy Council to support him in implementing it. As yet, nothing had been revealed to disturb the Palesmen, and the threat that Englishmen might be appointed to the judiciary in Dublin should have been sufficient to secure their support for Sidney.

Furthermore, the majority of senior posts in the army were vacant since Arnold had dismissed the Sussex appointees, thus leaving Sidney an opportunity to appoint supporters of his own. A trend was established when Sidney nominated St Leger for the Munster post, and he even solicited a knighthood for him so that his rank would be commensurate with the office. Sir Nicholas Bagenall, who was also chosen by Sidney for a seat on the Dublin council, had had long service in Ireland and was marshal of the army there until stripped of his office by Queen Mary because of his participation in the Dudley conspiracy. His support of the Dudley cause naturally endeared him to Sidney, and Bagenall had solicited Leicester 'sondrie tymes' for reappointment to the marshalship. The office was held in 1565 by Sir George Stanley, a Sussex supporter who had been denigrated by Arnold, and Sidney encountered little difficulty in persuading the queen to dismiss Stanley and restore Bagenall to the post. There was a danger here that Sidney would be accused of making Ireland a power base for Leicester instead of Sussex, and while this was probably his intention he was saved from dismissing many of Sussex's men by the fact that they had been previously discredited and removed from office. In fact, the only prominent member of the Sussex faction who still held office in Ireland was Sir William Fitzwilliam, the treasurer at war, but since he was married to Sidney's sister Anne and was himself a first cousin of Cecil's wife he was acceptable to the new lord deputy.[18] Thus everything appeared to favour Sidney when he took up office as lord deputy, and, while nobody expected that the task of reforming the country would be accomplished within three years, it was a reasonable prediction that the machinery for bringing this about would be assembled and in operation before he relinquished office.

Everybody concerned, including Sidney himself, realized that the most urgent task was to curb the the power of Shane O'Neill, but the deputy decided to postpone action in Ulster until he had reorganized the administration of Leinster and had established St Leger as president in Munster. Thus Sidney hoped that when he came to move against Shane he could give Ulster his undivided attention in the knowledge that both Leinster and Munster were safely under control.

Sidney's first action in Ireland was, therefore, to spur the judges to greater effort, and he forced them to extend regular sessions of assize to all the counties in Leinster. New sheriffs were appointed early in 1566, for Counties Leix, Offaly, Kilkenny, Carlow, Wexford and Meath, and, in spring 1566, Sidney himself accompanied the judges on their circuit through Leinster. The central administration was also reorganized as a result of which, according to the deputy, the volume of legal petitions increased drastically so that he 'daielie [received] more billes and letters in the fore-noon than [he could] reede in the after noone'. The military establishment was reviewed and new men were appointed to control the garrisons. The government of the forts in the midlands had been vacant since the dismissal of Sir Henry Radcliffe, and these were now entrusted to Francis Cosby and Henry Cowley, who were appointed constables of the forts of Maryborough and Philipstown. Francis Agard, a member of the Dublin council, was appointed seneschal over the eastern Wicklow region, and Robert Pipho was given control over the western part of Byrne country bordering on Counties Kildare and Carlow. Thomas Fitzwilliams was made seneschal of the Gaelic part of County Dublin. Of the old seneschals only Nicholas Heron was continued as ruler over the Kavanaghs, and even he was to be removed shortly and replaced by Thomas Stukeley. Thus there was a complete change in personnel, and men who owned their positions to the lord deputy were now in charge of the army. [19]

The changes did not stop with personnel. The lord deputy redefined the role of seneschal and no longer tolerated them ruling after the manner of Gaelic chieftains. Seneschals, according to the new directive issued by the lord deputy, were to govern 'as nere as may be according to common lawe . . . and to keep them [the native Irish] therewhiles in deutifull obedyence and cyvile quyett without permittinge eny more their brehon lawe to be used emongest them'. In this the lord deputy was complying with his instructions, and in his journey through Leinster in the spring of 1566, he accepted submissions from the various chieftains of the Gaelic areas of Leinster explaining to them the changes that he hoped to bring about. [20] Thus, by April 1566, arrangements were made for the administration of justice in Leinster, for controlling the Gaelic parts of the province, and for gradually drawing them within the common law.

So far everything had gone according to plan, and the deputy hoped that his arrangements for Munster would operate just as smoothly. He and the Dublin council formulated instructions for Sir Warham St Leger and forwarded them to London for approval. The instructions bore the stamp of Sidney's past experience in that they were largely derived from the instructions to the president of the marches in Wales. St Leger was proposed as president and was to be assisted by two Anglo-Irish lawyers, Robert Cusack and Nicholas White. The president, unlike his counterpart in Wales, was to be entrusted with the power of martial law and provided with a permanent following of thirty horse and twenty foot with authority to raise further troops in the province. The jurisdiction of the president was to extend over Counties Waterford, Limerick, Kerry and Cork, and the earldom of Thomond. The earls of the province and the bishops of Waterford, Limerick and Cork were appointed to serve with Cusack and White on the council, and the president and council were directed to conduct regular sessions throughout the province, thus fulfilling the function of justices of assize.[21]

The lord deputy recognized that some remnants of English law and administration still survived in Munster and that Counties Waterford, Limerick and Cork 'had and have sheriffs and such lyke officers', but he despaired of their exercising their offices effectively and saw the presidency as the vehicle for restoring civility to the province. The proposed instructions for St Leger are yet further proof of Sidney's determination to see both Ormond and Desmond over-ruled in their 'pretendid palatyne liberties without which yt is never to be lookid for that Mounstir shall be reformed'. The whole tenor of the instructions was directed against the tyranny of overlords, and one of the defined purposes of the presidency was to defend those unable to afford recourse to common law, or anybody 'like to be oppressed by maintenance, strength, power, degree or affynity of the parties adversary'.[22]

The frequency and vehemence of his protestations on this issue indicate that the lord deputy anticipated opposition to the presidency. The institution was, after all, being created without prior consultation with any of the concerned parties in Munster and without the sanction of parliament. Furthermore, the palatinate jurisdictions of both Ormond and Desmond were being entirely disregarded and were declared to be 'pretendid'. What the deputy had in mind was to play upon the differences between the earls of Desmond and Ormond in the expectation that neither party would want to be the first to oppose the queen's wishes. In this, he did not allow for the ingenuity of the earl of Ormond who objected to the person of Warham St Leger rather than to the creation of a presidency, thus hoping to delay the appointment and win time to deflect the queen from the proposed course of action. St Leger was a cousin of Ormond, but the relationship was one that the earl would have preferred to forget, since the St Leger family had claimed the title and lands of the Butlers in 1515, when the old Butler line had died out. Sir Anthony St Leger was, when lord deputy of Ireland, well aware of his claim to the Butler lordship, and this explains the antagonism between him and the ninth earl of Ormond. There is no evidence that Warham St Leger wished to pursue the dispute into a third generation, but Ormond argued that the representative of a family with such a record of opposition to the Butlers was not acceptable to him as president in Munster. [23] The earl went further and alleged to the queen that Sidney was in league with St Leger to bring about the downfall of the Butlers. Ormond's evidence for this was the arrest of his brothers on the charge of exacting coyne and livery contrary to law. The earl did not deny the charge, but thought it unjust that the loyal Butlers, rather than the disloyal Fitzgeralds, should be made an example of when the lord deputy sought to end the practice.

Ormond argued his case well and soon drew the queen over to his way of thinking. The earl's task was not difficult, since the queen had always been doubtful about the establishment of a presidency in Munster, lest it add to her charges in Ireland, and she needed little persuasion to revoke her earlier decision. St Leger's appointment was stopped, and the presidency in Munster was declared vacant until the queen should nominate a suitable candidate. Furthermore, the queen directed her deputy to favour Ormond in all his causes 'as reason shall require', and on the specific complaint over coyne and livery she ordered that the practice be tolerated among loyal subjects until such time as the less obedient had been disarmed. [24]

The lord deputy was astounded at this curb on his power and complained bitterly that those subjects who had briefly tasted justice were once more restored to their former condition, under which they had 'never herd of other prince than Ormond or Desmonde'. There was nothing for it, however, but to comply with the queen's wishes in the hope that she would be lured to appoint a new president. On a tour of Munster during the spring of 1567, the deputy supervised sessions of assize in each county, the first that the province had seen for many years, and at Waterford sat in judgement on the Ormond-Desmond feud. The lord deputy followed the queen's direction and decided against Desmond who then forfeited the bond of £20,000 which he had given in London as a guarantee that he would keep the peace. The dissatisfaction of Desmond with the verdict and his refusal to abandon coyne and livery did not augur well for the future peace of the province. In order to ward off future trouble, the lord deputy arrested Desmond, on a charge of intent to commit treason, and brought him prisoner to Dublin. Control of the Desmond lordship was left to the earl's brother, Sir John of Desmond, and a commission, composed of the lesser nobility of the province, was instituted to advise him and to see to the continued administration of justice pending the appointment of a president. [25]

So far, the actions of the lord deputy were in accordance with the wishes of the queen and should have gone a good way towards satisfying the earl of Ormond. Sidney was, however, increasingly frustrated because no president was being appointed, and he sought by other means to truncate the power of the lords of that province. He looked to the clause of his instructions that recommended him to seek the subjection of all chieftains holding land by Gaelic tenure and saw in this a means by which to deprive both Desmond and Ormond of their lordship over Gaelic septs. Work in this direction had been initiated by Sidney's predecessors, and, in June 1565, Donal McCarthy, chieftain of the mountainous region of south-west Munster, had surrendered his lands to the queen and was regranted them with the title of earl of Clancarr. Accepting this as a precedent, the lord deputy now recommended that the lesser nobility and gentry of Munster, notably Sir Maurice Fitzgerald of the Decies, Viscount Barry, Lords Roche, Coursey and Fitzmaurice, Sir Donagh McCarthy of Carberry and Sir Dermot McCarthy of Muskerry, should be severed from dependence on Desmond and receive their lands as 'free subjects owinge immediate service to your Majesty'. The deputy made no such blanket recommendation for the earldom of Ormond, but he did suggest that Sir Barnaby Fitzpatrick, baron of Upperossory, and O'Carroll, lord of Ely O'Carroll, should hold their lands independently of Ormond. Thus the deputy hoped, at least, to prepare the way for the arrival of a lord president in Munster.[26]

This, in fact, was Sidney's mistake because he revealed his intentions before he had the means to implement them, and without any assurance that the queen would appoint a president in Munster. Furthermore, the earl of Ormond was warned in advance and was in England seeking Sidney's recall. In his efforts Ormond solicited the aid of the earl of Sussex, in the hope that he would thus win the Norfolk faction to his side and so end the unanimity of the Privy Council on English policy towards Ireland. Sussex, during his term of office, had always enjoyed the support of Ormond and was, therefore, bound to give him a sympathetic hearing. The request for support was opportune, however, because it coincided with a particularly bitter outbreak at court between the earls of Leicester and Sussex. Leicester was using Sussex's past service in Ireland as a means of denigrating him and presented as evidence the descriptions provided by Sidney of the neglected condition of the country when he assumed office in Ireland. Sussex was taken aback at what he considered the complicity of Sidney with Leicester and availed himself of the opportunity provided by Ormond to launch an attack on Sidney's administration in Ireland. Thus the government of the country was reduced once more to the level of court intrigue, and Sidney was placed in the position of salvaging his reputation rather than pursuing his policy in Ireland.[27]

Now that the lord deputy had been frustrated in his effort to draw Munster under effective government control, there was nothing for it but to concentrate his energies against Ulster. Nobody in England could deny the urgency of curbing the power of O'Neill, and success would have enhanced Sidney's reputation in relation to that of the earl of Sussex. On his departure for Ireland in October 1565 the lord deputy had had assurances from Sir James Croft, the marquis of Winchester, and Sir William Cecil that they would give every support on council to bring about the overthrow of Shane. Even the queen despaired of ever winning Shane's subjection by persuasion and noted 'how farr different his deeds . . . be from that which he ought to be, or by his writings, letters and messages wold seme to be'. She was, nevertheless, willing to give one last chance to negotiations and was dissuaded from this only by the lord deputy's graphic description of the overweening pride and ambition of Shane who was alleged to have boasted that he 'never made peace with [the queen] but by her own sekyng'.[28]

The deputy's letter certainly galvanized the support of the Privy Council, and Cecil reported that 'every man's mind and judgement was inclyned to the extirpation of that proud rebel'. The secretary himself was confident that Shane's 'head shall be from his shulders before any crown can be made redy to make hym ether kyng or erle', but the queen was less sanguine. Instead of accepting the deputy's advice, Queen Elizabeth dispatched Vice-Chamberlain Sir Francis Knollys to Ireland to discover if Shane O'Neill might be removed by 'any other waye . . . than by open and actuall war'. Knollys was in full agreement with the lord deputy's assessment and endorsed also the method of attack that had been outlined by him. It was essential, according to Knollys, that garrisons be established in Ulster to wear down the power of O'Neill, and he recommended the first of these for Derry as a means of breaking O'Neill's domination of the O'Donnell lordship. Knollys strongly favoured the lord deputy allying himself with Shane O'Neill's enemies in Ulster, and he further recommended that ships be provided to cruise the north-east coast to prevent the arrival of Scots reinforcements to Shane. All of this, wrote Knollys, should precede an incursion into Ulster from the Pale.[29]

This was the scheme eventually decided upon in England, and the queen sanctioned £6,000 for the war. Extra troops were assigned to Ireland, under the command of Edward Horsey and Humphrey

Gilbert, and an expeditionary force of seven hundred, under the command of Edward Randolph, was sent to Lough Foyle by sea to establish a garrison. Thus the way was prepared for the lord deputy to march with the army through Ulster (17 September-12 November 1566), join Captain Randolph at Derry and provide him with reinforcements and provisions for the winter. It was not his purpose to track down O'Neill's army, but rather to destroy his country and encourage the chieftains in Ulster who were enemies of Shane. Callough O'Donnell was restored to the lordship of *Tir Conaill,* of which he had been deprived by Shane, and O'Hanlon, O'Reilly, McMahon and Maguire were all persuaded to forsake O'Neill. The lord deputy likewise received the submission of O'Connor Sligo and promised to establish him as an independent lord in his country. From Sligo the army proceeded to Athlone and from there returned to Dublin through Leinster.[30]

This was certainly a dazzling achievement, and Ireland stood in awe and admiration of the lord deputy. Shane O'Neill's prestige was greatly damaged by his failure to make a stand against the invading army, which passed through the heart lands of his country by his principal house at Benburb. Furthermore, much corn was destroyed, and Shane was forced to raze fortifications lest they fall into enemy hands. An even greater loss for Shane was being deprived of his *ur-ríghthe,* and the English ships cruising the coast prevented him from obtaining Scots reinforcements. It was clear, in the winter of 1566-7, that Shane O'Neill had suffered a major reverse, and that he could only recover his position by ousting the garrison at Loughfoyle and by reasserting his dominance over the O'Donnell territory. Fortune favoured him in the first of his objectives, since an accidental fire destroyed the fort at Derry and forced the garrison to withdraw to Dublin. This was more than offset, however, by the crushing defeat inflicted by the O'Donnells on Shane's army at the battle of *Fearsat Mór,* May 1567. The demented Shane, desperate for reinforcements, sought support from his bitter enemies, the Mac Donnells of Antrim, who, on 2 June 1567, hacked him to death at a dinner brawl. His head, 'pickled in a pipkin', was forwarded to Dublin and added to the embellishments over the gates of Dublin castle.[31]

The death of Shane O'Neill was particularly fortuitous for the lord deputy who was quickly losing the support and confidence of the queen and Privy Council. The government had continued to support the military campaign in Ulster, but at the expense of the remainder of the lord deputy's programme. The queen, as was noted, had vetoed the appointment of St Leger and had failed to nominate an alternative president of Munster. The lord deputy's request that an Englishman be appointed as master of the rolls was likewise ignored, as was his plea to have a court of star chamber instituted in Dublin. Neither was a chancellor appointed until May 1567 when Cecil, after innumerable petitions from the lord deputy, persuaded Dr Richard Weston, the aged dean of the court of the arches, to accept the position in Dublin. It was evident to all that the remuneration offered for administrative and legal positions in Ireland was not sufficient to attract English lawyers, but the queen was unwilling to concede higher stipends. Thus the lord deputy was frustrated in his ambition to see the common law in force throughout the island, and, despite exhaustive efforts in Ireland, he saw the success and fame that he had hoped for receding quickly. Instead, largely because of the efforts of Ormond and Sussex, his administration was becoming the subject of much criticism in England. It was this which forced Sidney to exclaim:

> I fynd my lot the strangest that ever lyghted on generall, servyng either Chrystyan or hethen prince [since] I . . . that desygned probably, proceded paynfully and ended hapely can not fynd that I am well alowed of.[52]

With the death of Shane O'Neill the lord deputy's hopes of fame and reward were revived. The queen forgot her earlier reservations about Sidney's rule in Ireland and was now effusive with praise for him and favourable towards further action in Ulster. Cecil was even more enthusiastic and wanted immediate action in securing Ulster for the crown. The lord deputy was by now sufficiently experienced to place little trust in any such promises and was, in any event, well aware that he no longer enjoyed the undivided support of the Privy Council. Furthermore, nothing had been conceded on the presidency of Munster which was so basic to Sidney's programme. Thus, instead of placing his trust in promises, the lord deputy requested a temporary recall to England so that he might reformulate his programme for the government of Ireland and secure assurance of support from the Privy Council. The lord deputy outlined a temporary scheme for garrisoning Ulster, and Humphrey Gilbert was appointed as governor of the province until Sidney returned. The commission that had been appointed to oversee the government of Munster was continued in office, and the lord deputy hoped that he would be able to persuade the English government to take decisive action in appointing a president. The lord deputy was thus able to depart for England on 9 October 1567, leaving Sir

William Fitzwilliam and Chancellor Weston to act as lords justices
in his absence.[33]

It can be said that in October 1567 Ireland was more peaceful and
prosperous than it had been for many years. The Pale had certainly
benefited from Sidney's two years in office, and common law
procedures were once again in operation there and were enforced
over an extended area, including Counties Leix, Offaly and
Kilkenny. The seneschals were likewise effective, and some form of
quarter sessions had been introduced into the Gaelic parts of
Leinster. In Ulster, Shane O'Neill had been overthrown, and the
province was governed by English military forces pending the
introduction of English colonies there. For the other provinces
Sidney had negotiated treaties with several of the lesser lords and
chieftains and had promised them letters patent for their lands in
return for an annual rent to the queen. To this end a group of Irish
lords, including O'Connor Sligo, John O'Reilly, Ross
McGeoghegan, O'Carroll, Patrick Fitzmaurice of Lixnawe and
Hugh O'Neill, accompanied the lord deputy to the English court.
Their presence indicated that Sidney was still determined to win
official sanction for his social policy and would seek a reindorsement
of his programme.[34]

The London government must have been quite satisfied with Sir
Henry Sidney's progress in Ireland, but the deputy himself was
conscious that he had not succeeded in his objectives. The overthrow
of Shane O'Neill and the improved conditions in the Pale were both
largely due to the deputy's efforts, but nothing had been achieved
towards creating the new institutions that Sidney considered so
essential for maintaining order in the outlying regions. Had these
been instituted, it is likely that Sidney would have resigned his post
in the knowledge that he had made a lasting impression on Ireland.
Now that he had won his recall to England, in October 1567, he
made it quite clear that he had no interest in serving in Ireland
unless there was a firm guarantee that the government would
support his propositions for the establishment of provincial
presidencies and the introduction of English colonies in the outlying
areas.

The deputy's resolve was strengthened by the waspish remarks of
both the earls of Sussex and Ormond who wished to detract from his
achievements. Sussex pointed out that it was the Mac Donnells, and
not Sidney, who had killed Shane O'Neill, while Ormond charged
the deputy with neglecting Munster and turning a blind eye to the
damage inflicted by Sir John of Desmond on the earldom of
Ormond. These accusations irritated Sidney, and he was further

displeased that the queen did not grant him any mark of honour for the services rendered.[35] This explains why, in May 1568, Sidney asserted that he would not be resuming his duties in Ireland and was confident that he would be appointed instead as treasurer of the queen's household. The queen thought differently and proclaimed, in April 1568, that she would not consider any replacement for Sidney as governor of Ireland. Thus Sidney was in a particularly strong position to dictate his terms to the queen when she called upon him to resume his duties in Ireland.[36]

The lord deputy's bargaining power was increased by the fact that he still enjoyed the support of many on the Privy Council who recognized their opportunity of dealing conclusively with the Irish situation. The earl of Leicester was, understandably, vociferous in supporting the policies outlined by his brother-in-law, and had stated, in 1566, that 'hit ys hie tyme to loke to that countrey and nothing in respect of her honor as sourlye behoveth more her Ma[jes]tie to deale substanaly in than in Ireland causes'. Sir Francis Knollys was undoubtedly in favour of pursuing the policy that he had previously endorsed, and the aged marquis of Winchester consider the time right for a forceful subjugation of Ireland.[37] The most enthusiastic advocate of an aggressive policy in Ireland was, however, the secretary, Sir William Cecil. It appeared to Cecil that the time was now at hand to draw Ireland to civility, and he considered that the full implementation of Sidney's programme would go far beyond his immediate objective which was to have Ireland pay its own way. He recognized the overthrow of Shane O'Neill as a major achievement, but he argued that the area would relapse into its former condition if some action were not taken to maintain control over the province. The secretary had, with the aid of maps, familiarized himself with the natural and political geography of Ulster, and he displayed a formidable knowledge of the Gaelic institutional system. He claimed that the security of the province could be guaranteed only by the expulsion of the Scots from Antrim and the establishment of colonies of Englishmen in their place. For the remainder of the province he recommended that the O'Neill overlordship should be ended and the lands over which Shane had ruled divided among the various members of the O'Neill sept and the heads of those septs which had been subservient to the O'Neills under the Gaelic disposition. Each individual was to hold a compact area from the crown in return for an annual rent, and it was to pass to his eldest son according to the law of primogeniture. To this extent, Cecil's proposals were a modification upon the surrender and regrant scheme, with the essential difference that the proposed arrangement favoured the lesser lords rather than the overlord under the Gaelic system. It was realistic also in that he recommended that the entire province of Ulster should first be declared crown property by act of parliament, and he acknowledged that the scheme could operate only when supervised by an English military presence in the province. The secretary advised that fourteen forts should be constructed to house garrisons of soldiers. The garrisons were to be located strategically so as to preserve the position of each lord who surrendered, and the garrisons on the coast were to aid the English colonists and end the Scots penetration of the province. Furthermore, Cecil recommended that the lord deputy should reside for some years at Armagh, to oversee the work, and should then be replaced by a military governor, or even a lord president, of Ulster.

Many of the ideas originated with Sidney, who must have been greatly encouraged by such enthusiastic support. The document drawn up by Cecil indicates the intelligent way in which he approached his responsibility for Ireland, and the fact that he dispatched a map maker, Robert Leith, to draw accurate maps of the relevant areas of Ulster augured well for the future. For the rest of the country, Cecil favoured the institution of presidencies in Munster and Connacht, but he made it clear that he expected that these agencies of government would be self-financing. The secretary was convinced that much land in those two provinces was by right crown property – either by escheat, by descent from extinct noble houses, or by the fact that it was monastic land – and he hoped that the presidents would establish proper title to this land and use it for maintaining themselves or for the support of English colonies in these provinces. Cecil's recommendations were, therefore, more than an endorsement of Sidney's programme, and it was becoming clear that colonization would play a more significant role than had originally been intended. It is significant that many proposals for the colonization of Ulster were being directed to Cecil from both Ireland and England, which suggests that others besides privy councillors were willing to support the final subjugation of Ireland.[38]

It certainly appeared to Sidney that he would have strong support at council level in implementing his programme in Ireland, and he was satisfied to resume duties when the final arrangements had been made for his return. The fact that he again petitioned the queen that he be continued as president in Wales suggests that he anticipated no difficulty in putting the new machinery into operation, and he expected that once installed it would be able to operate without him.[39] The London government displayed similar optimism, and much of the summer of 1568 was devoted to compiling fresh instructions for Sidney, and to the consideration of bills for the proposed Irish parliament. In his new instructions, Sidney was commissioned to bring Ireland to obedience, and was directed to summon parliament and enact bills that would further this process and increase revenue in Ireland. The underlying theme was financial; Sidney was to look more carefully to the leasing of crown lands and was to cut back on expenditure, particularly military expenditure. Ireland was now relatively quiet, and it was expected that the size of the army would soon be reduced. Ulster was, for the moment, exempt from these stringent measures: the queen looked forward to the final extinction of Scots from the province and instructed that the O'Neill lordship should be broken up either by force or persuasion. Queen Elizabeth refused to authorize all of the building programme suggested by Cecil, but she did approve of fortifications for Carrickfergus, Armagh and Olderfleet, and looked to the establishment of colonies on the north-east coast. Restraint marked the queen's recommendations for the remainder of the country, but she did authorize presidencies for Munster and, tentatively, for Connacht and encouraged the reclamation of crown land. The general purpose of her deputy's service, wrote the queen, was 'to have an universall obedience . . . by order of justice'. To this end she advised that bills be enacted for the construction of churches and the establishment of schools and a university, all at the expense of her subjects in Ireland. Thus she expected that the inhabitants of the country 'now ruyned and for lacke of lawe and justice leading a barbarous and sauvage lief, without knowledge of God or of us' would be brought to civility.[40]

It was evident from the instructions that the queen, no less than her advisers, recognized that there were two roads to civility; one through persuasion and education, the other through the more forceful methods that they intended to employ in Ulster. The secretary took it upon himself to recruit suitable candidates for the provincial presidencies, and legislation had been agreed upon for the organization of a system of education that would further the work of reform.[41] Thus the lord deputy was free to deal with the more urgent business in Ulster. Sidney set sail directly for Carrickfergus and devoted the months of September and October 1568 to organizing the northern province. He reminded the Gaelic chieftains of Ulster, notably Turlough Luineach O'Neill, of their subservience to the crown and, in renewing compacts with them, extorted a promise of an annual rent of 1d per acre. The lord deputy then turned his attention to the suggested fortifications in the province, but he insisted that the three authorized fortifications were insufficient for the control of the province and recommended eight, to be garrisoned with two thousand men. He foresaw that the queen would consider such an undertaking too costly, and he proposed that she should finance merely the construction of the forts while 'the nobilitie and principal gentlemen of England' would undertake to garrison them with a colony of two thousand men who would occupy the lands of north-east Ulster. The queen was unmoved by this suggestion, and Cecil reported that it was 'better lyked than thought lykly'. [42] Sidney was undaunted and persisted with his scheme for colonizing parts of Ireland with the support of private individuals in England. Thus a new chapter had opened in Irish history, and the ensuing experience served as a precedent not only for future plantations in Ireland but for colonization also in the New World.

4

The programme in action:
Colonization

Sidney's suggestion of 30 November 1568 was startling not because it recommended colonization as a means of bringing Ulster to subjection but rather because it provided greater scope for colonization than had originally been intended. Even the queen, as early as 1559, had acknowledged the propriety of expelling the Scots from north-east Ulster and substituting 'some number of English people' aided by 'some faythful captaynes or rulers'.[1]

Neither time nor money had then favoured the settlement of colonies in Ireland, but the English government continued to accept its desirability, and it is likely that the possibility of undertaking this task attracted Sidney to service in Ireland. It is important to remember that Sidney had spent the years 1553-6 as an emissary of Queen Mary in Spain, and would, most probably, have become acquainted there with the activities of the Spanish *conquistadores* in the New World. Furthermore, those Englishmen who wrote on colonization counted Sir Henry Sidney and his son Philip among their supporters, and both men were to invest money in English overseas ventures of the 1570s and 1580s.[2] While we can only speculate on the extent to which Sidney's views on the government of Ireland were influenced by his knowledge of Spanish practice in the New World, it is a fact that the first practical proposals for organizing colonies in Ulster coincided with the appointment of Sidney as lord deputy of Ireland. Furthermore, after every campaign through the provinces Sidney wrote of the desirability of settling English colonists not only in Ulster, but in strategic areas throughout the land. It was he, for example, who drew the government's attention to the trade pursued by Spanish merchants with the Munster towns, and he stressed that the southern lords obtained their arms through this source. This argument became more frequent during the 1570s when relations between England and Spain began to deteriorate. Sir Humphrey Gilbert, as well as Sidney, foresaw the possibility of Spain using the dissatisfaction of the Munster lords to further their own anti-English aims, promising 'to restore them to their ancyent tytells of honner, lybertie and papistrye'. Those of Gaelic origin, claimed Gilbert, were even more susceptible to foreign allurements because 'all nacyons doe naturallie mislike forraigne subjectyone ... all conquered people obeying rather for feare than throughe love as may p[ar]tlie appeare by Naples, Myllanne, Cecill [Sicily]'. Thus Gilbert was openly advocating what had frequently been suggested by Sidney and his followers, that the government should encourage colonization in the strategically dangerous Gaelic areas as well as in north-east part of Ulster inhabited by Scots intruders.³

It is true that Sidney and Gilbert desired to see loyal colonies settled along the Munster coastline, with fortifications constructed to ensure their security in the event of war. The lord deputy was equally anxious to see foreign craftsmen introduced into the towns of the Pale to encourage trade and industry there. One possible source of craftsmen, in 1567, was the Low Countries, and Sidney recommended that some of the Protestants who had fled to England from Flanders should 'be plantyd in Irelande'. A colony of refugees, estimated at forty families, was eventually settled at Swords, County Dublin, where they made 'diaper and tickes for beddes', as well 'as excellent good lether of deer skynnes goate and shepe felles as good as is made in Southwark'.⁴

Even more important in Sidney's view was the settlement of small colonies of Englishmen throughout the country, but especially in the vicinity of garrisons. The settlers would thus enjoy the protection of the garrisons and would, in turn, provide for the garrisons in times of crisis. The lord deputy envisaged such settlements as oases of civility in a desert of barbarism, and it is likely that he expected the colonists to act as sheriffs, justices of the peace and members of parliament. It was certainly to further such settlements that Sidney availed himself of every opportunity to declare confiscate the lands of any rebellious lord. A bill for the attainder of James Fitzgerald, the White Knight, who had died in rebellion in 1570, was immediately brought before the Irish parliament by the lord deputy. Furthermore, the activities of the map maker Robert Leith were concentrated upon those areas where it was hoped that land would become available for settlement. Afterwards Sidney prided himself

on how 'greedily were those lands sought for', and on the subject of
the White Knight one government official expected that 'the lands
being disposed to assured and well ordered men it will take away
occassion of stryff betwixt the Butlers and Geraldyns'.[5]

It was Sidney also who recognized the possibility of attracting to
the country individuals whose forebears had conquered land which
had since been lost to the Irish. The most notable of such colonizers
was Sir Peter Carew, of Devon, who claimed that his ancestors had
held land in Leinster and Munster which had been encroached upon
by trespassers for many generations. Carew was highly acceptable to
Sidney not only because their interests coincided, but also because
he was a renowned Dudley supporter and had suffered loss of
property and exile as a result of his complicity in Wyatt's rebellion.
Since 1554 he had adventured on the Continent, having fought on
the Huguenot side in the French civil wars, and returned to England
after the accession of Queen Elizabeth. His interest in Ireland was
purely material, but he received every encouragement from the lord
deputy who persuaded him, in 1568, to return with him to Ireland.[6]

Every facility was provided for Carew in searching out his title to
the barony of Idrone in County Carlow and to the manor of Maston
in County Meath. Idrone was an area held by the Kavanaghs who
were in turn subjects of Sir Edmund Butler, brother and heir to the
earl of Ormond. Such a claim raised the ire of the Butlers, and the
landowners of the Pale were equally disturbed by Carew's claim to
the manor of Maston which was the property of Sir Christopher
Cheevers, one of the more important gentry. In the light of this
hostility, Carew and his lawyer, John Hooker, argued that they
would not get a fair trial from an Irish jury. The lord deputy
intervened and had the case heard before himself and council sitting
with the judges of the bench. The verdict went in Carew's favour,
and the episode illustrates the lengths to which Sidney would go to
promote colonization in Ireland. Carew was satisfied to sell his title
to Maston to Cheevers, but he took up residence in Idrone and
instituted legal proceedings against Sir Edmund Butler for an
adjoining tract of land 'cauled the Dullough'. Afterwards, Carew
was appointed captain of the garrison at Leighlin Bridge, which lay
in the midst of his barony, and the government expected that he
would, in time, provide for the garrison, thus reducing the defence
budget. The arrangement, according to Carew, was in keeping with
'thorder devised and purposed for the plantynge of Englishe men yn
this countrie for the makinge and buyldying of townes which shalbe
replenyshed with all sortes of English artyficers'.[7]

Another area on which English colonies might be settled was the land of the monasteries in the outlying areas which had escaped the closure orders that followed upon the Reformation Parliament. Mention of the crown's title to such lands had been made by Cecil in his recommendations on Ireland in 1568, but the lord deputy needed no reminding of the possibilities. Even before his return to England, in 1567, Sidney had requested for himself a fee farm of all the monastic lands in Connacht. In return he offered to pay a rent of three hundred marks, promised to maintain the garrison at Athlone at his personal expense, and undertook to build a bridge over the Shannon at his own cost. The petition was rejected, and the lord deputy saw this as a curb on his colonization ambitions since he had expected 'never to have won gaine but fame'. After his return, in 1568, Sidney renewed his efforts to have Englishmen settled on the monastic lands, and a bill declaring monastic lands in Munster and Connacht to be crown property was passed by Sidney's parliament.[8]

Even before this, Jacques Wingfield was authorized by the deputy to discover 'what parcells of the queenes Majesties revenus within the counties of Corke and Lymeryck' were available, where he 'and other of Englysh byrth should thereof become tenants'. The lands in question were most probably monastic property which had hitherto been rented to such as the earl of Desmond but which was now reserved for 'Englishmen and such as be civilly brought up to be planted thereabouts, that by ther example others might be brought to embrace the good orders of this realm, and the obedience of the lawes thereof'.[9]

It is evident from what has been said that Sidney was determined to establish colonies of Englishmen throughout the country. Most of his projected settlements were relatively small, and he expected to introduce them gradually without causing any major disturbance of the indigenous population. What he proposed for north-east Ulster was different, in that he anticipated settling a colony two thousand strong there which would involve removing much of the existing population, recruiting colonizers in England, transporting them to the proposed settlement, and supporting them for at least a year until their first crop would be harvested. Such a massive undertaking could not have been got under way without long preparation, and even then the outcome would have been most uncertain, particularly in view of the usual gap between resolution and execution in sixteenth-century England.

That considerable thought, planning and recruitment had already taken place is quite certain, but it is difficult to discover the details of the proposed settlement in Ulster because of the deliberate concealment of the government's intentions prior to the death of

Shane O'Neill. The experience of the Leix-Offaly plantation had convinced the government, and particularly Sidney, that a purely military settlement was unworkable. [10] It was accepted, however, that a close liaison should exist between the colonizers and the army, and particular attention was paid to the recruitment of officers for the military campaign against Shane O'Neill. The captain of Carrickfergus, the existing English outpost in north-east Ulster, was William Piers who was quite acceptable to the lord deputy since he was strongly recommended by Leicester as 'valiant and given to serve' and had previously served under the command of Ambrose Dudley, earl of Warwick. [11] With the war in France at an end, Sidney was in a position to take command of many others who had served under Warwick but were now unemployed. Thus Sidney was assured of the loyal support of men who had known active service in an alien environment, and who were adherents to the Dudley family. The three captains, Nicholas Malby, Edward Horsey and Thomas Leighton, who accompanied Sidney to Ireland had participated in various conspiracies to further the Dudley family, had afterwards served in France under Ambrose Dudley and were, in 1565, recommended by the Dudleys for service in Ireland. [12] Their experience was quite standard for those in charge of the military enterprise in Ulster in 1566-7: Edward Randolph, or Randall, who commanded the fortifications at Derry, had been a participant in Wyatt's rebellion and had suffered exile during Queen Mary's reign; William Winter, who was in charge of the naval side of the Ulster campaign, had actually been arrested in 1554, as a result of his participation in Wyatt's rebellion, but was later released and served under Ambrose Dudley at Le Havre; Edward St Loe, who was second in command to Randolph, also belonged to a family noted for their allegiance to the Dudleys. [13] Most of these were landless adventurers who might have relished the opportunity of obtaining land in Ireland, but they were not suited to the actual task of colonization because they did not have control of tenants in England who could be persuaded to send their sons and relatives to occupy land in Ireland. It was evident, however, that such men would give enthusiastic support for a military campaign the end purpose of which was colonization, in the hope that they themselves would benefit from the spoils.

The appetites of the officers of the campaign of 1566-7 must have been whetted considerably when they discovered that the would-be colonizers were acquaintances of theirs, and in some cases former fellow conspirators. The first we hear of a formal proposal is in May 1565 when Sidney recommended the adoption of 'Capt Peers hys oppenyn ... to inhabit betwene them [the Scots] and the sea whereby with some shipping all hope of succor shalbe cut from them'.[14] He can only have been referring to an undated document entitled 'The Ulster Project' with the name of William Piers on the reverse side, which was probably presented to some members of the Privy Council when Piers was received at court prior to March 1565. This project revealed that a corporation of twelve had already been constituted for the purpose of settling a colony of '4,000 inhabitants of her naturall subjects' in the province of Ulster. The members of the corporation sought from the queen a loan of £20,000, the command of five hundred horse and one thousand foot, and the use of one galley, two brigantines and the royal ship *Phoenix*. With these resources they promised to oust the Scots from the province, to re-establish O'Donnell in his lordship of *Tir Conaill* and support him with a fortified garrison at Loughfoyle, and then, with the aid of O'Donnell, to overthrow Shane O'Neill and any other Irish chieftain who refused to acknowledge the queen. The corporation would in return have, from the queen, title to all lands lying eastward of the river Bann with authority 'to make estates in fee simple' among their followers.[15]

Not the least interesting aspect of the document is that the strategy outlined was that eventually decided upon by Sidney and Knollys and adopted by the government.[16] This suggests that Sidney was the author, since he would certainly have been pondering methods for subduing Ulster at the time that the document was compiled. The visit of Captain Piers to court could be explained by the necessity for specific details, but it is likely that Piers, because of his special competence in Ulster affairs, was one of the corporation of twelve. The fact that the *Phoenix* was requested specifically suggests that its master, William Winter, was associated with the venture. Winter was certainly acquainted with both Piers and Sidney and, more to the point, was willing and able to invest in speculative ventures, such as Hawkins's slaving voyage of 1562 and Frobisher's three voyages during the 1570s.[17]

We can only speculate about the association of Sidney, Piers and Winter with the corporation, but there is more concrete evidence of the participation of some English gentry. When Sidney launched his attack on Shane O'Neill there accompanied him 'many more gentlemen ... who being none of the army ... came over to serve this journey' into Ulster. One of these, Edward Vaughan from Wales was killed and another, a servant of Leicester, injured, but the principal personnel seem to have had interests other than fighting. Their leaders, according to Sidney, were 'Sir Arthur Champernoun,

Mr. John Champernoun his eldest brother's sonne and heire, and Mr. Philip Butsid, and divers other gentlemen, yeomen, and seamen of the west of England, desirous to take lands, and to inhabit in the north parts of Ireland'. It was, most likely, these who sponsored the colonial enterprise of 1565.[18]

The obvious common denominator of the group is their place of origin, Devonshire. We cannot establish conclusively the identity of those who accompanied the Champernouns and their cousin, Philip Budockshide of Butshed, but they were related to other notable West Countrymen who also appeared in Ireland in the 1560s – Humphrey Gilbert, Sir Peter Carew, Sir Richard Grenville and Edmund Tremayne. We can be virtually certain that Gilbert was one of the original corporation since, in 1567, he had become recognized as their official agent. The queen supported, and Sir Francis Knollys proposed, that Gilbert be appointed military commander in Ulster to enable him 'joyning with his frendes of the west . . . to plant habitacon there of Ynglishe men with reasonable conditions', and to lure 'artisans and sea fysshers to plant uppon the Ban', at Strangford and Lough Foyle. When Champernoun revisited Ireland in July 1567 he went 'to see . . . the contrey' and to have 'furder conference' with Gilbert on the subject of colonization. The recommendation of Knollys was in fact accepted, and when Sidney departed for England in October 1567 he left Gilbert in charge of the Ulster garrison.[19]

It is obvious that the government wanted full co-operation between the soldiers and the colonizers. This was a realistic expectation in view of the fact that the colonizers, no less than the army, were noted adherents to the Dudleys, spanning from Wyatt's rebellion in 1554, in which the Carews and Champernouns were conspicuously active, to the wars in France, where many of them had volunteered to serve under Ambrose Dudley. Furthermore, they had displayed the same adventurous spirit as the soldiers and representatives of this closely knit group, as also their neighbours and acquaintances Drake and Hawkins, had participated in most recent military or exploratory enterprises ranging from Florida to Hungary, but most notably on the Huguenot side in the French Wars of Religion.[20]

How many or which members of this group came to colonize in Ulster in 1566 is not certain. All the evidence does signify, however, that it was some of their number who sponsored the 'Ulster Project', and, while some others may have joined them, it was the western gentlemen who showed most anxiety to carve out lands for themselves in Ulster and to lead four thousand of their Devonshire

tenants to inhabit there. They were particularly suited to the
purpose not only because of their close relations with the army in
Ulster, but also because of the proximity of Devon to Ireland, and
the availability of shipping at Dartmouth to make the crossing
possible. The fact that so many of them belonged to the Dudley
faction suggests that Sidney was the principal organiser and
probably the author of 'The Ulster Project'. There is further
evidence to show that he wished to expand the scope of the
enterprise by inviting English merchants to join in the expedition. It
was noted in the first chapter that merchants from Westchester and
Bristol traded with the Irish in Ulster and availed themselves of the
valuable salmon fishing in Lough Foyle and the mouth of the Bann.
Now that a colony was about to be established, Sidney was anxious
that provision should be made for the settlement of merchants, and
he had been sued for 'the fyshyng of the Ban and other waters in that
provynce . . . by Valentine Browne and by the Chestrys merchants of
Brystall, both suffycyent men'. Browne was favoured by Sidney
because he had had military experience at Berwick and would
therefore be 'able to do good in thys cuntre more wayes than one'.[21]

The other natural wealth that north-east Ulster provided was
timber, and it appears that some businessmen in England were
enticed to join in the colonization venture so that they might exploit
this resource. Two representatives of English business concerns
appeared in Ireland in the years 1566-7, and both displayed
particular interest in the woods of the Dufferin, County Down. One
of these, Thomas Lancaster, was an agent of the earl of Leicester
who had mining interests at Skeddagh in Cumberland and wished,
on behalf of that company, to obtain cheap Irish timber 'at fyve
shellings the thousand after London byllett'. It is evident that the
lord deputy had been previously consulted on the matter and had
been promised 'for the xxiiiith part of a parte that he should be
one of your companye'. The other, John Denton, who described
himself as a merchant-tailor of London, was representing 'the
companie of mineralls in the north'. Cecil appears to have been a
member of this company, but the guiding hand seems to have been
that of Lionel Duckett, alderman of London, who again was assured
by Sidney that he would be facilitated in obtaining wood and coal
for the company's mines in the north of England.[22]

The various details suggest that Sidney's was the master mind
behind the colonization project, and we can get a reasonably clear
idea of the procedures that he hoped to follow. He expected the army
to clear the way for a settlement of Ulster, and, like Cecil, he wished
to break up the former O'Neill lordship among the lesser chieftains

and the collateral branches of the O'Neill sept. The new arrangement was to be upheld by the garrisons that he hoped to establish in stragetic locations, and it is evident that he foresaw the captains of garrisons fulfilling the same role as the seneschals in the Gaelic areas of Leinster. It appears, therefore, that the lord deputy expected continued government support for the garrisons, but he was confident also that the soldiers would be able to obtain sustenance from the crown lands in the province. This explains why, in 1567, it was proposed to 'cause speciall inqre and survey to be made of all abbey lands and all demeane lands belongyng to the earldom of Ulster'. Some of these lands were also to be disposed of to English settlers who would act as a reserve force for the garrisons and be a model of civil living to the Irish. The lord deputy also hoped that merchants and artisans from England would establish permanent towns at the mouths of the Rivers Bann and Foyle. [23]

It is evident, therefore, that, as far as the O'Neill lordship was concerned, Sidney was consciously limiting himself to a restricted programme. The alternative to this was 'to banysh them quyte and unpeople the soyle by inducement of colonyes', but while he considered this 'optable and fesyble' he admitted that it would necessitate an expensive and sustained military campaign which the queen was unlikely to support. [24] The intensive settlement of Englishmen was, therefore, to be confined to the area east of the Bann which was 'no parte of Tirone'. There was already a strong military presence there in 1567, and the lord deputy expected that the soldiers would force out the Scots settlers and push those of Irish origin to the west of the Bann. The land would thus be left vacant for the Devon group, each member of which Sidney expected would 'aventure to take iii or iiii hundred or moor mete men, having thereof some artificers, some husband men, and having victells of the Q. Mary for vi months to go into Ulster, and to gett some portion of land there and to have it to them selves by state of inheritance'. Besides victuals, he advised the colonizers to bring 'some large porcon of otes and barley' for sowing, as well as implements 'as if they shoulde imagine to finde nothinge here but earthe, and in dede litell els shall they finde savinge only fleshe, and some beasts for caring of the grounde'. It is clear that Sidney did nothing to disguise the difficulties involved, but he was assured that the effort would be well rewarded, since he estimated that gentlemen 'for one yeres charge, and that no greater than they should be at by lyving in England, may purchase to them and to their heirs for ever a competent and sufficient lyveng'. [25]

This certainly shows that Sidney envisaged the Devon group

carrying the major brunt in the colonization venture. The spoils in Ulster were not to be exclusively theirs, however. Cecil wanted to allow 'any subjects in Ireland' to join in the venture, and all wanted the earl of Kildare at 'his owne chardge' to assert his title to Lecale in County Down. Besides these, it was expected that all redundant soldiers in Ireland, especially those who were 'good husband men, plowe wryghtes, kart wryghtes and smythes', should be given the option 'eyther to take habitation yf they be hable, or els to staye and serve there under sotche gentlemen as shall inhabyte there'. After the landed settlement was secure, it was expected that the English merchants would follow up, 'intrenchyng themselves' in suitable locations with a view towards the eventual development of 'haven townes' in Ulster.[26]

This effort is important, therefore, in that it indicates the sources from which aid was expected in establishing colonies in Ireland. Since Ireland's principal commodity was land, it was hoped that the gentry, and more particularly the landless younger sons, would be attracted to colonial ventures in Ireland. The Leix-Offaly experience had made it clear that little could be expected of soldiers as colonizers, but it was hoped that some of the soldiers already in Ireland, and especially those on pensions, would be absorbed into the colony. The third group that was expected to involve itself in Irish colonization was the merchant class, particularly the wealthier merchants in London, who had company interests that might be furthered by access to Irish raw materials, and merchants in the western towns of England that had existing trading interests in Ireland. It is significant that Sidney succeeded in attracting the attention of Lionel Ducket to Ireland, since he was one of London's leading merchants and was to become lord mayor of London in 1573. More important was the fact that he was one of the foremost among England's early overseas adventurers, as well as being prominent in the formation of companies. He had, for example, joined with William Winter and Sir Thomas Lodge in financing John Hawkins's first slaving expedition in 1562, and in 1568 was appointed governor of the Company of Mines Royal. He was thus previously acquainted with some of those who were sponsoring colonization in Ireland, and it is probable that he was related by marriage to Thomas Leighton of Shropshire who, as was mentioned, accompanied Sidney to Ireland in search of his fortune. In thus bringing about an amalgam of merchant and gentry interests, Sidney was anticipating the coalition that backed the development of English enterprise and empire during the later sixteenth century.[27] In forming a corporation to direct the colonization in

Ulster, those responsible were employing a method that was becoming increasingly popular in English business organization, and that was to be used in the major plantation enterprises in Ireland and North America. For these reasons the Ulster venture can be seen as a major advance in English colonial practice. That is was regarded as such in England is indicated by the moral, if not financial, support that it obtained from so many privy councillors; William Cecil, Sir James Croft, Sir Francis Knollys, the earl of Leicester and the marquis of Winchester all made it known that they approved of the method by which 'the realme of Ireland wilbe well mayneteyned without any charge to the queene's majestie out of this realme with some yerelie profite'.[28]

It appears that the colonization venture would have got under way had the queen been willing to continue a garrison in Ulster. Now that Shane O'Neill had been defeated and the immediate threat to the Pale had been removed, she refused to finance the construction of forts and to increase the military strength in Ulster. The ardour of the West Countrymen dissipated when it became clear that crown support was not forthcoming, and by June 1570 Sidney reported that 'none will come from home, but uppon some certen gaine and assurance to them and their successors', and also 'some entertaignement to begin withall'.[29] It was in recognition of the fact that the 'Ulster project' had aborted that Sidney, in 1568, called upon Cecil to persuade 'the nobilitie and principall gentlemen of England' to undertake the task of colonizing north-east Ulster.

Cecil too was alarmed at the waning prospects of a self-supporting colony and feared that the effort of the previous years would now be lost. In desperation, he recommended as colonizers those lieutenants and captains who had formerly served in Ireland, but the lord deputy dismissed the suggestion on the ground that soldiers were too poor 'either to fortifie themselves in strength, or to get out the frutes of the earthe'. The last hope for a privately sponsored colony was Sir Thomas Gerrard, of Lancashire, who actually made the journey to Ireland. His demand for the command of five hundred royal troops ensured rejection by the queen, and so Sidney was forced to accept Cecil's suggestion that lands in Ulster should be granted to retired or redundant soldiers.[30]

A precedent for a private-soldier colony had already been established by Sir Nicholas Bagenall – the marshal of the army in Ireland – who maintained an outpost at Newry and controlled the surrounding country-side. Now that all else had failed, Sidney proposed that Captain Nicholas Malby should settle in McCartan country, that Sir Peter Carew and one Henry Palmer should similarly take up posts by the sea-coast, and that some of the captains on pension should join them on the understanding that they would enjoy 'some helpe to beginne with'.[31] Thus Sidney's ambition was limited to securing the sea-coast and excluding the Scots mercenaries. He was still convinced that 'thinhabitants presentlie thereof of the Irisherie will never be good subjectes', and he advised those who wished to undertake the task of colonizing 'to fortifie, inhabit, and to mayntene tillage that within tyme may beare the chardges'. More volunteers came forward, such as Thomas Chatterton and his brother, of Wiltshire, who tried to settle in O'Hanlon country, and Captains Thomas Browne and Thomas Borrow who first settled in south County Down, and later sought a grant of the Ards peninsula.[32]

The government was none too enthusiastic about these offers, because the volunteers lacked the resources necessary for a successful plantation and required too many privileges from the government to compensate them for their effort. The grants were never officially sanctioned, but the government was happy to continue the colonizers in Ulster to maintain an English presence there until such time as a comprehensive settlement might be made. Nothing was done, however, to maintain the position gained by the English west of the River Bann, and thus Turlough Luineach O'Neill, who had succeeded Shane as lord of Tyrone, was able to build up his position, particularly by importing Scots mercenaries. The rise of Turlough eventually convinced the government to resume the conquest of Ulster. The colonizers who came in 1572 were confronted by a more formidable Irish resistance than had existed earlier, but they could also benefit from the knowledge and experience of people, such as Chatterton, who had settled in Ulster. Furthermore, they could draw upon the experience gained from the experiments of 1565-7, and from the attempts to settle colonies in Munster during the intervening period.

The government, as was noted, was anxious to settle Englishmen along the coast of south-west Munster, but little action was taken because of the greater urgency in dealing with Ulster. It appears that the lord deputy intended the president of Munster to make arrangements in that province, which would explain Sidney's anxiety to secure St Leger's appointment. If such was the case Sidney was not disappointed, since, from the outset, St Leger set himself to gaining a foothold in the province. His being dismissed from office did little to frustrate his purpose, and it appears that by 1569 he had already organized a settlement in Kerrycurrihy, an area west of Cork City. This manor seems to have come into St Leger's possession by virtue of the fact that the earl of Desmond while detained in England was dependent on St Leger's hospitality, and thus became considerably indebted to that family. The transfer of the manor settled the debt, and Sir Warham seems to have added to it by laying claim to church land in an adjoining area called Tracton. From this base it was hoped to win over and colonize a considerable part of south-west Munster. Furthermore, as we saw, Jacques Wingfield wished to emulate St Leger by gaining title to church land in Munster on which he hoped to settle English colonists, while Peter Carew also had longing eyes on Munster. It was St Leger, however, who continued as the organizer in chief in Munster.[33]

By February 1569 St Leger had made a significant settlement at Kerrycurrihy and had been joined by Richard Grenville who had brought at least 106 followers to Munster with him, among them the adventurer Thomas Stukeley. Official benediction was given to the enterprise when Grenville was appointed sheriff of County Cork, and the selection of Sir John Pollard to replace St Leger as president in Munster is a further indication of government support. Pollard, was, like Grenville, from the West Country, an avowed supporter of the Dudleys, and could not have been ignorant of the plans for colonization in Munster. Pollard, as it happened, was forced to reject the office due to ill health, but the arrival in Munster, in 1570, of Edmund Tremayne, who had come to join Pollard, provides us with some evidence of their intentions. Edmund Tremayne was a younger brother of the twins Nicholas and Andrew Tremayne, of Devon, who had been hailed as heroes after their deaths in battle at the siege of Le Havre. He claimed to have been left greatly in debt by his brothers, and his purpose in coming to Munster was 'to set to work to ease that burden broughte by those debts', so that he might 'hold up that familie, and in myne old daies to eat myne own bread in mye own house'. The only prospect for enrichment that Munster had to offer him was land, and it appears that he had hoped to join with Pollard and 'my cousen Grenfelde [Grenville]' in 'the worthiest enterprise that ever was attempted'. Tremayne, however, had no resources of his own, and when Pollard, and the prospects of an office in the Munster provincial council, failed him, he gladly accepted the post of personal secretary to Sidney, and was thus removed from the Munster scene.[34]

St Leger, however, was not so dependent on Pollard and following the example of 'The Ulster Project' had formed a corporation to undertake the colonization of south-west Munster. The official agent of the newly formed body, and one who was to feature prominently

in all attempts at colonization in Ireland up to 1576, was Jerome
Brett, probably an employee of the St Leger family since he too was
from Leeds, Kent. The other members, besides St Leger and
Grenville, were Edward St Loe, Thomas Leighton, Humphrey
Gilbert, Jacques Wingfield, Gilbert Talbot, son of the earl of
Shrewsbury, and one Mr Evenfeld. Froude, writing in 1870, cited
evidence that is no longer to be found, purporting that a 'number of
gentlemen . . . twenty seven in all', chiefly from Somerset and Devon
– 'Gilberts, Chichesters, Carews, Grenvilles, Courtenays' were
participants. Even without the Froude statement, it is evident that
the West Country group, who had originally involved themselves in
north-east Ulster, had now shifted their interests to the richer lands
in Munster. St Leger was the only real outsider, and even he was a
cousin of the group through a cadet branch of the family that had
settled in Devonshire. That the government in Dublin approved of
the switch in interest is indicated by the transfer of Gilbert, in
October 1569, from command of the forces in Ulster to colonel of the
government troops in Munster.[35]

Again following the example of 'The Ulster Project', the leaders of
this expedition sought support from English merchants. The most
extravagant assertion of merchant involvement comes from a
Spanish spy in London who claimed, in June 1569, that 'a company
of thirty of the richest of the London merchants had also made an
agreement with the queen that they will conquer a certain part of the
country [Ireland] the lordship of which shall belong to them on
payment of a tribute, and they are already preparing an expedition'.
There is little outside evidence to substantiate such an allegation,
but the presence in Munster, between 1571-4, of Edward Castelyn, a
London merchant, suggests that it contains an element of truth.
Castelyn had varied interests, being a merchant-adventurer, and
afterwards was to become a member of the Muscovy Company in
1580, and a founder member, in 1575, of the Society of Mineral and
Battery Works. He claimed that he had been invited to Munster by
his 'deare ffrende Sir Warham Sentleger, Knight, three years past
[January 1571] to repaire into this parties here to drawe traffique of
marchandiz wheare souiche neede ys'. Another Englishman, John
Corbine, a London shipowner-cum-pirate, was present in Munster
in 1567 and also supported the idea of a coastal colony to eliminate
the Spanish trade in that area.[36]

These two references constitute proof of some merchant interest in
the Munster colony. Furthermore, the various petitions by Brett and
Gilbert gave full play to the mercantilist advantage of channelling
Munster produce into the English, rather than the Spanish, market,

and to the control that England might exercise over transatlantic traffic. Attention was also devoted to the possibility of finding mineral wealth in Munster, and, without any obvious reason, expectations were high that gold and silver would be found in abundance. This, added to the survey for minerals conducted by John Denton in Munster in 1567 and the presence of Castelyn from 1571-4, suggests that those who founded the Society of Mineral and Battery Works may have backed the venture; Cecil, Leicester and Sidney, as well as Castelyn, were members of that society, as was Francis Agard, a member of the Dublin council. There is also evidence of some exclusiveness in the enterprise, because when John Denton sought to survey the woods and mineral wealth of Munster on behalf of Lionel Duckett he was arrested for three months by St Leger 'for non other cause than that dyvers sormises were devised'.[37]

It would appear, therefore, that the pattern of organization followed closely upon that of 'The Ulster Project'. The most aggressive element was the gentry who hoped to gain land in Munster, but they were also successful in arousing interest in the scheme among English business circles. The government in Dublin was obviously favourably disposed towards the infant colony at Kerrycurrihy, and some at least of those holding high political office in England were regarded as supporters. Sidney was satisfied that 'great good' would 'cum of the offer made by the gentlemen to inhabyte Munster', and the organizers were so confident of Cecil's support that in 1573 they wanted his eldest son, Thomas, to be put in charge of the enterprise. The organizers, however, met with difficulty in persuading the queen to grant them support, which was also the chief obstacle in the way of 'The Ulster Project'.[38] Their approach was different in that they themselves offered to raise three thousand men in England who would eventually settle on the lands, but who would serve initially as soldiers in the queen's pay 'at tenne thousande markes yerlye under her ordynary allowance'. The organizers saw that there were two stages in colonization: winning the land from the indigenous inhabitants and inhabiting it with English settlers. They differed from the leaders in Ulster in that they would have the same people perform both functions, but not even this convinced the parsimonious queen that further expenditure was warranted. She preferred to compromise with the Gaelic chiefs in south-west Munster rather than authorize a complete conquest of Munster,[39] and therefore the plans of St Leger and Brett were stillborn.

The failure of this effort was important in that it made would-be colonizers look for alternate means of raising finance. In 1573 Sir

John Perrott, who succeeded to the presidency in Munster and who favoured colonization in that province, recommended 'an extraordinary course be taken to have monny', since England would not provide money 'for reforming of the disordered partes of this realme'. This suggests that it was he who was behind the revival of the project in 1573, when an offer was made to Cecil (by then Lord Burghley) to renew the effort at plantation in Munster. The anonymous author and 'J[erome] B[rett]' were the organizers, and they wished the letters patent to be issued in the names of Mr T[homas] C[ecil], the captain of the guard, Mr Thomas Gorge and 'Myself'. Other interested parties were named as St Leger Mr J[erome] B[rett] and Sir John of Desmond 'who ys in deed the pryncypall mocyoner of the sewete'. The inclusion of Sir John of Desmond is interesting, and indicates that the Fitzgeralds had no objection to English colonies in the province, provided that it was their enemies to the south-west who lost their lands. The new device for raising working capital was that two of the members would mortgage their lands in England and put the money to use in organizing a colony in Ireland. Nothing came of the offer, but it is significant that the financial method suggested by the anonymous author was that employed by the earl of Essex in his effort to colonize north-east Ulster.[40]

The St Leger exploit is thus important because it highlighted the difficulties involved in colonization and forced future colonizers to consider the problem of raising money before they set out on their venture. It was significant also in that the infant settlement at Kerrycurrihy struggled along until the 1580s when it did become the basis for the Munster plantation. Most of those who wished to join with St Leger in the 1560s and 1570s renewed their interest when land became available after the confiscation of the Desmond estates and were then rewarded for their earlier efforts. A study of this unsuccessful attempt is important also because it gives us an insight into the minds of those who wished to profit from the exercise, and it shows that the motives of the colonizers were not completely in accord with the wishes of the government.

Every petition for letters patent for land in Munster stressed the 'profit and comoditie' that would accrue to the government as a result of a settlement in Munster. They emphasized the fact that their request was in accord with the government's wishes to have a settlement on the Munster coast as a means of preventing the Spaniards from trading in the province. Their request, however, far exceeded the desires of the government, since they wanted title to all the coast and a monopoly of fishing rights from Ross to the Blaskets,

with a right to trade with any country not at war with England.
Besides this they wanted title to all the lands held by the Gaelic Irish
in Munster, naming specifically the lands of the earl of Clancarr
[McCarthy Mor], the McDonoughs, the O'Callivans, the
O'Sullivans, the O'Driscolls, the Mahonds [Mahoneys] and the
McSwynes. Their pretext for this was that most of these had joined
in rebellion with James Fitzmaurice Fitzgerald in 1569, and were
thus liable to lose their lands. [41] What they did not acknowledge was
that the rebellion had, in part, been provoked by the claims of St
Leger and Sir Peter Carew to land in south-west Munster. Instead of
lamenting the rebellion, they welcomed it as an opportunity for their
own enrichment. That they hoped to provoke further rebellions in
the province is suggested by their claim to all lands that should fall
to the crown 'within the space of tenne yeres . . . by office, attaynder
or otherwise'. What they were really looking for was authorization to
establish themselves as freebooters, and they made their request
appear attractive by the assertion that 'thies contries now possessed
by disobedient people assistinge everie rebellion to the disglorie of
god and greate dislike of your Maiestie shalbe inhabited by naturall
Englishe men'. The fact that they also wanted power for 'the
chieften of the company' to 'institute and ordeyn any wholsom and
necessary lawes' for the colony, and the right to exercise martial law
throughout the entire province of Munster, suggests that what they
really wanted was freedom from the traditional restraints of English
society. [42]

The other attraction that Ireland held was an opportunity for
quick enrichment and advancement. This is clearly evident from
their desire to be exempt from trading restrictions and to have
authority to wage war as a means of acquiring land. Besides this
they wanted a right to exploit the timber on their lands which they
obviously regarded as a quick cash crop, and for the land itself they
requested 'lycense to allynate or dispose by will or otherwyse any
parte or parcell of the premisses to any sufficient Englishman that
shall enhabit there'. When this was denied them they still pleaded
their right to return at will to England and 'not to be made as it were
banished men from their naturall country'. These claims must have
done much to convince the Privy Council that the members of St
Leger's company were not so much concerned with becoming 'the
lanterne and countenance of all cyvilitie within that province' as
with earning a quick penny in Ireland and, thus enriched, returning
to England leaving their lands to any willing English lessee. [43] In the
light of this information the government could place little credence
in their promises to build towns and fortresses at their own expense

and to pay an annual rent and feudal dues to the crown. This lack of confidence may explain why letters patent were never drawn up for St Leger and his company, and the government chose to compromise with the Gaelic chieftains rather than let loose a group whose hope was that the Irish propensity to rebel would soon entitle the queen to the entire country and, thus, present themselves with an opportunity for personal enrichment.

Since the arrangements for the proposed settlement in Munster were less confidential than those for Ulster, we can get a better idea of the type of colony that it was hoped to establish there. The organizers had no objections to continuing 'the naturall inhabitants of that coontrey' as cultivators of the soil, so long as they should have a 'sufficient noomber of Englishmen for the guarde and defence of suche as shall manure and inhabit the lands'. The government, however, would have preferred a completely English settlement, and, therefore, St Leger's company contracted to introduce three thousand Englishmen whom they hoped to impress and hire in Cornwall, Somerset, Gloucestershire and the counties of South Wales. Some of the organizers expected to raise recruits from among their own tenants, but they expected to conscript the majority in the designated counties. [44] The colony of three thousand was to be composed of three distinct elements. The first group was to consist of fifteen hundred men aged between twenty-five and thirty-five years, 'brought upp as servants in husbandry', whom it was hoped to continue as farm labourers in Ireland with a prospect of obtaining a copyhold of sixty acres of land after three years' service. The second group was to consist of seven hundred and fifty married men between the ages of thirty and fifty 'having no freeholdes in England and being mete to have husbandry holdes of iii ploughlands [360 acres]' in Ireland. The third group was to consist of tradesmen, including ploughwrights and fishermen, who were to receive wages and enough ground to feed three cattle and two horses or to sow gardens.

Thus we can see that the intention was to reconstruct in Ireland a society modelled on that of England. The eight or ten gentlemen who organized the project would obviously become the squires, each having a large manor occupied by farmers, labourers and tradesmen divided in the ratio of two labourers to one farmer to one tradesman. Any other gentleman who was 'disposed to go and inhabit in Ireland of his owne charges' would obtain one plough-land for every two men 'brought up in husbandry' that he brought with him, but his manor was not to exceed forty plough-lands [4,800 acres] which he would divide into copyholds and leases at his pleasure. There was, as yet, little talk of constructing nucleated settlements, but we see in this the first effort at designing the ideal colony, an activity that became more common in England as the sixteenth century progressed.[45] It is evident that they hoped to lure to Ireland those who were under-employed in the English country-side, and the prospect of obtaining a copyhold of sixty acres of fertile land would certainly have tempted many labourers in England who were living at subsistence level. They, no less than the organizers of the company, were being presented with a prospect of social advancement that would never have come within their grasp in England.[46] The freedom from social restraints, even at this level, was something that the government did not fully endorse, and it is significant that Cecil wished to have a restriction on the amount of land available to those who did not already occupy some land in England. It is evident, therefore, that the government was not convinced by the rhetoric of colonization and would have preferred it had the organization been in more responsible hands.[47]

The Munster effort failed principally because of problems in securing financial support to cover the initial cost. St Leger, following the example of 'The Ulster Project', requested a loan of £10,000 from the government and even offered as security lands in England valued at £15,000. Another desperate suggestion was that every parish in certain counties in England should supply either a horseman or a foot-soldier for the colony and support him for two years, the money to be repaid after the colony began to show a profit. This was, however, a cumbersome scheme, and never had any real hope of success.[48] The activities of the western gentry, however, kept alive the idea of colonization in Ireland and aroused people in England to the possible advantages to be gained. The Privy Council was still seriously interested as is indicated by the formation of a special committee to deal with Irish affairs. The first of these, appointed in December 1567, was composed of Lord Keeper Bacon, Sir Francis Knollys, Walter Mildmaye and William Cecil. In the next committee, June 1568, Leicester and Northumberland replaced Mildmaye and Knollys, while the majority of councillors devoted sporadic attention to Ireland. During the summer of 1571, following Sidney's return to England after he had resigned the deputyship of Ireland, 'many consultations' were conducted at council level 'to relieve her Majesty's excessive charges in Ireland, and yet to reduce that country into better order'. The subject under discussion was obviously colonization, and the appointment of a new subcommittee, in June 1571, composed of advocates of a rigorous forward policy – Sidney, Knollys, Croft and Secretary Sir Thomas

Smith – was a prelude to a more determined colonization effort. That the earl of Leicester was at one with them is indicated by his unqualified praise of the recent 'great efforts' of these Englishmen who 'at their own costs and charges have offered to carry numbers of people into that cuntrey and to plant them there with owt doing injurye to any man, but only to inhabytt such places as be lawfully and justly her Majestys'.[49]

This was undoubtedly the first blast in support of the offer made by Sir Thomas Smith to undertake the settlement of a colony in the Ards Peninsula in County Down.[50] Malby and Chatterton, as previously mentioned, were seeking grants, respectively of McCartan and O'Hanlon countries, and the tract of land sought by Smith was stretching from Belfast southwards into the Ards Peninsula. These were adjoining territories which in turn linked up with Bagenall's settlement at Newry, and it was envisaged that the network would constitute 'a wall to the English pale' and a protected coastline for north-east Ulster.[51] This was certainly following Sidney's overall scheme for Ulster, and a grant to Walter Devereux, earl of Essex, of the remainder of Ulster lying east of the River Bann was a further continuation of the policy. All of these attempts met with total failure, but they have attracted considerable attention from historians because of the support that they received in England, and because of their contribution to colonial theory and practice.

Sir Thomas Smith, as has been mentioned, was one of England's leading intellectuals. Having been professor of civil law at Cambridge he was afterwards employed as a public servant firstly as ambassador to France and then as a privy councillor (from 5 March 1571) and secretary of state (from 13 July 1572). His study of the classics had aroused his interests in colonization, and it may have been he who inspired one of his students, Richard Eden, to translate part of Peter Martyr's *De Orbe Novo* as a means of prompting Englishmen to emulate the Spaniards in the New World. He had certainly maintained an interest in Ireland and had always championed Sidney's efforts to promote colonization there. His absence in France had prevented Smith from taking an active part in any of the earlier ventures, but on his return he decided to set an example for his fellow councillors to follow, and had, by 16 November 1571, received letters patent entitling himself and his natural son Thomas to the Ards Peninsula. Like the earlier organizers, Smith joined with 'associates' with a view to establishing a colony of 'naturall Englishemen borne . . . at their own charges and perils'. Once the patent was issued, a broad sheet and, afterwards, a pamphlet were published soliciting support for, and stressing the propriety of, the expedition.[52]

Smith differed from the others in that he did not seek financial support from the government but depended rather upon his own prestige to attract private investors to speculate in the venture. For a start, he was confident of support from fellow council members, but especially from Leicester, Cecil, Sir James Croft and Sussex. There is evidence that Cecil invested in the venture, and the younger Smith considered that in undertaking the task he was in Leicester's service. Those who had been involved in the Munster exploit were favourably disposed towards the new venture. Sir John Perrott regretted that the Ards was so far removed from Muster, but Jerome Brett and Sir Peter Carew were not discouraged by distance and joined in Smith's enterprise.[53]

Such hardened campaigners were no doubt welcomed by Smith, and he appealed also to those, such as Sir Valentine Browne, who had earlier expressed interest in Irish colonization. Smith also attracted to Ireland newcomers, such as Edward Knollys, son of Sir Francis Knollys, and in his printed message he appealed particularly to the younger sons of the gentry to join with him and seek their fortunes. He intended that they should actually execute the mission, but he hoped for financial support from their seniors. The example of Smith himself was typical; he invested heavily in the enterprise but never visited Ireland himself, intending that his son should lead the expedition and thus win fame and fortune. It was his intention that 'other noblemen who better may' would follow the example, since neither he nor his son 'had lands or tenants enough to compel to it, nor authority to muster any man'.[54]

In this Smith was recognizing a difficulty that had similarly confronted St Leger, but he sought to overcome it by the novel method of the printed propaganda campaign. The pamphlet and broadsheet must have generated great interest throughout England, and Smith appealed to merchants to invest in his enterprise, as well as to younger sons of the gentry whom he called upon to muster tenants from their fathers' estates and lead them as colonists to Ireland. Professor Quinn has drawn our attention to the novelty of this device which served as an example for future colonization ventures in Ireland and the New World. In the short term it served Smith's purpose well, and between seven and eight hundred men assembled at Liverpool during the spring of 1572 awaiting embarkation to Ireland.

The second novel feature of this expedition, and one which was, likewise, to have importance for future colonization ventures, was the application of the terminable joint stock principle, hitherto used in trading ventures, to a colonization project. Smith, like St Leger, considered £10,000 to be the sum of money necessary for the exploit. This, he claimed, was sufficient for raising and providing for three hundred horse and four hundred foot for one yar, and for transporting them to Ireland and constructing fortifications there. After the year he expected that the colony, having established itself, would be self-sufficient. He calculated that each horseman should provide, or have subscribed for him, £20 which would entitle him to two plough-lands, while the £10 subscription expected of a foot-soldier was sufficient for one plough-land. Any non-participant who invested £16 13s 4d in the common stock (sufficient to support one foot-soldier for a year) would also have title to one plough-land, and if the expedition ran into difficulties there was provision for a call up of the same amount for a second year. The number that assembled at Liverpool suggests that there were enough people willing to invest in the venture, although there is little evidence of non-participants investing in the common pool. Sir William Cecil did subscribe £333 6s 8d, sufficient to entitle him to twenty plough-lands, while Sir Thomas Smith himself was the largest subscriber with £450 in stock. The only other individual whom we know to have invested was Sir John Thynne of Longleat, a pesonal friend of Smith, but it is likely that many others, such as the earl of Leicester, contributed to the common stock and left the organization to Smith. Most of the support, however, came from those sons and members of the gentry who were ready to provide men and money.[55]

Thus the financial and organizational obstacles had been overcome, when Sir Thomas Smith was reappointed as ambassador to France (10 December 1571) and was forced to leave the management to his incompetent son. Worse still, the expedition was objected to by Sir William Fitzwilliam, the new lord deputy of Ireland, who resented the fact that he had not been consulted, and feared that the exploit would foment a rebellion in Ulster for which he would he held responsible. The absence of the prestigious father and the delay due to Fitzwilliam caused many to withdraw or divert their energies elsewhere, thus defeating the ambition of Sir Thomas Smith to establish a colony in the Ards. The example of Sir Edward Mansell of Galmorganshire was probably quite typical. He, on the personal advice of Smith, 'joyned with a nombre of gentlemen and others' in readiness for the journey to Ulster but withdrew his support when Smith was delegated to France.[56]

Eventually only one hundred men reached Ulster, in August 1572, and these made little advance against Sir Brian McPhelim O'Neill,

chieftain of Clandeboy. By August 1573 they had almost lost their foothold, and the younger Smith was killed in that year by his Irish household servants. The father was undaunted, however, and equipped a supporting fleet of two hundred and fifty men in August 1573, but that never reached Ireland. Yet a third expedition of two hundred men was on its way in August 1574, this time guided by George Smith, brother to Sir Thomas, and the ubiquitous Jerome Brett. By this time Sir Thomas Smith had abandoned the joint stock idea and had developed a new concept of organization. Instead of himself trying to recruit individual settlers, he chose to entice men of substance to raise colonists from among their tenants. Every individual who provided one hundred foot-soldiers and fifteen horse-soldiers was entitled to one hundred plough-lands and would be designated lord of a hundred. Those supplying fifty foot-soldiers and twenty horse-soldiers were to receive fifty plough-lands and would become lords of half a hundred. Thus, according to his earlier calculation, he wished to attract only those who could afford to venture £1,300 or £900 initially, and these lords were then to accept responsibility for the fortification and defence of their lands and were to combine in the construction of the proposed central capital to be called Elizabetha. The scheme was based, almost entirely, on Roman methods of colonization, as were the provisions for the constitutional life of the colony. Some details, however, were to have significance for the future, especially the idea that the principal colonizers should undertake to construct castles on their lands.[57]
The enterprise did not have much appeal for the type of individuals that Smith was interested in attracting, and, of those who adventured, only his brother George Smith, Francis Cary and Edward Russell were of wealthy backgrounds. Names such as Jerome Brett, John Barkeley and T. Lancaster suggest that those with previous experience in Irish colonization were still interested, but the majority of those who contracted to join in the expedition were seemingly personal friends of Smith and men of little substance. The expedition fizzled out, therefore, for lack of support, and the last we hear of it is an offer by Essex, in April 1575, to integrate the Ards into his own territory of Clandeboy.[58]

We recognize a certain hollowness to this offer when we consider that the earl of Essex was unable to make good his own claims in Ulster. It is difficult to explain why Walter Devereux, earl of Essex, undertook the task of colonizing Clandeboy, but it is likely that he was persuaded by Sir Henry Sidney and the earl of Leicester with whom he was acquainted. He certainly entered into the project with almost a missionary zeal, and he was confident that success would establish him as a hero at Elizabeth's court and bring him from his relative obscurity on the march-lands of Wales to the centre of political life. The fact that he was a nobleman with important connections among England's landed society explains why younger sons of distinguished families accompanied him, rather than Smith and each brought along tenants from his lands as soldiers and colonists. Essex also enjoyed the support of previous colonizers in Ireland and enlisted the aid of St Leger, Sir Peter Carew and Sir Arthur Champernoun. Henry Knollys, son of Sir Francis Knollys and brother-in-law to Essex, was one of his principal followers, as were Lord Rich, Michael and John Cary, sons of Lord Hounsdon, and John and William Norris.[59] The earl was so confident of success that he mortgaged extensive lands in England and Wales as security for a loan of £10,000 for the queen, and he was thus saved the trouble of collecting money from private sources. With this he was able to employ officers and soldiers who had previously ventured or served in Ireland, among them Nicholas and John Malby, Edward Barkeley, Thomas Chatterton and Francis Drake, who was captain of a barque called the *Falcon*.[60]

Specific lands in Ulster were allocated to the individuals before they sailed, and it was expected that each adventurer would fortify his own lands and then introduce colonists and tradesmen from England. The expedition ran into trouble from the outset, beginning with a storm that divided the fleet, and continuing with the withdrawal of many adventurers after they had seen the inhospitable state of Ulster. Thus Essex was left to depend upon the support of the soldiers and was forced to plead for financial aid from the queen who loaned him additional money against further mortgages on his estates. 'I will not leave this enterprise', wrote Essex, 'as long as I have any foote of lande in England unsold'.[61] All was to no avail, and his time was spent in fighting the Scots, the Clandeboye O'Neills and Turlough Luineach O'Neill rather than in making a permanent settlement. Various devices were resorted to by the government so as not to sully the earl's reputation or leave him totally destitute, but they hesitated to appoint him to the lord deputyship of Ireland and strove to satisfy him with such empty titles as governor of Ulster and earl marshal of Ireland.[62] The only realistic aid that the government provided was to take over the payment of the troops, but what was required was a larger fighting force to pin down the leaders of the Ulster resistance and force them to subjection. This the government failed to do, and the only return for the total government expenditure of £21,250 was a sad record of atrocities, such as the murder of Brian McPhelim and his followers

at the Christmas feast, and the Rathlin Island massacre of July
1575, when John Norris and Francis Drake sailed to the island and
slaughtered the entire population, including women and children,
which they estimated as six hundred people. Thus the death of Essex
in Ireland in 1576 came as a relief to the government who availed
themselves of the opportunity to wind up the first phase of
colonization in Ireland.[63]

The campaign was ill conceived, badly organized and poorly
executed, but it was important in that it underlined the need for a
military conquest by government troops before a colony could be
introduced. Essex was, evidently, advised by Sidney, since the
locations that he chose for fortifications were those selected earlier
by Sidney for the defence of the province.[64] The earl of Essex was
therefore the only nobleman who responded to Sidney's call of 1568
to undertake the conquest of Ulster. His failure, however, proved
that the task had been somewhat ambitious, and the queen in her
efforts to bail him out had spent more money than if she had
financed the military conquest in the first instance. The outcome
was as Sidney had foretold, when he stated that military conquests
were 'no subject's enterprise a prince's purse and power must do
it'.[65]

This study of colonization ventures is important, therefore, in
showing how the English government were slowly groping towards
an efficient method of colonization. The knowledge that they had of
the Irish social and political system suggested to them that a
conquest might be accomplished without any great difficulty. There
were frequent references to the facility with which the Normans had
seized land in Ireland, and many of those who became involved with
the colonization ventures thought themselves to be resuming a task
that had been abandoned after the reign of King Richard II. This
thinking was perhaps best expressed by Sir Nicholas Wotton who
considered it 'a greate shame for us, that the crowne of England
having been conquerors yn Irlande these fowre hundred yeres wel
neere, cowde not all this whyle bringe that realme to a goode civilyte
and obedience, nor take sume honest comodity and profyte of that
countrey so goode and so fruytefull'.[66] Those, like Sidney, who knew
the country realized that the Irish, and the Scots in Antrim, would
provide strong resistance, and that the nature of the terrain would
favour the native population against English intruders. The
experience in Munster and Ulster certainly bore him out, but it took
the Essex failure to bring home to the officials in England the
enormity of the task that faced them.

The succession of failures, therefore, did not dissuade the

government from their course of action, but rather convinced them that the royal army should play a greater role, certainly in the initial stages. After the failure of Essex, Cecil speaking of Ireland emphasized 'how harde yt wear to reduce any province to conformytye without the specyall chargies and contenance of her Majestie'. Sir William Fitzwilliam, who was appointed lord deputy on Sidney's departure, was of the same opinion. He had resented both the Smith and Essex attempts at colonization because the plans had proceeded without prior consultation with him. The policy of colonization, however, met with his approval, 'as the best, so it were indeed and thoroughlie ron owte'; what he objected to were insufficient expeditions led by men who knew little of the country and proceeded as if 'taking of a ferm in Midd [Meath]'.[67] The setback suffered in Ulster was a great disappointment to Sidney also, but nevertheless he was not discouraged but rather deplored the lack of financial support from the government for

> the introduction of collonys of English and other loyal subjects, whereby a perpetuall inhabitation would have ensued to the recompense as well of that which was spent, as for a yerely and continuall profitt by rent and services, and strength of the country against all forreyne invasion.

Sidney was convinced that the resources at the disposal of Essex had been sufficient for the task in hand, and that if they had been well employed all Ulster would 'undoubtedlie' have been 'reduced . . . to as good obedience as the English pale',[68] The fact that Essex had failed, however, ensured that the government would never again call upon private individuals to aid in colonization in Ireland unless the project was organized and directed by the government. This meant that there was little prospect of resuming the task while the queen continued with her parsimonious attitude towards Ireland. On the other hand, the experiences of the 1560s and 1570s had convinced the English that they were dealing with an unreasonable people in Gaelic Ireland, and that no compromise arrangement was sufficient for reducing the area to civility.[69] The task of colonizing was, therefore, postponed rather than abandoned, and circumstances dictated that the work would be renewed in Munster sooner than expected. The government was then able to benefit from the experience that had been gained in the unsuccessful exploits of the previous decades.

The successive attempts helped also to make Englishmen aware of the possibility of advancing themselves in Ireland. At the outset, only the more adventurous were willing to gamble in Ireland, and of those only clients of the Dudley faction or confidants of Sidney. There was a gradual spread of interest, first at Privy Council level and afterwards throughout the country. Between them, the Smith and Essex enterprises must have aroused interest throughout all of England, and many prominent members of the political nation indicated support. There is evidence of merchant investment in the various ventures, but it was the gentry element who were most attracted by prospects in Ireland. The outlets for younger sons in England were certainly limited. Sir Thomas Smith attributed their predicament to the closure of the monasteries, but even more significant was the relative lack of military engagements during the early years of Queen Elizabeth's reign. Many lamented the peace as detrimental to the advancement of the adventurous, and there emerged a literary genre that looked nostalgically to the reigns of Henry VIII and Edward VI when the military profession was held in regard. Not so in Elizabeth's reign when, according to Sir Francis Walsingham, 'martial men presently bear no price'.[70] Ireland was the only theatre that presented prospects of independence to the landless, and this explains why so many persisted in their efforts to establish colonies there. Those who owned some property but who were frustrated by the social and economic restraints of English society recognized an opportunity of advancing themselves quickly in Ireland. There was a lull of interest, however, after the Essex débâcle, and many of those who had sought their fortune in Ireland looked further afield. This too is reflected in the investment pattern in England where the rate of company formation was accelerated greatly as members of the gentry disengaged themselves from colonization ventures in Ireland.[71] Interest revived again in the 1580s when there were renewed prospects of cheap Irish land, and the plantation in Munster attracted many of those who had been involved in the abortive efforts of the previous decade. It can also be demonstrated that many of the surnames associated with the early ventures in Ireland recurred in later plantations both in Ireland and Virginia, which goes to show that despite the failure of these colonies they certainly contributed towards the establishment of a pattern of conquest.

5

The programme in action:
Provincial presidencies

The means suggested by Sidney for reducing the feudal areas of Ireland to obedience and bringing them under the rule of English law was the creation of provincial councils modelled on those in the north of England and the marches of Wales. All historians are agreed that Sidney secured the appointment of the first provincial presidents in Ireland, but the point has also been made that the idea did not originate with him, that he merely implemented what had long before been suggested by others.[1]

It is true that Sidney was more a man of action than a theorist but it must be taken into account that the powers and functions of the presidents appointed by Sidney were more clearly defined and were far in excess of anything previously suggested for provincial governors in Ireland. The Palesman Sir Thomas Cusack, for example, had been a persistent advocate of provincial councils, but, as we shall see, the institution that he had in mind was far different from that created by Sidney. Cusack, and those of the Anglo-Irish nobility who supported his views, expected that the office of president would fall to a local lord or bishop, who would be joined by some lawyers to act as councillors. The president and council would then be granted a commission of oyer and terminer for the administration of justice in the locality. A president for them was a glorified lord-lieutenant of a shire; what Sidney brought into being was almost diametrically opposed to this.

That there could be such a divergence in expectations is explained by the history of provincial presidencies in the neighbouring island. In England, the provincial presidency, as an agency of central government on the local level, was something that had developed haphazardly from medieval institutions during the sixteenth century, and was still undergoing change until 1569. In Wales, for example, there was no provincial council in the modern sense until 1525, when Wolsey granted a commission of oyer and terminer to the officials of the court of Princess Mary, directing them to administer justice throughout Wales and the bordering shires.[2] The council was therefore merely an outgrowth of a royal household with special powers to curtail lawlessness in an unruly area. The early presidents in Wales were local bishops, and it was only with the appointment, in 1533, of Bishop Rowland Lee, a creature of Thomas Cromwell, that the office assumed a political as well as an administrative role: Cromwell saw in the presidency a convenient weapon for undermining the power of local lords.[3]

The council in the north of England experienced an even more chequered history. The north had always been of strategic importance because it bordered on Scotland. To guard itself against possible invasion from Scotland, the English crown had, through the years, courted the favour of the northern lords. It had become customary to appoint members of the leading northern families as wardens of the marches, thus encouraging them to use their forces for the defence of the realm. This practice was both necessary and desirable while a threat existed of invasion from Scotland, but it also encouraged the maintenance of private armies, and in less dangerous times the wardens – Percies, Cliffords, Dacres and Nevilles – used their forces and offices to pursue family feuds and rivalries. Even more dangerous for the state was the possibility of over-mighty subjects turning their weapons against the monarch. The Yorkists and early Tudors were keenly conscious of this danger and sought gradually to eliminate the office of warden of the marches and assert royal authority in the north. It was to this purpose that many castles, notably Berwick, came under royal control, and a permanent garrison was thus established in the north.[4]

The emergence of the king's council in the north was one aspect of this gradual assertion of royal authority. This council, like its counterpart in Wales, was an outgrowth of a royal household – that of the duke of Richmond – with special authority to administer justice.[5] It was not until the Pilgrimage of Grace, in 1536, that the government was able to exploit fully the split among the northern lords and use the council as an effective political as well as administrative force.[6] The powers of the council were then increased, as was the area of its jurisdiction. From then onwards no temporal lord holding estates north of the Trent held the office of president of the north, and even those holding lesser posts on the council tended to be parvenus, like Sir Thomas Wharton, who owed both lands and office to the crown. [7]

It is evident, therefore, that the political possibilities of provincial councils came to the fore only in the late 1530s, and the hand of Thomas Cromwell is clearly evident working behind the scenes. Bishop Rowland Lee in Wales, as was previously noted, was an appointee of Cromwell, as was Robert Holgate, bishop of Llandaff and subsequently archbishop of York, who was appointed president in the north, in June 1538. [8] It was Cromwell also who established the short-lived Council of the West (March 1539–circa June 1540), and Professor Elton asserts that Cromwell intended extending this method of government to other unruly areas of England. [9] The fall of Cromwell brought an end to these plans, and his arrangement in the West Country was actually reversed. Instead of an extension of the system of provincial councils, Tudor monarchs decided to place trust in the local nobility and appointed them lord-lieutenants of shires. [10] It is this which explains the diverging concepts of provincial government. The councils as defined by Cromwell, and as actually administered in Wales and in the north, represented the government's attempt at undermining particularism, while in most of England the government solicited support from the nobles in ruling the localities.

Even in Wales and the north, the local nobility did not despair of regaining their lost power, and some still cherished hopes that the provincial councils would benefit them. This was particularly true in the north, where successive dukes of Norfolk pressed for the appointment of themselves or their nominees to the presidency, in the hope that the Howards would replace the discredited Percies as the mediators between London and the north. [11] That this ambition was not altogether wishful thinking is suggested by the appointment, in 1568, of the earl of Sussex – after his resignation from the lord-lieutenancy of Ireland – to the presidency of the north. [12] Sussex was Norfolk's cousin as well as his most effective supporter. His handling of the Northern Rebellion of 1569 did not satisfy the government, however, and his recall, in 1572, marked the last hope of the old nobility of using the presidency to further their own ends. [13]

When we consider that some of the English nobility expected – despite evidence to the contrary – that provincial councils would not prejudice their local power, it is not surprising that the Irish feudal lords lived under a similar delusion. Provincial councils, as a remedy for the unruliness of the Irish localities, was first suggested in the 1530s, and we can safely assume that what the English government

envisaged were institutions similar to those devised by Cromwell for
the better government of provincial England. No attempt was made
to implement Cromwell's programme in Ireland, and the Irish lords
remained convinced that participation in a provincial presidency
would enhance their standing in the eyes of the crown, without in
any way diminishing their local power. The earls of Kildare had,
before their downfall in 1536, used the lord deputyship of Ireland to
further their own ends, and there was every reason to believe that
now provincial councils would likewise come under feudal control. It
was thinking such as this which explains why the earl of Desmond,
in his frequent negotiations with the government in the 1560s,
supported their suggestions for a provincial council in Munster. The
earl agreed to assist 'all manner of counsells' and requested the
queen to establish 'some counselles in the remote part of your said
realme as is seen to have been established in the north parts of your
realm of England and in Wales'.[14]

A council for Munster, with the archbishop of Cashel as
president, was mooted in 1548. In 1552, Sir Thomas Cusack
suggested three provincial presidencies, to be located at Limerick,
Galway and Armagh.[15] We can be certain that Cusack envisaged
local noblemen filling these posts, as he did in 1563 when he
suggested that Shane O'Neill might be appointed president of
Ulster. Another Palesman, in 1563, proposed four councils, one to be
located in each of the earldoms of Ormond, Desmond and
Clanricard and a fourth in Ulster. The first three were to be presided
over by the respective earls, while the earl of Kildare, who had title
to extensive land in Ulster, was to be president in that province.[16]
All of these proposals suggested that the establishment of provincial
councils would strengthen the position of the Irish lords if they
conceded to the more effective administration of justice.

No action was taken on Cusack's proposals other than the
appointment of commissioners in Munster 'to assist and mayntein
such as shall governe well in their severall chargs and to reforme and
represse such others as shall do the contrary'.[17] As was previously
noted, the various commissions sent to Munster succeeded in
restoring peace to the province, but on their departure for Dublin
chaos generally broke forth again. Commissions clearly provided no
final solution to the instability of provincial Ireland, and continued
strife encouraged Lord-Lieutenant Sussex to seek an alternative.

Sussex looked to provincial presidencies as the solution to the
problem, but the institutions that he favoured had nothing in
common with those proposed by the Anglo-Irish other than the
name. He was the first to state openly that the presidents should be

Englishmen, and that local nobles should merely hold seats on the various councils in Munster, Connacht and Ulster. It was the primary purpose of Sussex to hold down the country militarily. This explains why he wanted provincial presidents to be military men backed by troops to aid them in maintaining order by force. He suggested that the presidents of Munster and Connacht should each have forty troops at his disposal, and the president of Ulster – the unruly province – was to be supported by an army of four hundred men.

This, therefore, was the first time that the reality of provincial councils was brought home to the Anglo-Irish lords. The lord-lieutenant recognized that the implementation of his proposals would be costly, but he was confident that the new expense would be met by a tax levied on the principal landholders, added to the fines and forfeitures of the provinces.[18] Sussex never had an opportunity of bringing his plans to fulfilment, but many of his suggestions were eventually integrated into Sidney's programme.

It has been noted in the third chapter that Sidney was more ambitious than Sussex and wanted to achieve the final subjugation of Ireland, thus reducing the cost of Ireland to the crown and creating office and opportunity for the English adventurers in Ireland. This meant extending English influence throughout the entire country, and Sidney saw the vigorous execution of justice by provincial presidents as the best means of accomplishing this in all areas, except the Gaelic lordships which first required the use of force. The example of Wales was undoubtedly before the lord deputy's mind, and he wanted to emulate Bishop Rowland Lee who had been the first effective president in Wales. Sidney was proud of the order of Wales and the way in which the people welcomed English justice – 'a better people to governe, or better subjects to their sovereign Europe holdeth not' – and he gave full credit to the presidency for this satisfactory condition. Many others were converted to this view, and, as late as 1601, Bishop Lee's manner of dealing with the Welsh was recommended as the best method of governing the Irish.[19]

Ireland, in Sidney's opinion, suffered from the same problems that had plagued Wales in 1536, and so he prescribed the same remedy. The explicit purpose of Thomas Cromwell in reconstituting the Welsh presidency was, according to Penry Williams, 'to eliminate the various anomalies in English government and to sweep away the pockets of local power independent of the crown'. In 1561, when Sidney assumed office in Wales, this political purpose had been largely achieved, and only the palatinate county of Chester – a crown possession – and the chartered towns retained any jurisdiction independently of the council. The presidency had largely succeeded in emasculating the marcher lords, and all areas had been reduced to shire ground. The common law prevailed everywhere, and the president and council had little work besides settling local disputes, and the purely administrative tasks of supervising military affairs, and overseeing the proper functioning of justice. This explains why Sidney was able to delegate his authority as president of Wales while he served as lord deputy in Ireland.[20]

Sidney was clearly convinced that the Welsh experiment had been a total success. This explains his enthusiasm for introducing similar institutions in Ireland to bring local independence and palatinate jurisdictions to an end there also. He voiced these views even before his appointment to the lord deputyship of Ireland, and his opinions remained unchanged throughout his life. In 1576, when his efforts were meeting with strident opposition, he exclaimed that 'so long as any subiecte hath any jurisdiction pallatyne . . . there will hardly be any sounde and perfect reformacion in Munster'.[21]

We can now see that the English concept of provincial government was completely different from that envisaged by the Irish feudal lords. Sussex saw in the institution of presidency a convenient, if expensive, means of maintaining order in times of crisis. Sidney agreed with and elaborated upon this idea, and saw provincial presidencies fulfilling a political and economic as well as a purely military function. He, like Sussex, realized that expense would be involved – he estimated pay and diet for a president, his staff and fifty soldiers at £1,916 10s 10d – but again like Sussex, he was confident that 'in short tyme' the investment would reap dividends.[22] The expense was to Sidney's mind justified since he saw the presidency as the solution to all of Ireland's problems.

> By this the fisshing now used by the Spaniards and ffrenchmen may be converted to the comen – welth of that realme and fermid to the Queen's advantage. By this rich mines now hidde and lost may be lokid into and gainefully usid to the Quenis use. By this lands and goods may yerely for offence excheat to th Queene, and finally this done, why shuld not the Quenes Majesty, being the naturall soveraign of the realme, have subsidy of the people ether ordinary or extraordinary as well of those captaines who now usurpe auctority over them. But without planting of severall counsells to be resident in severall placs yt is not possible to bring this to passe.[23]

It appears from this that Sidney envisaged the provincial presidents in Ireland having as broad a jurisdiction as the lords proprietor were to enjoy in the American colonies in the seventeenth century. He accepted, however, that the primary purpose of the presidency was 'the xecution of the lawes in those countrees' with 'lyke authoritee for hering and determining of cawses as the president and counsell have heere in England for the marches of Wales'.[24]

This explains why the instructions drawn up by Sidney and the Dublin council, in February 1566, for the guidance of the president of Munster were modelled on the instructions to the president in Wales. The president and council were made responsible for the administration of justice throughout the province, including the two palatinate counties of Tipperary and Kerry. They were granted commissions of oyer and terminer and gaol delivery, and the council, when in session, had all the powers of an assize court. The president and council were further granted authority to exercise martial law 'where other ordynary administration of justice and by lawe can not have place'. Fifty troops from the standing army were put at the president's disposal, and, in an emergency, he was authorized to levy further men from the province 'as to his discrecon shall seeme convenient'.[25] It is quite evident that Sidney intended that the president should overrule everybody in Munster, and when we consider the deputy's persistant efforts to abolish coyne and livery it becomes obvious that he wanted the president to have the only military force in the province.

Ormond quickly recognized that the presidency constituted a threat to his power base. It was largely through his instigation, as has been noted previously, that the appointment of Sir Warham St Leger was revoked by the queen. It is probably that Desmond also saw himself threatened, but he may have fostered the hope that the president would at least help him in his feud with Ormond. If such was the case, his dreams were shattered during Sidney's visit to Munster in 1567. The lord deputy decided the case in Ormond's favour and adjudged that Desmond should pay £20,000 in damages to Ormond. No less alarming for Desmond were the attempts by Sidney to abolish the dependency of Munster's lesser nobility on the Fitzgeralds. The culmination of Desmond's troubles was Sidney's taking him into custody in 1567, and the subsequent arrest of the earl's brother, Sir John of Desmond, in 1568, must have convinced the Munster Fitzgeralds that the government was conspiring with Ormond to bring about the downfall of their house.[26]

It was, therefore, evident to all, both Butler and Fitzgerald, that Sidney was determined to use the presidency as a political weapon

to undermine their power; Munster was brewing with dissatisfaction. In view of this, the queen's recall of St Leger, and her
failure to appoint a replacement, was extremely ill advised. Sidney,
in arresting Desmond, was deliberately removing the most
intransigent opponent to the presidency, and he had every hope that
Sir John of Desmond would be more compliant. No president was
appointed, however, and even Sidney's interim arrangement for the
administration of the province by commission was defeated by the
order from London, under pressure from Ormond, that Sir John of
Desmond should likewise be arrested. This added to Fitzgerald's
dissatisfaction, and a political void was left in the earldom itself.
This void was soon filled by the earl's rival for power, his cousin
James Fitzmaurice Fitzgerald, who was 'by the lyking of the
countrey men theare and those his factyon made ruler of thearles
territoryes'. What little hope there had been of forcing the
Fitzgeralds to co-operate with a president in Munster was now
dissipated, since Fitzmaurice realized that his usurpation of power
could be made good only so long as he successfully opposed the
introduction of a presidency to the province.[27]

This course of events shows how the Munster Fitzgeralds were
virtually forced into opposing the presidency. Both Desmond and
Ormond now recognized that the Munster presidency was designed
by Sidney to undermine their source of power. Ormond was able to
defeat the deputy's purpose in London, and Desmond thus became
convinced that the government was aligning itself with Ormond
against himself. The continued detention of Desmond and Sir John
of Desmond in England presented the usurper Fitzmaurice with an
opportunity to strengthen his position. The real mistake, however,
was that of the queen in leaving the presidency vacant for so long,
allowing Fitzmaurice and the other opponents of the presidency to
prepare for war.[28]

The queen's reason for neglecting the Munster post was
principally financial. She argued that the stipend to the president
should be reduced from that promised to St Leger. Sidney called
incessantly for a replacement, but the queen chose to ignore his
pleas. Finally, during his visit to England in 1568, the lord deputy
was given an assurance that a candidate would be chosen from a list
supplied by him, but again financial obstacles delayed the
appointment. Cecil was committed to appointing a president in
Munster and continued to press the issue after Sidney had returned
to Ireland, in September 1568, favouring for office, from among
those suggested by Sidney, people with experience of the presidency
in Wales. By November 1568, Cecil had persuaded the queen to

agree to two councils, one in Munster and one in Connacht, and the candidates agreed upon were Sir John Pollard for Munster and Sir Edward Fitton for Connacht. Once again the queen had last minute financial reservations, and Pollard, unwilling to accept a reduced stipend, had himself excused from accepting appointment. [29]

By then rebellion in Munster had got totally out of hand, and the time was past when a president would have proved effective. Instead of a president, Sidney, in September 1569, appointed Humphrey Gilbert as colonel of the province to restore order by force of arms. From then until February 1571, when Sir John Perrott was appointed president in Munster, the province was ruled exclusively by martial law. A commission composed of those of the principal landholders in the province not engaged in rebellion and of the mayors of the Munster towns, together with Sir Warham St Leger and Richard Grenville – both occupied in colonization in the south-west – was appointed to advise and support Gilbert, but this was merely a concession to placate local feeling. Gilbert was granted power of martial law over the entire province, with the sole exception of lords and captains of countries, and he had authority, with the advice of any one commissioner, to proclaim as an outlaw or rebel anybody within the province 'that is a notorious offendor or malefactor or shall wilfully refuse to come to answer the lawe'. Again with the advice of one commissioner, Gilbert was authorized to levy and billet troops, to impress galleys and to exact purveyance from the country. The colonel was empowered to wage war on anybody whom he considered an enemy and to demolish the castles of any 'rebel or suspect person'. The culmination of the document was an all-embracing clause which declared it 'lawful for him to annoy in every way any such malefactor by fire and sword according to the quality of the offence, and to use any kind of punishment upon the suspected person for the furthering of her Majesty's service for the better understanding of the truth'. [30]

These extraordinary discretionary powers were authorized by Sidney without sanction of parliament. Gilbert exercised little restraint in wielding his authority and quickly cowed Munster into submission. Fitzmaurice remained in rebellion until 1573, but his supporters fell away so rapidly that the lord deputy could exaggerate that he had become ' a bush beggar not having 20 knaves of all sortes to follo hym'. Sidney was so pleased with this progress that he considered, in January 1570, that Munster was again ready to receive a provincial presidency; 'the iron is now hot, apt to receive what prynt shall be stryken'. [31] The lord deputy did not admit, however, that while harsh government had achieved the appearance of peace in Munster, there was no guarantee that the province would not revert to its former condition when the pressure was relaxed. It appears, in fact, that the Munster lords, even those who stood to benefit from Sidney's innovations, found their first taste of direct government most unsavoury and resolved to resist having to sample more. It was also evident that Gilbert was closely associated with the colonization efforts in south-west Munster, and Sidney's appointing St Leger and Grenville on the commission to advise Gilbert was a most impolitic move. Gilbert may have achieved outward conformity, but rebellion continued to smoulder beneath the surface.

When, in February 1571, Sir John Perrott assumed office as president of Munster, he was forced to continue Gilbert's work. Fitzmaurice was still at large, and two full years of Perrott's brief sojourn in Munster (February 1571–September 1573) were principally devoted to quenching the last embers of rebellion. This ensured that the presidency became associated in Irish minds with the atrocities of Gilbert, and there is little to suggest that Perrott's rule was anything more lenient.

Perrott was issued a set of instructions quite similar to those drawn up for St Leger, with the significant difference that Tipperary was declared exempt from his jurisdiction. He was, however, provided with no legal assistance and he was himself able to devote little of his time to the administration of English justice. The lord president recognized this shortcoming, and he requested a colonel for Munster so that he himself could 'deal with the place of the presidentship'. Even the Dublin government admitted that Perrott was primarily a military officer when they sent a special commission to the province, in August 1571, to settle civil suits there. [32]

Even when he did conduct sessions, Perrott secured convictions by common law as easily as Gilbert had by martial rule. He reported, in May 1571, that he had 'helde sondrie cessions and at some of them there have ben executed for treasons and felonies 28 or 30 at the tyme', a rate that he consistently maintained during his tenure of office. In November 1572, he boasted that he had just executed twenty on charges of treason in Cork, and, in the following June, sixty more were convicted and executed in the same city. In April 1573, he estimated that, besides those he had slain in battle, he had 'kylled and hanged both by the lawes of this realm, and also by the mershall lawe, of the rebells and their ayders about the number of 800 persons'. This total was of itself sufficient to convince all Munstermen that the establishment of a presidency did not serve their best interests. It was becoming clear to them that common law could be no less tyrannical than martial law when juries were forced to bend before the will of a president. What made it even worse was that Perrott had no regrets about his behaviour and recommended it to others: 'a man maye easily shewe gentlenesse when he will, and truely whiles I have dealings heare, my meanyng ys not to rule by intreaty for that (in my judgment) hath of longe tyme hurtt this nacon'.[33]

Their first experience with a provincial presidency came, therefore, as a shattering blow to the Munster lords. As an instrument of government, it was far different from anything they had preconceived, and, despite the fact that many of them were nominated as members of the council, they were unable to curb the wishes of the president. Ironically, the institution as it materialized did not live up to Sidney's preconception either. The fact of the matter was that Perrott was primarily a military officer completing the task of Humphrey Gilbert. It was only in the short interval between the submission of Fitzmaurice, in February 1573, and the resignation of Perrott, in September of the same year, that the presidency functioned as Sidney had intended. During this short interval, Perrott devoted himself to substituting royal justice for local custom and Gaelic law. The president had earlier proclaimed illegal the practice of brehon law, the continuation of coyne and livery and the maintenance of troops other than those kept by a lord as his personal retinue. Perrott now attempted to enforce his proclamation and stipulated that all men in the province should be booked and accounted for, and all bards, rhymers and 'carroughes' (gamblers) should abandon their occupations or be put in the stocks. The wearing of Gaelic dress, particularly in the towns, was proscribed, in consequence of which Perrott jocosely remarked 'I am assured to have no wyfe in these parts'.[34]

The purpose behind these actions was to symbolize the advent of a new order. Perrott was satisfied that Munster was approaching the same level of civility as Wales and reported to the queen in July 1573 that 'the plough . . . dothe . . . now laughe the unbrydeled kearne and roge to skorne, the poore doo praye for your highnasse, and the rest such as be hable for the warr . . . do now honnor you only, and are sworne to your Majesty'. The president was confident that this happy state would continue as long as Desmond was kept imprisoned and a president remained in Munster. Neither of these conditions was complied with. Perrott resigned his office on 22 November 1573, and no replacement arrived in Munster until July 1576. The earl of Desmond, who some months earlier had been returned to Ireland, escaped from his Dublin prison on the day of

Perrott's departure and reclaimed his lands, liberties, castles and privileges in Munster. Perrott despaired of his achievements and complained that the earl of Desmond was 'a man rather mette to keepe Bedlem then to come to a newe reformed countire'.[35]

This turn of events certainly did much to cancel out the achievements of Perrott, and there was little prospect of a new appointment as long as Sir William Fitzwilliam continued as lord deputy in Ireland. The return of Sidney to Ireland in 1575 meant that there would be renewed efforts to bring Munster into conformity with his idea of civility. Provincial councils were still accepted by Sidney as the best method of winning the compliance of the outlying areas to central authority. The new lord deputy considered Perrott 'the most complete and best humoured man to deale with that nation that I know lyving' and asserted that 'if Mr. Perrott had continued till my arrival and maintained the course still held while he was there I should have found Munster as I left Wales'. From the reappointment of Sidney as lord deputy until the arrival of Sir William Drury as lord president in Munster, in July 1576, the government in Dublin pressed consistently for the re-establishment of provincial councils in Munster and Connacht, since there was 'no other way to defend Ireland from forreyn foes, nor to suppress the natyve rebellys'.[36]

The lord deputy made it clear that he wished to strengthen the position of the lesser landowners in provincial Ireland at the expense of the greater lords, in the hope that those dependent upon government support would favour provincial councils. It was to prepare the way for the reintroduction of presidents that Sidney set out, in December 1575, on a tour of Munster and Connacht. At Cork, the lord deputy held court for six weeks, where he was attended by the lords and gentry of the province, both Anglo-Irish and Gaelic-Irish, accompanied by their wives and families. The landowners promised to forego their practice of retaining idle men, and they offered fealty and homage to the queen, and, after some persuasion, agreed to pay rent to the crown instead of the military support that they had formerly provided. In return, the lord deputy promised that a president would be appointed in Munster to keep order in the province – thus rendering unnecessary the maintenance of private armies – and he guaranteed the lesser nobility that their lands would be free from further interference by the earl of Desmond if they paid the annual rent due to Desmond as their overlord. The lord deputy also contracted to appoint sheriffs to execute English law, and he set the example by conducting sessions during his visit. In settling disputes between neighbouring lords the lord deputy acted with impartiality and leniency, and thus did much to restore the confidence of the lesser landowners in the crown. His attitude towards loose and masterless men was harsh, however, and most of those executed at the Cork sessions fell into this category. Furthermore the deputy issued a proclamation demanding that all landowners submit a list of their dependants on the understanding that 'any ... found unbooked [would be] used as a felon or vagabond'. The lord deputy did likewise in Thomond where the chief landowners consented to bear 'the charge of a provost marshall of myne appointment ... for that the countrie swarmed of idle men'.[37]

It is evident that the lord deputy intended the president in Munster to continue with the threefold task of reducing the jurisdiction of the great lords, eliminating masterless men who might serve in private armies, and winning a rent from the landowners to cover the cost of the presidency. The earls of Desmond and Thomond could do little to oppose this policy and were forced to comply with the new regulations. In Thomond the lord deputy made it clear that the surrender and regrant arrangement, by which ownership of the lands in the lordship was vested in the hands of the earl, was not to his satisfaction. He encouraged the collaterals of the O'Brien family, as well as the heads of the lesser septs - 'captains and lords of large territory' - , to pursue in court their claims to freehold status, thus undermining the greatness of the earl. The lord deputy also took prisoner a brother of the earl of Thomond, chose Sir Daniel O'Brien, the earl's chief opponent, as sheriff of the county 'and appointed some other of the countrie birthe to be sergeaunts, cessors and other meane officers'. Thus the lord deputy was exploiting the divisions within the O'Brien lordship, and the earl was left with no option but to accede to his wishes. The same tactic was employed by the lord deputy in the Desmond lordship, and the earl was unable to oppose his wishes lest he be identified with the rebellious James Fitzmaurice Fitzgerald who was then in exile. The position of the earl had also been weakened by the Fitzmaurice rebellion, and Desmond was, ironically, dependent upon the lord deputy to win the acquiescence of the lesser nobility to pay him an annual fixed rent. The baron of Lixnawe, for example, had, since the Fitzmaurice rebellion, resisted all attempts by Desmond to claim rent from him, and it was only on the lord deputy's persuasion that he conceded an annual rent of 240 marks and 120 beeves.[38]

Equally significant was the fact that the earl of Ormond and the lords residing within the Butler lordship did not attend at either the convocation at Cork or Galway where the new arrangements were agreed upon. Instead Ormond paid his respects to the lord deputy at Limerick and lingered only to negotiate a conciliation between himself and the baron of Upperossary. Thus he made it clear that no lord president would have jurisdiction within the earldom of Ormond, without a protracted legal argument. On the other hand the lands of Ormond were not exempt from the lord deputy's censure. Sidney described the earldom of Ormond as 'the sinke and receptacle of innumerable cattle and goods stolen', and he made great play of an English forger of Spanish coins finding refuge within the liberty of Tipperary. The lord deputy also pleaded for the independence of Upperossary and O'Carroll and called for an end of the palatinate of Tipperary: 'so long as any subiecte hath any jurisdiction pallatyne ... there will hardly be any sounde and perfect reformacion in Munster'.[39]

The lord deputy had clearly outlined his intentions of changing the social structure in Munster in favour of the lesser landowners. It is evident that the government was better informed on conditions in Munster than it had ever been before, and direct contact had been made with most of the gentry of the province. This store of knowledge was put at the disposal of Sir William Drury who arrived, in July 1576, to take over the post of president in Munster. Drury was well suited to the post since he had a long military career behind him and was also familiar with the workings of a provincial council, having served on the council in the north. His task in Munster was facilitated by the preparatory work of the lord deputy, and his role was clearly defined. Thomond was, for the first time, declared to be under the jurisdiction of the Munster president, but the earldom of Ormond was declared exempt from his rule.

In his various sessions, Drury concentrated on the indictment of masterless men and boasted that he had executed four hundred in less than two years. Drury also tackled the practice of coyne and livery and indicted Desmond, Viscount Barry, Sir Cormac Mac Teigh McCarthy and Sir Edmund Butler for contravening the proclamation prohibiting the practice. The president made direct contact with the lesser landholders and had them pay rents to their overlords in lieu of the military exactions that they had previously rendered.[40] This accomplished, Drury set himself to extracting rents from the lords to cover the cost of maintaining a provincial council. This met with considerable opposition, but most lords were compelled to succumb to Drury's wishes. Desmond refused to pay anything, initially, and even went to the extreme of offering his lands to the queen, in return for a rent of £2,000 a year, until his eldest son would be of age. This was not what Drury required, and the earl was forced to accede to the president's wishes. The demise of Desmond as an independent magnate was symbolized by Drury's conducting a session at Tralee – the centre of the palatinate of Kerry – against the earl's wishes, and the earl was compelled to disband his army 'except 20 horsemen to attend upon him' and to 'put all his lands . . . unto a certain rent'. [41]

The landholders of Thomond had no recourse other than to yield to Drury's demands since he first deprived them of their castles. Viscount Barry also conceded defeat and contracted to pay an annual rent of £150, and McCarthy Reagh promised to pay £250 a year. By March 1578 Drury claimed that he had come to a settlement with all the lords of Munster, except those of County Tipperary, and they has assured him of an annual rent of £1,170 6s 6d towards defraying the annual expenditure of £3,815 on the presidency. This still left a considerable deficit, but with sheriffs active in all the counties of the province it was expected that wardships and forfeitures would bring a substantial revenue to the crown. The monastic lands were not ignored, and Drury estimated that these alone would yield £1,119 17s 5d in rent to the government. [42]

The presidency was obviously a major threat to the position of the Munster lords since it not only required them to abandon their private armies but expected them to make a sudden adjustment from being warlords to becoming landlords in the English sense. Direct contact had, as yet, been made only with the tenants in chief, but it was obviously the government's intention to regularize the payment of rent down to the lowest level, thus ending uncertain exactions. Drury, for example, was collecting evidence on the revenues claimed by such as Lord Roche from his tenants, with the specific purpose of highlighting the injustice of exorbitant rents and services. [43] Such a challenge to their position was obviously resented by the Munster lords, but they showed themselves capable of making the adjustment. Furthermore, the landowners were now promised security in their estates, and this must have had particular appeal to the Gaelic chieftains of the south-west who had hitherto been threatened by Carew's claims on their lands, and by the ambitions of English colonizers in Munster. The government had at this stage abandoned its hopes of a major English settlement in the province, and Drury intended to grant leases of monastic lands to local lords rather than to English adventurers. It appeared, in 1576, that Munster would be brought to conform with the English model of civility by gradual means rather than by force. Only the earl of

Desmond was totally opposed to what was happening, and he had no option but to conform with the wishes of the president. Munster was well on the road to reform and would probably have continued on that route were it not for the fact that Drury was called upon, in 1578, to act as lord justice in Dublin to replace Sidney who had resigned from office. The presidency in Munster was again left vacant, and the province was left open to the invasion from the Continent led by James Fitzmaurice Fitzgerald. The earl of Desmond availed himself of the opportunity to throw off the shackles placed on him by the president and joined with Fitzmaurice in rebellion. Defeat for Desmond and his followers meant confiscation of property, with the result that colonization rather than persuasion eventually changed the character of the province. It is significant that many of the lesser lords who had surrendered to Drury remained loyal to the government during the Desmond rebellion and persisted as a prominent, though reformed, element among the landowners in Munster into the seventeenth century.

The presidency of Connacht, first instituted in December 1569, evolved much more closely to the Welsh model than its counterpart in Munster, and so more nearly fulfilled Sidney's expectations. The fact that southern Connacht and Thomond, the areas over which the president gained control initially, were low lying areas and the lordships much less militarized than in Munster goes a long way towards explaining this. It is also significant that the two earldoms of Thomond and Clanricard were of relatively recent creation, and the earls still depended on crown support to maintain themselves against their local rivals. Of equal significance is the fact that the presidency of Connacht was held uninterruptedly by the same man, Sir Edward Fitton, from December 1569 until March 1574, and the local opposition to the presidency was thus denied an opportunity to mobilize as had been the case in Munster.

Fitton, a dependant of Burghley, was selected for the office after it had been rejected by Sir Andrew Corbet, a member of the council in Wales. Nothing in his background particularly qualified Fitton for the post, but he, unlike Perrott, was provided with legal assistance in the person of Ralph Rokeby, who had seen service on the council in the north. Robert Dillon, a Palesman with a knowledge of the Irish language, was appointed as second justice. None of the instructions to the successive presidents of Connacht has survived, but it is likely that they enjoyed the same powers as their Munster counterparts. We know that Fitton enjoyed power of martial law, but no extra troops were appointed for his support since his base at Athlone was already provided with a garrison. This meant that the Connacht council was much less of a drain on resources than the Munster presidency proved to be. The only extra expenditure involved in Connacht, initially, was a stipend of £133 6s 8d for the president, £100 for Justice Rokeby, £66 13s 4d for the second justice and £12 for the clerk of the council.[44]

The first task facing the presidency in Connacht was the shiring of the province, beginning with those areas most amenable to control, the earldoms of Thomond and Clanricard and the lowland area immediately west of Athlone, which was constituted into the county of Roscommon. Work on this project had been initiated by Sir Thomas Cusack, earlier in 1569, and was resumed by Fitton on his assuming office.[45] By 4 January 1570, Fitton had completed a circuit of Counties Galway and Roscommon, where he conducted sessions and received the ready submission of the chief landholders. He took pledges and recognizances valued at £9,000 as an assurance of their good conduct, and insisted that each accept responsibility for the behaviour of his dependants. In this he was following the example of Gilbert in Munster. The chief landholders were to provide

books of the names of such men as ar undre them and the soldiers and such as they wyll undertake to be answerable to lawe, and the resydewe that none wyll booke and undertake ffor are accepted for ydle persons and a provost marshall appoynted to truss upp such as be thought the canker of this comon welthe, namely horseboyes, woodkerne and proclamed rebells that wyll not come in to any government.

It was made clear that Fitton was opposed to the practice of coyne and livery, and Gaelic laws and customs were prohibited as was evidenced by his insistence that all who submitted themselves should symbolically 'cut ther glybbes which we doo thynke the ffyrst token of obedyence'.[46]

In all of this Fitton and his council received surprising co-operation from Clanricard, whom he found 'a very good and honorable subject, and redy and willing to wyne with us in the furtherance of her majestyes servyce and to leave all unreasonable exactions and lewd yrysh customs'. The explanation for this, as previously mentioned, was that Clanricard was dependent on government support, and he may have originally seen Fitton as an ally against his local rivals. The earl may have had no objection to being disarmed himself as long as his opponents were similarly treated. We must consider also that Clanricard and Thomond, unlike the earls of Desmond and Ormond, did not have any claim to palatinate jurisdiction or other such privileges and so had less to lose than their Munster counterparts.[47]

What did irritate the western earls, however, and what became an issue between them and the president was Fitton's selection of sheriffs. The president, quite naturally, sought candidates for office who were not dependants of the great lords, and who could thus be relied upon to select impartial juries. The obvious candidate in County Galway was John Burke, cousin and rival to the earl of Clanricard. Burke represented the branch of the family that had been passed over when Henry VIII had created the first earl of Clanricard in 1541. Since then his forebears and he had persisted in opposing successive earls, and it was natural that he should now jump at the opportunity of becoming a curb on the earl's power. Even more invidious, from Clanricard's point of view, were the special privileges accorded by Fitton to John Burke. His lands were declared exempt from the earl's control, he was granted occasional stipends by the government to encourage him in his work, and, most offensive to Clanricard, he was by virtue of his office granted power of martial law.[48]

It was evident from the beginning that Clanricard opposed this appointment, but there was nothing he could do to prevent it other than complain to the queen. The earl of Thomond was less patient when Fitton tried a similar device for County Clare. The sheriff appointed there was Tadhg O'Brien, son of Murrough O'Brien, the rival to Conor O'Brien who had been created earl under the surrender and regrant policy of Henry VIII. The appointment was totally unacceptable to the earl of Thomond, and he reacted to it by refusing to meet with the president when he visited him in early 1570. A struggle ensued which signalled the beginning of a general opposition to the presidency in Connacht.[49]

Fitton could do little to impose his will on the earl of Thomond and called upon the government to provide him with military support. He wrote to Cecil that 'power is the thinge must brydle them, and justice must comfort them, for by the one alone they will grow desperate and notwithstanding the other they will continue insolent'. Rokeby was even more pessimistic and denied that justice had, as yet, any role in Connacht.

> Yt ys not the maze [mace] nor the name of a lord president and councell that wyll fframe them to obedyence, yt must be ffyer and sword, the rod of God's vengeance that must make these cankerd sorts and stubborn mynds to yeald for feare ... yt must be

valiannte and coragious captaynes and hardy soldiers that must
make a way for law and justice in these remote parts or els fare
well Ireland.[50]

Some military support was forthcoming from the government, but
this defeated the earlier achievements of the presidency. Those who
had previously welcomed the orders of the president relieving them
from the military exactions of their lords, now found themselves
supporting government troops instead. As rebellion spread
throughout Connacht, the need for troops grew greater, and the
presidency that started as a purely administrative body came to
resemble the Munster presidency. Even Fitton admitted that the
troops were a 'heavy burden' on the province, and some landowners
thought it 'as good to spend theym selves and defend their libertie
... as to yealde theym selves to bondage'. Clanricard also
complained bitterly of the discretionary powers of the president,
especially that of martial law, and he instanced the execution of one
of his supporters as illegal being 'contrary to a statute of this realm
that prohibiteth any subject worth 40s per annum in freehold or £10
in chattell to be executed but by Her Majesty's common laws'. The
complaints were to no purpose, however. As resistance grew stouter,
the authority of the presidency increased accordingly, until, by July
1576, Lord Deputy Sidney granted powers to the president of
Connacht little short of those granted to Gilbert, in 1567, for
Munster.[51]

There were factors other than military ones that contributed to
the estrangement of the Connacht lords from the presidency, not
least of which was the religious policy of Fitton. There was a clause
in the instructions to successive lords president in Munster, as well
as to the lord deputy of Ireland, advising them to further the
Reformation in Ireland. As we have seen, however, the government
tended to turn a deaf ear to such advice. The language barrier was
an insurmountable obstacle to the course of the Reformation, and it
was quite evident that molesting existing church practices was futile
so long as the government could not provide preachers fluent in the
Irish language to undertake a missionary campaign. Fitton,
however, placed religious enthusiasm before prudence, and on his
very first circuit through Connacht he 'visited sundry and many of
the ydolls and ymags in their churches and comytted them to the
ffyer, and expulsed and discharged sondry of the ffreres of Athenry
and Kylconnell'. Similar depredations on places of worship
characterized his early rule in Connacht, and had he not desisted he
would have galvanized the Irish of the province against him.[52]

The measure initiated by Fitton which occasioned most anxiety among the landholders of the province was his dividing the counties into plough-lands with the purpose of using the plough-land as a unit of taxation. By May 1571, after a survey had been conducted of Thomond and Clanricard, the president divided them respectively into 160 and 200 plough-lands, and demanded an annual payment of one mark from each plough-land. The outbreak of hostilities prevented him collecting the tax, but the purpose remained in his mind, as can be seen from a document forwarded to Burghley, in 1574, providing him with a comprehensive list of the chief landholders of Connacht and the capacity of each to pay taxes. [53]

The departure of Fitton for England, in 1574, brought the scheme temporarily to a standstill but activity was renewed in Connacht, as in Munster, when Sidney was reappointed lord deputy in 1575. The lord deputy extended his tour into Connacht and conducted a convocation of the landowners of Connacht similar to that held earlier at Cork. The lesser chieftains of Thomond – O'Loughlin, two McNamaras, McMahon and several of the O'Briens – had been received by the lord deputy on his journey to Galway, and the fact that he did not have them join him was the first indication that Thomond was to be in future ruled by the president of Munster. The earl of Thomond, however, did attend the deputy when he held court at Galway, and the earl of Clanricard was in constant attendance. The bishops of the province as well as the lesser lords of Clanricard – O'Kelly, O'Flaherty, Bermingham and several Burkes – all paid their respects to the deputy, and the chieftains of north Connacht, who had hitherto been relatively free from English interference, came and submitted to the deputy. These chieftains – McWilliam Burke of Mayo, the head of the sept of Clandonnells, O'Malley and many others – surrendered their lands to the deputy and bound themselves by oath and indenture to hold them from the queen in return for specified rents. As he proceeded to Athlone, on his return journey, the lord deputy received all the lords and chieftains of the Roscommon region, principally O'Connor Don, O'Connor Roe and McDermott. On his return to Dublin, the deputy received submissions from O'Connor Sligo and O'Rourke who offered to pay rent to the crown in return for security of tenure.

All of this indicates that the lords and chieftains of Connacht were coming to realize that their positions would be in jeopardy unless they arrived at an accommodation with the government. The fact that Sidney wished to secure submissions from the north of the province shows that he wanted the presidency in future to extend its jurisdiction to that area, and this explains why Thomond was transferred to Munster when Drury took up office there. [54]

The best remembered action of the lord deputy at Galway was his sanctioning the demarcation of Counties Galway, Mayo, Roscommon and Sligo, thus preparing the way for English law. Sheriffs were appointed in the newly designated shires, and one Robert Damporte was installed as provost marshall in Clanricard's territory to 'apprehende and execute the thieves and destroyers of the countrie'. Much of the deputy's time at Galway was devoted to conducting sessions of assize, and 'loose and masterless men' were again executed summarily. The principal concern of the deputy, however, was in treating with the landowners of the province and curbing the power of the great lords. The deputy promised to grant independence to O'Shaughnessy, whose lands lay on the borders of Thomond and Clanricard, and he set out to remedy the situation within the lordship of Clanricard where, according to Sidney, the earl's 'friends and followers fare well and the rest go to wreck'. The earl's two sons, John and Ulick Burke, who had been the cause of considerable disturbance were taken prisoners to Dublin. Clanricard was deprived of his two strongest castles, and the deputy imposed a fine of £2,000 to be levied on the lands of the earldom for the repair of Athenry which had been destroyed in the recent rebellion. [55] The lords in the other counties of the province were almost totally Gaelicized, but the lord deputy hoped that by their surrenders they would be persuaded to accept English governmental institutions. All of them were bound by indentures, but none of the grants was finalized pending an inquisition that would determine the freehold rights of the lesser lords and chieftains. Thus the lord deputy ensured that he would not repeat the errors of the surrender and regrant policy, and where that scheme was in operation, as in Thomond and Clanricard, he strove to remedy its inequities. Thus at the end of this tour the lord deputy stated that:

> I am and ever have beene of opinion and holde the same for an infallible principle, that the discipacion of the great lordes and their countries by good distribucion into maney hands is a sounde way of proceadinge to the perfecte reformacion of this unhappie and cursed estate. [56]

The basis for the reorganization of Connacht had been laid by Sidney, and he expected that the provincial council would continue with the task. To this end he called for the appointment of the earl of Essex or some other suitable person as president of Connacht. No appointment was made immediately, and the settlement that the deputy had made was threatened when Clanricard's sons escaped to Connacht and attempted to rouse the province. The lord deputy headed west on first news of the revolt, and he consolidated his previous arrangements by taking hostages from the landowners of the province. By this means the rebellious Burkes were isolated and were forced to depend on imported mercenaries for support. The government could boast of the loyalty of the landholders of the province 'as well principall gent as the rest', and Sir Nicholas Malby who was appointed colonel, and subsequently president, of the province with command of three hundred troops had little difficulty in suppressing the revolt.[57]

Malby was familiar with Ireland, having served with Essex in Ulster, and was able to combine toughness with moderation in insisting that the Connacht landholders comply with his wishes. He compelled each landholder to contract to pay certain sums of money and provisions to the president annually and to maintain a specified number of the president's troops. Thus, while Malby was primarily a soldier, he never lost sight of the principal objective of revolutionizing the landholding system in the province. By 1577, the principal men of Connacht had come to accept the presidency as final and were prepared, if reluctantly, to provide money for its support. Under this arrangement a revenue of £1,137 had been raised in Connacht, and further revenue was expected from monastic and concealed crown land that had been surveyed by Lancelot Alford who, in 1576, had accompanied Sidney to the province. The settlement made between Malby and the landholders was known as a composition and pointed the way towards the Composition of Connacht of 1585 that went much further in bringing conditions in the province to conform with English practice. As far as the reform of Connacht was concerned a pattern had certainly been devised between 1565 and 1576.[58]

From what has been said, it appears that provincial presidencies as they evolved in Ireland were a more forceful instrument of government than either the council of the north or the council in the marches of Wales. The presidencies were both established by decree, even though parliament was in session at the time, and the discretionary powers of the presidents far exceeded those of their counterparts in England. In the English situation provincial councils enjoyed merely administrative and political roles, but in Ireland a fiscal function was added. Furthermore, it was the stated policy of the president to resume whatever land could be shown to be crown property. This involved much more than monastic land, and there is plentiful evidence to support the view that presidencies were stalking horses for colonization. St Leger had been the first choice for the Munster post, he afterwards served on a commission with Gilbert to rule the province, and both were actively involved with colonization in the province. It is significant also that Richard Grenville, St Leger's principal partner in colonization, was appointed sheriff for County Cork in 1569. The Connacht presidents were also active in confiscating land for the crown, and Fitton proclaimed, in 1572, that enough property was forfeited to the queen 'to mainteane at the leaste, half a hundred gentlemen of good calling with everie one xx followers at least, and everie one to have honest men's lyvings'.[59]

It is true, however, that their intention in this matter was to introduce pockets of Englishmen in strategic places, and the true purpose of altering the land distribution in the provinces was never lost sight of. The fact of the matter was that Englishmen could hardly conceive of a society without nobles, and they merely wanted to curb the powers of the existing lords and force them to comport themselves as their English counterparts did. Thus when it appeared that the forward policy might drive the Irish nobles to revolt there were those in English government circles who wished to leave the lords unmolested. One such was Sir William Fitzwilliam who opposed provincial presidencies in principle even though he was lord deputy of Ireland. The earl of Sussex was likewise uncertain about the form of provincial councils that emerged and favoured moderation. Sussex admitted that the earl of Clanricard was 'not so perfect a subject as he ought to be and as earls be in England, and the like I believe of every earl in Ireland in matters that touch themselves, and yet I think he and they be obedient and ready otherwise to all services to the crown'. His advice, therefore, was to bear some falts with them for the time, than either by ruining or discrediting of them to leave a worser sort of people to domyne at their licentious wills'. When, with the rebellion of James Fitzmaurice Fitzgerald, it appeared that the forebodings of Sussex would come true, there were those who favoured strengthening rather than weakening the position of the Anglo-Irish lords. Such advice was presented to the government in November 1568 when it was suggested that the size of the army should be reduced and the defence of the country entrusted to the nobility, especially Ormond and Kildare, who were also to participate in government 'that they be not made strangers to the matters of the state there'. For the outlying areas it was proposed that the nobles 'be principallie trusted within their severall countries and lymitts'. Much the same proposal was made in 1573 when it was suggested that the role of lord deputy should be confined to 'manage causes of justyce and lawe', and 'to have the sword put into the hands of the . . . lords of Ireland as therles of Ormond and Kildare'. These illustrate the fact that the English government had no intention of overthrowing the Anglo-Irish lords, and it was with some difficulty that Sidney was allowed to pursue his policy of curbing their powers.[60]

It was the persistence of Sidney, both in Ireland as lord deputy and in England as adviser to the Privy Council, that won government acceptance for the idea of provincial councils. Their unique task was in the breaking up the large landholding units and the strengthening of lesser proprietors who would correspond with the gentry in England and act as a counter-weight to the great lords. This, it was hoped, would facilitate the spread of English justice in the provinces, and thus end the disturbed conditions. With all the power in the hands of one individual, it was argued, a lordship was 'unfitt ever to be reduced to a countie and sheire, for what shall any sherif have there to doe where one man ruleth all, where there be no freeholders nor consequently any lawfull jurie as in this government there cannot be'.[61] This, therefore, was the official objection to the lordships of Ormond and Desmond as well as to the more Gaelicized earldoms of Thomond and Clanricard. The work of the presidency was frustrated in Ormond by the influence of that earl and in Desmond by rebellion that led to confiscation and plantation. It is ironic, therefore, that the scheme met with its greatest success in the lands west of the Shannon. This was explained by the fact that both the earldoms were ruled consistently by a president and were not given an opportunity to mobilize their forces against the government. The few insurrections that did occur were limited in extent, because the allegiance of the landowners was forced by the terrifying system of suspended penalties: the taking of hostages and recognizances. By these means the sway of the president was extended also into the almost totally Gaelicized northern part of Connacht, and these areas were eventually brought to conformity also by forceful persuasion rather than colonization. As a result of the success of the programme laid down by Sidney, Connacht, and not Munster, remained as a bastion of the Anglo-Irish into the seventeenth century.

6

The breakdown:
Elizabethan attitudes towards the Irish

We have so far confined ourselves to the practical side of the Elizabethan conquest and have largely ignored the legal and ethical considerations raised during the implementation of the programme.

As to the feudal lordships, the government was merely seeking to reintroduce the English law into areas that had once been subject to the crown. In seeking to accomplish this, use was made of the same administrative machinery that had been employed by the London government to undermine the power of the lords in the outlying areas of England and Wales. Thus the government could justify their actions by referring to the precedent 'by the which pollicie Wales was sometimes reformed and brought to subjection'. Lord Deputy Sidney might have sought by legal means – such as a writ of *quo warranto* – to deprive the lords of their palatinate jurisdictions, but instead he refused to recognize the grants without documentary evidence. The official assumption was that private jurisdictions had outlived their usefulness, and it was thought that what the crown had once granted it could now revoke, particularly if there was evidence that the lords had exceeded their authority. Thus, by drawing attention to the inequities of Irish feudal society the government officials were presenting a case for the abolition of palatinate counties.

It is true that the powers vested in the provincial presidents in Ireland were greater than those enjoyed by their counterparts in England and Wales. The government was able to justify entrusting its officials with the power of martial law by pointing to the unruly conditions prevailing in provincial Ireland, and more especially to the continued practice of coyne and livery by the Anglo-Irish lords.

Again there was nothing novel in this, since the seneschals in Leinster, and even the sheriffs in most of the counties in Ireland, had previously enjoyed the right to exercise martial law. Moreover, it was argued that such power would be recalled when it was deemed to be no longer necessary, and the way was ready for the free exercise of English law. In the words of Captain Thomas Lee:

> martial law is very necessary, and (in my opinion) ought to be granted to all governors of remote and savage places where your majesty's laws are not received . . . until such time as the people shall become civil, and embrace the laws, and peaceable living.[1]

The draconian system of suspended penalties that was used by the presidents in Munster and Connacht could also be justified by reference to English practice since, at the end of the fifteenth century, similar measures were used by the government to guarantee the loyalty of the English aristocracy.[2] Thus the ambition of the government was not to overthrow the Irish feudal lords, but rather to compel them to comport themselves as their English counterparts did and open their territories to the free administration of English law. It was regarded as unreasonable to oppose the efforts of the government, and any Anglo-Irish lord who did so ran the risk of suffering the same penalty as a rebellious English lord would have done – indictment for treason and confiscation of property.

The problems raised by colonization were much greater, however, since it involved establishing title to property and clearing the indigenous population from the lands they and their ancestors had occupied for hundreds of years. The first of these problems presented little difficulty to the English legal mind. England, after all, had established title to most of Ireland by right of conquest during the Norman offensive of the twelfth and thirteenth centuries. Even though the native Irish had reoccupied much of this land in the counter-offensive of the fourteenth and fifteenth centuries they had never established legal title to it, and could therefore be declared trespassers on land that really belonged to the crown or to the descendants of the original conquerors. It was by right of conquest, for example, that Peter Carew claimed title to the barony of Idrone, and he intended to pursue a similar claim to more extensive lands in south-west Munster. Again it was by right of inheritance, from the long-extinct line of the earls of Ulster, that the queen claimed the lands in that province, and the posthumous act of attainder of Shane O'Neill merely reiterated the crown's title. Sir Thomas Smith, for example, was granted title to lands in Ireland as 'parcel of the county of Ulster in Ireland' to hold from the crown as heir to the earldom of Ulster by service of a knight's fee, and Essex likewise sought a patent for 'the dominion of Clandeboy [etc.] . . . in the earldom of Ulster'.[3] There was, in fact, only one attempt to colonize lands to which legal title had not been established, that of St Leger in south-west Munster, and in that case it was hoped to have the lords who resisted attainted as rebels. The accepted legality was, in the words of Spenser, that 'all is the conqueror's as Tully to Brutus saith'. Legal technicalities were certainly sufficient to satisfy Gilbert's conscience in asserting claims to land in Ireland, and he was happy to report that the Irish were 'so apte to offende as it is very likely that by justice theye will make your highnes in small time owner of all the rest'.[4]

Not all colonizers were as callous as Gilbert, but even those who were squeamish about availing themselves of legal flaws were satisfied that better use would be made of the lands by the English settlers than had been made by the native inhabitants. Smith was satisfied that no injury would be inflicted on the native inhabitants 'yf the desolate and desert growndes be made inhabited and plentiful', and similar statements were made by all colonizers to further justify their acquisition of land in Ireland. This argument became so commonplace that Sir John Davies, in proposing the plantation in Ulster at the beginning of the seventeenth century, could state categorically of the Gaelic Irish that:

> if themselves were suffered to possess the whole country as their septs have done for many hundred of years past, they would never (to the end of the world) build houses, make townships or villages or manure or improve the land as it ought to be; therefore it stands neither with Christian policy nor conscience to suffer so good and fruitful a country to lie waste like a wilderness.[5]

Thus, the legal question involved in establishing title to land was easily answered to the satisfaction of the queen's, and England's, conscience, and the colonizers were satisfied as to the equity of their actions when they referred to the consideration of land utility. How to treat the indigenous population was a more complex question since it could not be answered by recourse to precedent. The Normans had driven off merely the ruling elite from the lands they conquered and had retained the majority of the inhabitants as tenants and cultivators. The Anglo-Irish descendants of the earlier conquerors followed the Norman example. They clearly regarded the struggle in Ireland as a conflict between cultures, Gaelic and

English, but while they considered the Gaelic system of government to be tyrannical, hence barbarous, they did not consider those living under Gaelic rule to be incapable of being civilized. On the contrary, they held that once the Gaelic chieftains were overthrown and Gaelic law abolished, the native inhabitants, thus liberated from thraldom, would be accepted as subjects under English law. Even the Statutes of Kilkenny (1366), which some historians have labelled apartheid legislation, allowed for a procedure by which Irishmen could be granted the same legal status as English subjects. The fact that native Irish in the sixteenth century were being freely accepted as tenants to land within the Pale proves the persistence of these attitudes among the Anglo-Irish.[6]

As long as this remained the accepted ideology the scope for intensive colonization in Ireland was limited. The Anglo-Irish view won acceptance even among English privy councillors such as Sir James Croft who hoped that 'the wyld people [in Ireland] may be brought by degrees to be apt to erect such lawes and ordinance as be used in the English Pale'. Croft's original hope had been that the heirs to Gaelic lordships, once educated at grammar schools, would draw their subjects to obedience and civility. Thus, Croft was unwilling to countenance stern measures against any inhabitants in Ireland other than the Scots in Ulster, whom he regarded as intruders and 'not in case to receyve any good orders'.[7] This too was the queen's thinking on the matter. She recognized that the Scots, who inhabited lands in north-east Ulster, were interlopers and not her subjects and could therefore be forcibly removed with impunity. She directed, however, that the native Irish population there should be 'well used', and on the subject of the Essex expedition she stated specifically that 'our meaning is not that the said Erle nor any of his company shall offend any person that is knowne to be our good subject'.[8] Both Essex and Smith promised to observe this limitation, but Essex's assurance that he would not 'imbrue' his 'hands with more blood than the necessity of the cause requireth' was somewhat short of convincing.

Essex did follow the queen's instructions by concentrating his energies against the Scots settlement in Ulster. It was with the intention of breaking their power that he mobilized the nocturnal expedition to Rathlin Island, in 1574, which succceeded in slaughtering the entire population of the island, to the estimated number of six hundred people.[9] The earl was frustrated by the queen's directive that he should not molest the Gaelic–Irish inhabitants of Ulster, and when the local chieftain, Sir Brian McPhelim O'Neill, broke his compact with Essex he considered 'all this to fall out to the best . . . so in the manner of their departure and breach of their faiths they have given me just cause to govern such as shall inhabit with us in the most severe manner, which I would not without evil opinions have offered if their revolt had not been manifest'. One of the lieutenants of the expedition, Edward Barkley, was glad of the opportunity to extend stern rule over the Irish, and he wrote that the inhabitants of Ulster would be commanded by the queen or starve. Barkley gave a graphic description of how they had driven the Irish from the plains into the woods where they would freeze or famish with the onset of winter, and concluded with the smug observation: 'how godly a dede it is to overthrowe so wicked a race the world may judge: for my part I thinke there canot be a greater sacryfice to God'. Smith was equally pleased at the Irish resistance, and interpreted it as 'the best token that can be that God will prosper this doing when he castith his feare in them before whom he wold have reduced in to good order'.[10]

The most extreme action of the enterprise took place at a Christmas feast in 1574, when Sir Brian McPhelim O'Neill, his wife and kinsmen were seized by Essex and two hundred followers slaughtered. This massacre went beyond the original instructions of Queen Elizabeth, but it is significant that the attitude of the London government had hardened sufficiently to countenance the actions of Essex. The queen even commended his service in Ulster and was satisfied that her instructions had been complied with,

> because we do perceive that when occasion doth present you do rather allure and bring in that rude and barbarous nation to civility and acknowledging of their duty to God and to us by wisdom and discreet handling than by force and shedding of blood; and yet when necessity requireth you are ready also to oppose yourself and your forces to them whom reason and duty cannot bridle.[11]

It appears, therefore, that the Essex experience had convinced the queen and her advisers that the Gaelic-Irish were an unreasonable people, and that they, no less than the Scots intruders in Ulster, might be slaughtered by extralegal methods.

Similar extreme action was taken by Gilbert against those who opposed the colonization effort in Munster. When the expected resistance occurred, Gilbert was, in October 1569, appointed as military governor of Munster with almost unrestricted power of martial law.[12] Thereafter war in Munster became total war, and Gilbert extended his action to 'manne, woman and childe', so 'the name of an Inglysh man was made more terryble now to them than the syght of an hundyth was before'. [13] The pamphleteer, Thomas Churchyard, who accompanied Gilbert to Munster, justified the slaughter of non-combatants on the ground of expediency. Their support, he claimed, was essential to sustain the rebels 'so that the killyng of theim by the sworde was the waie to kill the menne of warre by famine'.

Even in accepting former rebels to mercy, Gilbert displayed the utmost cruelty and inhumanity. All who submitted were compelled to demean themselves utterly before him, to take an oath of loyalty to the queen and to provide pledges and recognizances as an assurance of their future loyalty. The true impact of the severity is brought home by his practice described graphically by Churchyard:

> that the heddes of all those (of what sort soever thei were) which were killed in the daie, should be cutte of from their bodies and brought to the place where he incamped at night, and should there bee laied on the ground by eche side of the waie ledyng into his owne tente so that none could come into his tente for any cause but commonly he muste passe through a lane of heddes which he used *ad terrorem,* the dedde feelyng nothyng the more paines thereby: and yet did it bring greate terrour to the people when thei sawe the heddes of their dedde fathers, brothers, children, kinsfolke and freindes, lye on the grounde before their faces, as thei came to speake with the said collonell.

Churchyard recognized that some would criticize this conduct, but he justified it by asserting that the Irish had been first in committing atrocities, but more especially on the ground of efficiency 'through the terrour which the people conceived thereby it made short warres'. [14]

The significant factor is that both Essex and Churchyard, in acknowledging the possibility of criticism of their actions, were admitting that what they were about was innovative. The Norman lords were not known to have committed such atrocities in Ireland, and there is no evidence that systematic execution of non-combatants by martial law was practised in any of the Tudor rebellions in England. It is obvious that Gilbert and Essex considered that, in dealing with the native Irish population, they were absolved from all normal ethical restraints. The questions that we must pose are how, at the mid-sixteenth century, the Irish, a people with whom the English had always had some familiarity, came to be regarded as uncivilized, and what justifications were used for indiscriminate slaying and expropriation?

One important consideration is that this was probably the first time since the original Norman conquest that large numbers of Englishmen came into direct confrontation with the Gaelic Irish in their native habitat.[15] Various lords justices had first been screened through the English Pale and had been prepared for the cultural shock before encountering the native Irish. Few English emissaries actually penetrated deep into the Gaelic areas, and no lord deputy had ever made such comprehensive tours through the country as Sidney. Even more to the point is the arrival of colonizers, such as the younger Smith, Essex, and St Leger directly by ship to the proposed site of the colony, thus totally escaping the gradual acclimatization that approach through the Pale would have effected.

Another important consideration was the peculiar nature of Catholicism in Gaelic Ireland. That the Irish were Christian was never doubted by the Normans or their successors, but it was always recognized that Christianity in Gaelic Ireland did not fully conform to Roman liturgical practice, and that many pre-Christian traditions and customs were only slightly veneered by Christianity. Criticism of unorthodox practices was frequent, but deviations of this nature were not uncommon in medieval Europe and two systems – an episcopal church on English lines in the Pale and environs, and an Irish-speaking loosely structured church in the Gaelic areas – continued to tolerate each others presence.[16] This arrangement was accepted by the Anglo-Irish but not by those adventurers who joined Sidney in Ireland. These were, for the most part, extreme Protestants; many of them like Carew, had fled England in Queen Mary's reign and associated themselves with the exiled English divines on the Continent.[17] They were hypercritical of Catholicism in the Pale, but religious observance in Gaelic Ireland was so remote from anything they had previously experienced that they branded the native Irish as pagan without question.

The groundwork for this view had been laid by the Anglo-Irish who had, over the centuries, attributed certain vices to the Gaelic Irish which, they claimed, were fostered by Gaelic law. The most famous of such tirades was the 'Counter-Remonstrance' of 1331, but the accusations were repeated with a certain regularity down through the years, even into the sixteenth century. A Palesman was clearly the author of the unpublished pamphlet 'On the Disorders of the Irishry' issued in 1572. In this, all the customary accusations were levelled at the native Irish, and Gaelic law was declared 'contrary to God his lawe and also repugnant to the Queens Majesties lawes'. Even more severe was the assertion that the 'outwarde behavyor' of the Irish made it 'seme' that 'they neyther love nor dredd God nor yet hate the Devell, they are superstycyous and worshippers of images and open idolators'. The author was probably aware that much of what he said was rhetorical, and clearly his purpose was to impress upon the government the idea that the Anglo-Irish were the only true representatives of civility in Ireland and therefore deserving of support. Literature of this nature served, however, to prepare the minds of Englishmen for the worst, and many of those who came to Ireland saw what they had been conditioned to expect. [18]

What the English adventurers encountered in the remote areas of Ireland was taken as confirmation of the assertions of the Anglo-Irish, leading many to despair of Christianity there. Edmund Tremayne found religion 'totally lacking' in Munster, and refused to declare the Irish

> ether Papists nor Protestants but rather such as have nether feare nor love of God in their harts that restreyneth them from ill. Thei regarde no othe, thei blaspheme, they murder, commit whoredome, hold no wedlocke, ravish, steal and commit all abomination without scruple of conscience.

The most startling features were the decay of the churches, which Tremayne found were 'onlie like stables', and the ignorance of the 'priests and ministers of their owne race werse than shepherds'. [19] Sir Henry Sidney, a moderate Protestant, wrote an equally astonished report of the state of religion in Munster in 1567.

> Swerlie there was never people that lived in more miserie than they doe, nor as it should seme of wourse myndes, for matrimonie emongs them is no more regarded in effect than conjunction betwene unreasonable beastes, perjurie, robberie and murder counted alloweable, finallie I cannot finde that they make anny conscience of synne and doubtless I doubte whether they christen there children or no, for neither finde I place where it should be don, nor any person able to enstruct them in the rules of a Christan, or if they were taught I see no grace in them to follow it, and when they dye I cannot see they make any accompte of the woorlde to com.

The clear implication is that Sidney considered himself to be dealing with people who were essentially pagans. He, like Edmund Spenser, was arriving at the conclusion that while the Irish professed to be Catholics they had no real knowledge of religion.

> They are all Papists by their profession [wrote Spenser] but in the same so blindly and brutishly informed for the most part as that you would raher think them atheists or infidels. [20]

The English adventurers of the 1560s and 1570s thus had little difficulty in satisfying themselves that the Gaelic Irish were pagans, and this became an accepted tenet of many Englishmen. Lord Deputy Mountjoy, for example, was convinced that 'the poore people' of Ulster 'never had the meanes to know God', and he described one of the Gaelic chieftains of Ulster as being 'without any knowledge of God, or almost any civility'. [21] That such views could be offered without explanation in 1602 is a measure of the success of the colonizers of the previous generation in propagating them.

We must now ask why it was so important to the English adventurers to convince themselves that the Gaelic Irish were pagan? The first point to note is that the English recognized a distinction between Christianity and civilization, and believed that a people could be civilized without being Christian but not christianized without first being made civil. It was admitted that the Romans had been civilized despite being pagans, and sixteenth-century Englishmen were not ignorant of the existence of civilizations beyond the boundaries of Christian Europe. Supremacy was claimed for western civilization because it combined the benefits of Christianity with those of civility. To admit that the native Irish were Christian would, therefore, have been to acknowledge them as civilized also. By declaring the Irish to be pagan, however, the English were decreeing that the Irish were culpable, since their heathenism was due not to a lack of opportunity but rather because their system of government was antithetical to Christianity. Once it was established that the Irish were pagans the first logical step had been taken towards declaring them barbarians. The English were able to pursue their argument further when they witnessed the appearance of the native Irish, their habits, customs and agricultural methods.

We must bear in mind that of the group of adventurers who flocked to Ireland many were widely travelled and some well read. There is evidence that a few of the West Countrymen had fought on the Continent, even against the Turks in Hungary, while others had travelled to the New World. [22] All were interested in travel and adventure, and they had, through their exploits and reading of travel literature, such as the English translation of Johann Boemus (1555), familiarized themselves with the habits of peoples who were considered barbarians by European standards.[23] It was natural that they should now strive to assimilate the Irish into their general conception of civilization. One early example of this was Sidney's comparing the Ulster chieftain Shane O'Neill with Huns, Vandals, Goths and Turks.[24] Sidney was certainly well versed in travel literature, and it is significant that the translator Thomas Hacket, in dedicating one of his works to Sidney, associated Sidney's task in Ireland with that of the Spaniards in the New World when he praised 'such as have invented good lawes and statutes for the brideling of the barbarous and wicked, and for the maintayning and defending of the just'.[25]

What is significant is that many of the colonizers came to Ireland with a preconception of what a barbaric society was like, and they found features in Gaelic life to fit this model. The ultimate hall-mark of barbarism was the practice of cannibalism. While the Irish were seldom accused of cannibalism, we do find Sidney referring to Shane O'Neill as 'that canyball', and Sir John Davies, some fifty years later, asserted that those living under Gaelic rule 'were little better than Cannibals who do hunt one another'.[26] An aspect of Gaelic life that attracted much more attention was the practice of transhumance which the English took as proof that the Irish were nomads, hence barbarians.

In the travel literature that was read by sixteenth-century Englishmen nomadic people were considered to be at the opposite pole of civilization from themselves. Johann Boemus, for example, found the Scythians, and their offshoot the Tartarians, to be the most barbarous people in the world because they 'neither possessed any grounds, nor had any seats or houses to dwell in, but wandered through wilderness and desert places driving their flockes and heardes of beasts before them'.[27] This view became entrenched in the English mind and was repeated in the introduction of almost every sixteenth-century pamphlet dealing with travel and exploration. This explains why the practice of transhumance so readily caught the Englishman's attention in Ireland.

Sir Thomas Smith who sponsored a colony in Ireland, even though he never visited the country himself, was particularly vehement against the 'idle followyng of heards as the Tartarians, Arabians and Irishe men doo'; thus categorizing the Irish with those whom he considered to be at the lowest level of civilization. Spenser went even further and took the practice of transhumance as proof that the Gaelic Irish were descended from the Scythians because he

thought the practice to be after 'the manner of the Scythians as ye
may read in Olaus Magnus et Johannes Boemus, and yet is used
amongst all the Tartarians and the people about the Caspian sea
which are naturally Scythians'. Here was evidence to satisfy Spenser
that the Irish were indeed true barbarians, and this notion also
became entrenched in the minds of sixteenth-century Englishmen.
Fynes Moryson, writing at the end of the century, stated as a fact
that 'some of the Irish are of the race of Scythians, comming into
Spaine and from thence into Ireland'.[28]

The Irish were also declared to be exceedingly licentious. Incest
was said to be common among them, and Gaelic chieftains were
accused of debauching the wives and daughters of their tenants:
'even himself, his household and all his traine when pleaseth himself
. . . useth both wife and daughter by himself and his followers with
all abomination'.[29] By thus building up a catalogue of abuse the
English convinced themselves that the Irish were barbaric as well as
pagan. Gilbert certainly treated them as if they were a lower order of
humanity, and Carew considered one of his purposes in Ireland to
be 'the suppressing and reforming of the loose, barbarous and most
wicked life of that savage nation'. An increasing number of people
attributed beastly characteristics to the Irish, and Barnaby Rich
argued against those who thought English conduct in Ireland 'too
seveare' by pointing out that the Irish preferred to 'live like beastes,
voide of lawe and all good order', and that they were 'more uncivill,
more uncleanly, more barbarous and more brutish in their customs
and demeanures, than in any other part of the world that is
known'.[30]

The English colonizers certainly went further than the
Anglo-Irish in denigrated the Gaelic Irish, and, what is more
important, they put their conclusions to a different purpose. It
appears that the principal aim of the Anglo-Irish in decrying the
vices of the Irish was to instil themselves with confidence in their
rather precarious position, and to impress upon the English that
they, being the only civilized people in the country, should be
supported militarily and financially in their struggle for survival.
The underlying assumption was, however, that the depravity of the
Irish was caused by environmental factors, and the Anglo-Irish
repeatedly called upon the English government to aid them in
reforming the Irish. In 1572, for example, the Palesman Rowland
White argued against the contention that the Irishmen were 'so
naturallie rooted' in savagery 'that to aulter their condicions semith
impossible'. On the contrary, said White, the Irish were 'reasonable
men and see thruth', since 'the manner of the man' is due 'rather to

his educacion than to his naturall disposicion'.[31] Some Englishmen
of the sixteenth century adhered to this view as, for example, the
aged clergyman Robert Weston who served as lord chancellor in
Ireland. He acknowledged that 'ignorance ... is the mother and
nurse of those fowle babes', and to dispel this ignorance he
recommended the sending to Ireland of ministers of religion to save
'many thousand souls ... that else would perish'. Weston claimed
that such 'would work a willing and a more perfect obedience in all
subjects than any fear of sword or punishment can do', thus
suggesting that there were those who preferred the sword to the
pulpit as a means of bringing the Irish to obedience. That he was
fighting a lone battle is indicated by the outburst of Lord Deputy
Fitzwilliam in 1572:

> this people ... hath been long misled in beastly liberty and
> sensuall immunity so as they cannot abide to hear of correction,
> no, not for the horribelest sins that they can commit. Till the
> sword have thoroughly and universally tamed (and not meekened
> them) in vain is law brought amongst them: nay dangerously is
> the bridle thereof shaked towards them ... this makes them all
> tooth and nail ... to spurn, kick and practice against it.[32]

Fitzwilliam spoke for the young aggressive men who had been
influenced by the ideas of the Renaissance. Once these had been
persuaded that the Irish were barbarians they were able to produce
a moral and civil justification for their conquest of Ireland, and
turned their back on the Aristotelian notion of reform. Although
most of the colonizers avowed that their long-term purpose was to
convert the Irish to Christianity, they made no effort to accomplish
this end, contending that conversion was impossible so long as the
Irish persisted in their barbarous way of life. All were agreed that
their immediate object should be the secular one of drawing the Irish
to civility. Proclaiming this responsibility, Smith asserted that God
'did make apte and prepare this nation ... to inhabite and reforme
so barbarous a nation as that is, and to bring them to the knowledge
and lawe were both a goodly and commendable deede, and a
sufficient work of our age',[33] adding that it was England's civic duty
to educate the Irish brutes 'in vertuous labor and in justice, and to
teach them our English lawes and civilitie and leave robbyng and
stealing and killyng one of another'.

In Smith's view the English were the new Romans come to civilize
the Irish, as the old Romans had once civilized the ancient Britons.

This I write unto you as I do understand by histories of thyngs by past, how this contrey of England, ones as uncivill as Ireland now is, was by colonies of the Romaynes brought to understand the lawes and orders of thanncient orders whereof there hath no nacon more streightly and truly kept the mouldes even to this day then we, yea more than thitalians and Romaynes themselves.[34]

In accepting this idea, Smith was abandoning the notion of the Anglo-Irish that the native Irish were enslaved by their lords and were crying out for enlightenment and liberation. The Irish, in his view, were indeed living under tyranny, but were not yet ready for liberation since they were at an earlier stage of cultural development – the stage at which the Britons had been when the Romans had arrived. They needed to be made bondsmen to enlightened lords who would instruct them in the ways of civil society. In his major writing, *De Republica Anglorum,* Smith claimed superiority for England over all other nations, even the ancient Romans, on the ground that bondsmen were by the sixteenth century virtually unknown in England since all the inhabitants were fit to become freemen. Now that he looked at the Irish situation, it was logical that he should recommend that the Irish, whom he considered to be barbarians, should be made subservient to the colonizing English so that, through subjection, they could come gradually to appreciate civility, and thus eventually achieve freedom as the former British bondsmen had done.[35]

It is probable that the Roman parallel was used by Smith to enable him to justify his own actions in Ireland. This approach had already been taken by writers of the Italian Renaissance, such as Machiavelli, who contrasted medieval 'babarism' with old Roman 'civilization' in order to justify the eradication of the last vestiges of this barbarism. This anti-medievalism was easily transmitted by English Renaissance scholars, such as Smith, and further transformed when applied to the Irish who were considered even more 'barbarian' than their medieval monkish counterparts. This explains why the Roman allusion appears so frequently in sixteenth-century writing on Ireland. Edmund Spenser repeated, almost verbatim, the sentiments of Smith when he remarked that:

the English were at first as stout and warlike a people as ever were the Irish and yet you see are now brought to that civility, that no nation in the world excelleth them in all goodly conversation.

Almost fifty years later Sir John Davies, in urging his

contemporaries to complete the conquest of Ireland, again alluded to the Roman general Julius Agricola who had civilized 'our ancestors the ancient Britons' who had hitherto been 'rude and dispersed, and therefore prone upon every occasion to make war'.[36] It was only by retaining such a concept that cultivated men could allow themselves to bring other people to subjection, which was one purpose of English colonization in Ireland.

Thus Walter, earl of Essex, assured the Privy Council that he 'never mente to unpeople the cuntrie Clandyboy of their naturall inhabitauntes, but to have cherished them so farre fourthe as they woulde live quiett and deutifull'. It was his intention certainly to eliminate the military caste in Gaelic Ulster by having them 'executed by martiall lawe whensoever they be founde ydell and weaponed'. Otherwise he wanted the natives retained as cultivators of the soil, 'and the more Irishe the more profitable so as the Englishe be hable to master them'.[37] Sir Thomas Smith also envisaged the Irish husbandman continuing to occupy land in his colony and even being instructed in the English methods of cultivation. This, however, was to be done under the strict supervision of those who would undertake the task of colonizing. It was no part of his plan that any native Irish should 'purchase land, beare office, be chosen of any jurie or admitted witnes in any reall or personall action, nor be bounde apprentice to any science or arte that may indomage the Queenes Majesties subjectes hereafter'. They were to be allowed to 'beare no kind of weapon nor armoure', and the only benefits he had to offer them were that their 'plowing and laboure' would be 'well rewarded with great provision', and that they would be free from 'coyne, lyverye or any other exaction'.[38] What Smith and Essex really wanted to accomplish was to drive out the ruling elite and retain the majority of the population as docile cultivators. Smith, and afterwards Spenser and Davies, pointed to Roman precedent to justify this, and they considered the example to be pertinent because England was now the new Rome, the centre of civilization.

We can see clearly that Smith had developed a sense of cultural process which could be used as a rationale for reducing the Irish to servitude and, if they resisted, for slaughtering and dispossessing them. No other colonizer in Ireland articulated this view as clearly as he did, but there is evidence that all had a sense of cultural superiority to the Irish. Essex professed his mission to be 'groundid on Her Majesty's commiseration of the natural born subjects of this province over whom the Scots did tyrannise', but when the same subjects refused to accept the substitution of a new form of servitude for the old, he had no scruples about slaughtering them. [39]

Sidney too seems to have had a vague sense of a cultural process and at least approached a concept of cultural classification when he observed and compared the three segments of society that confronted him in Ireland – the Gaelic world, feudal Ireland and the 'civilized' society of the Pale. It was clear to the lord deputy that Irish feudal society was preferable to Gaelic Ireland, but he was equally conscious that feudal society in Ireland was more independent and authoritarian than its English counterpart, and was still at a stage of development beyond which England had advanced. Gilbert was even more emphatic on this point and condemned the independence of the Irish feudal lords, warning against the danger for 'a prince to have his subjectes greatly followed for themselves, as may partlie appear by Nevell earll of Warruicke, by the prynce of Orrainge in the lowe countryes, and by the ffaccions betwene the howse of Bourbon and Gwysse in Ffrance'. [40] It seemed to Gilbert that the Irish feudal lords were at a stage of development similar to that prevailing in France and the Netherlands but from which England had evolved. Others saw this as an intermediary stage between total licence, as in Gaelic Ireland, and final, if reluctant, acceptance of a centralized state, as in England. We get an example of this thinking, in 1607, from Sir John Davies, the then attorney-general for Ireland, in his recommendation that Hugh O'Neill, earl of Tyrone, be deprived of control of his tenants and be reduced 'to the moderate condition of other lords in Ireland and in England at this day'. Davies reminded his readers that 'when England was full of tenants-at-will our barons were then like the mere Irish lords, and were able to raise armies against the crown; and as this man was O'Neal in Ulster, so the Earl of Warwick was O'Nevill in Yorkshire, and the Bishopric and Mortimer was the like in the Marches of Wales'. [41]

The evidence is admittedly scattered, and no individual writer stuck consistently to one point of view, but we can state confidently that the old concept of the Irish as being socially inferior to the English had been replaced with the idea that they were anthropologically inferior and were further behind the English on the ladder of development. The old world had lacked a sense of history and hence a concept of social process and development, but the widening horizons of the articulate citizen of sixteenth-century England, both intellectually and geographically, slowly eroded the old idea of a static world. [42] It was only natural that the aggressive men who sought their fortunes in Ireland should try to fit Gaelic society into their expanding world view. But what provided

Englishmen with a growing sense of confidence and pride spelled disaster for Gaelic Ireland, which was now seen as a cultural throw-back that must be painfully dragged to modernity. In the minds of these adventurers, it no longer held true, as it did under the Statutes of Kilkenny of 1366, that an Irishman could be accepted under English law. To do so, said Spenser, would be as absurd as to 'transfer the laws of the Lacedemonians to the people of Athens'. Laws, according to Spenser,

> ought to be fashioned unto the manners and condition of the people to whom they are meant, and not to be imposed upon them according to the simple rule of right, for then . . . instead of good they may work ill, and pervert justice to extreme injustice.

The central theme of Spenser's *A View of the Present State of Ireland* was, therefore, that 'the common law . . . with the state of Ireland preadventure it doth not so well agree, being a people altogether stubborn and untamed'. The Gaelic law, which Spenser saw as fashioned unto the manner and condition of the people, could not, however, be tolerated, since it was opposed to all civility. The only solution was to forbid the practice of Gaelic law and subject the Irish by force so that they could then by 'moderation' be brought 'from their delight of licentious barbarism, unto the love of goodness and civility'.[45]

It is only when we appreciate this reasoning that we can fully understand the attitudes and policies of Sidney and his adherents in Ireland. The lord deputy was critical of feudal society in Ireland, but argued that it was capable of being reformed and made to conform with the English model of civility. In the words of William Gerrard, one of Sidney's subordinates, the native Irish could be subdued only by force, but the 'degenerate' English by 'the rodd of justice' for 'in theim yet resteth this instincte of Englishe nature generally to feare justice'.[44] Sidney was more moderate and even argued that those areas of Gaelic Ireland which were within easy reach of Dublin and had had some contact with civility were amenable to justice: extreme action was reserved for Gaelic Ulster and the Gaelic areas of south-west Munster.

The English Privy Council seems to have reasoned similarly, as is suggested by their confining St Leger's claims to the Gaelic areas of Munster. It was the Gaelic Irish who were the true barbarians and only force could draw them to civility. Sir William Fitzwilliam admitted that 'nothing but feare and force can teach dutie and obedience' to 'this rebellious people'. The same view was held by Sir

John Perrott who prided himself on his stern rule while lord president in Munster, and concluded that 'there ys no waye better then to make those wylde people . . . to feare, so they be not kepte in servile feare'. Essex too 'put litell difference betweene the Irishe and the Scott saving that the Skott is the less ill of disposition, more inclinable to civility though more dangerous'. The Irish were thus categorized as the most barbarous of peoples, and Englishmen argued that it was their duty and responsibility to hold them down by force so that through subjection they could be gradually uplifted and thus prepared for liberty.[45]

We cannot, however, attribute to the English complete originality in this. Many of the conclusions at which they were arriving about the Irish had already been come to by the Spaniards in their thinking on the Amerindians. Professor J. H. Elliott has argued that the Spaniards had come to consider the indigenous population of the New World as culturally inferior to themselves, and were, like the Elizabethans in Ireland, approaching a concept of cultural classification.[46] It can be established that many of the English associated with colonization were familiar with Spanish thinking, and it is quite probable that their attitudes and actions were influenced by Spanish precedents.

The most potent Spanish influence was undoubtedly communicated by Richard Eden's partial translation of Peter Martyr's *De Orbo Novo*. Eden was well known to the group of West-Country adventurers who came to Ireland in the 1560s, and Sir Thomas Smith had been Eden's tutor at Cambridge which is sufficient reason to assume his familiarity with the translation. Sidney was also acquainted with the work and may have had more direct acquaintance with Spanish colonial theory while he served in Spain, 1553-6, in Queen Mary's service.[47] In any event, it is difficult to imagine how any of the adventurers in Ireland could have been ignorant of Eden's work. It is more than likely that Champernoun, St Leger and the others saw themselves as *conquistadores* subduing the barbaric and pagan Irish just as their Spanish counterparts were bringing the Amerindians to subjection.

Smith certainly recognized that his venture in Ireland was being compared by others with colonization in the New World. He voiced no objection, other than the fear that his exploit would be tainted by association with the none too successful Anglo-French venture of 1563, and that he and his son would be 'accompted deceivers of men and enterprysers of Stowelies [Stukeley's] voiage of Terra Florida, or a lottarye as som evill tongues did terme it'. Essex acknowledged a parallel with Spain and expected 'that within two yeares, you shall make restraint for the Englishe to come hither [to Ireland] without license as at this date it is in Spaine for going to the Indyes'.[48] Leicester, too, appears to have been influenced by Spanish thinking and admitted that his attitude towards the Irish was influenced by the information that he had of the treatment meted out to other 'barbarous' peoples. He argued that since the Irish were 'a wild, barbarous and treacherous people, I would deall as I have hard and redd of such lyke how they have byn used'. In this he was, seemingly, suggesting that since the native Irish were barbarians there was no reason why the Spanish precedent should not be followed. Leicester's many statements make it clear that he favoured a tough policy for Ireland, and his sentiments come remarkably close to those of Richard Eden who recommended that Englishmen emulate the example of the Spaniards in the New World.[49] If Leicester was, in fact, influenced by the Spanish experience he acknowledged the debt by implication rather than overtly. Less hesitantly and despite their hatred of the Spaniards, other Englishmen occasionally cited Spanish actions to justify their own extreme measures in Ireland. Davies, for example, when justifying the transplantation of natives during the course of the Ulster Plantation cited the precedent of 'the Spaniards [who] lately removed all the Moors out of Granada into Barbary without providing them with any new seats there'.[50] It is evident, therefore, that the English were aware of the severity of the Spaniards in dealing with those who did not measure up to their standards of civility, and it appears that this knowledge strengthened the English in their conviction that they were justified in their own harsh treatment of the native Irish.

Thus, not only those who had practical experience in Ireland, but also those who observed events from a distance were satisfied as to the rectitude of English actions in Ireland. Croft, who as late as 1561 had advocated a moderate policy, was convinced by the new argument and became one of the principal advocates of colonization. Likewise Leicester, who in the early 1560s had favoured the Anglo-Irish of the Pale and had even supported the acceptance of Shane O'Neill to mercy, by the 1570s had closed his mind to moderate views. Not even the actions of Essex were harsh enough for Leicester who asserted that Essex

> must determine to become such a man as must show himself of such valor in his own person as must bring feare and terror to his enemyes which is not heard of yet . . . temporising warres are to be used with civill and expirt men, but savages and those rurall

raskells are only by force and fear to be vanquished.[51]

Even when considered in retrospect, there were few sixteenth-century Englishmen who voiced regrets about their actions in Ireland. Sir William Gerrard, who was appointed lord chancellor of Ireland in the late 1570s as the first great burst of colonization was being brought to a halt, thought it would have 'bene better . . . yf tenne yeares past the governor had put on determynacon to subjecte the whole Irishrie to the sworde'. When Richard Beacon discussed the actions of Richard Bingham, who, when president in Connacht, did 'proceede against offendors without observing the usuall ceremonies of lawe', he justified them by reference to Roman precedent, and he saluted Bingham who 'by his singular art and skill in military discipline as an other Cesar suppressed at the last Vercingetorix and the rebelling Gaules'. Fynes Moryson also defended Bingham against those who criticized him as a tyrant and asserted that 'those who best understood the Irish nature found nothing so necessarie for keeping them in obedience as severitie, nor so dangerous for the increase of murthers and outrages as indulgence towards them'. Sir John Davies agreed with these sentiments and drawing upon English experience in Ireland laid it down as a general principle that:

> a barbarous country must be first broken by a war before it will be capable of good government; and when it is fully subdued and conquered if it be not well planted and governed after the conquest it will eftsoons return to the former barbarism.[52]

It is clear from what has been said that the English concept of civility was derived from Renaissance thinking, but the English notion of barbarism was confirmed and reinforced to such an extent, as a result of their Irish experience, that the words Irish and barbarian became virtually interchangeable. Archbishop Parker, for example, when speaking of the people in the north of England feared lest they 'should become too much Irish and savage'.[53] It is obvious, therefore, that there was no longer any hope of conciliation in Ireland, since the English, convinced that it was their civic responsibility to subdue the barbarians, could never draw back. The acceptance of this ideology meant also that the Anglo-Irish in Ireland came under censure from the English because of the prevalence of Gaelic practices in their areas. Sir William Gerrard, for example, deplored the degeneracy of the lords of the Pale who for 'the most parte with delight, yea even in Dublin, speak yrishe and greatlie are spotted in manners, habyte and condicons with yrishe staynes'. As chancellor, he set himself 'to purge thenglish enhabitannts of the yrishe staynes' which meant depriving them of control of the principal administrative and legal offices and substituting Englishmen instead.[54] Thus the acceptance of the new ideology and the contemptuous attitude that accompanied it had alienated the Anglo-Irish as well as the Gaelic Irish, from the English government with the result that a virtual breakdown in relationships had occurred.

7

The breakdown:
Irish reactions to the Elizabethan conquest

The Gaelic Irish were slow to appreciate the threat inherent in the Elizabethan conquest and as a result were late to respond to the challenge. Furthermore, because of the dispersed nature of Irish society, there was little effort to form a cohesive opposition, but there is evidence of a growing hatred of the new English throughout the country and at all levels of Gaelic society.

This change in attitude is difficult to measure, but it is evident that Shane O'Neill, in the 1560s, did not recognize the determination of the English to undermine his position and had little understanding of political realities. He resented the invasion of his territory, certainly, but he regarded the English intruders no differently from his traditional enemies such as the MacDonnells or the O'Donnells. Even on his visit to the court of Queen Elizabeth, in 1562, he behaved as if he were an equal with the queen rather than her subject, while his ambition to become prince of Ulster, and his expectation that Queen Elizabeth would endorse him as such, was contrary to the political currents of the time.[1]

The Irish annalists, likewise, displayed a startling ignorance of political reality. Every reference to Sir Henry Sidney in the *Annals of the Four Masters* is complimentary towards him, and the authors obviously did not appreciate that it was he who advocated the conquest of Ulster. The entry for 1575, for example, ironically credits Sidney with restoring peace to Ulster and banishing 'to England the earl of Essex who had invaded Ulster and acted treacherously towards Con, the son of Calvagh [O'Donnell] and Brian the son of Felim Bacagh [O'Neill]'. The writers were correct on their facts but completely misinterpreted the evidence, since they failed to understand that Sidney's dissatisfaction with Essex was motivated by the earl's failure to pursue colonization to a successful conclusion. Another example of political naïveté is the entry for the year 1568 in the *Annals of Loch Cé* where the unsettled conditions that enveloped northern Connacht shortly thereafter are attributed solely to the death of the local chieftain, Ruaidhri Mac Diarmada, while the activities of Sir Edward Fitton are ignored as contributing to the disorder.[2]

The *filí,* writers of bardic poetry, had a better understanding of sixteenth-century politics, but few of them saw fit to recommend a coalition of Gaelic chieftains against the common foe. Instead, they left political decisions to their betters and praised them in whatever actions they undertook whether it was directed against the English or a neighbouring lord. The principal concern of the *filí* was their continuance as a privileged order, and if this entailed eulogizing a lord who had compromised with the English they had few scruples about doing so, unless that lord refused thereafter to entertain poets. This pragmatic turn is best illustrated by Maoilín Og Mac Bruaideadha in a poem addressed, in the 1570s, to the earl of Thomond, where he threatened to report to the government that Thomond persisted with forbidden Gaelic practices unless the earl provided him with patronage. The poet Lochlann Og O Dálaigh did not resort to blackmail, but he too accepted the anglicization of Thomond as final and hoped merely that his patron, Donal O'Brien, would not desert him despite *breath dlighidh gnáthchúirte Gall* 'the legal sentence of the common court of the foreigner'. Even more cynical was Tadgh O Dálaigh who in 1618, recognizing that the Gaelic order was at an end, requested patronage from Sir George Carew claiming that he, unlike some of his fellow poets, had never used his pen against Carew:

> Ní hionann as merdha mhé
> 's a lán eile dom aicme:
> a chruth fhíal go dtenn dtresa
> ríamh ad chenn ní[r] chuires-sa[3]

O Dálaigh was exceptional in the seventeenth century because by then many poets, especially those who had fled to the Continent, admitted that they had lost their opportunity in the previous century to promote resistance to the Elizabethan conquest. They tried then, but too late, to make good the deficiency by composing poetry aimed at kindling a spirit of rebellion in the soul of Ireland. Thus *Fúbún fúibh a shluagh Gaoidheal* is one of the few sixteenth-century poems that is uncompromising in its call for united resistance to the English.[4] Despite this general failure of Gaelic Ireland's *literati* to take a political stand, we can trace a growing resentment towards the new English in the abusive vocabulary employed by Irish writers to describe them. The annalists were careful to distinguish them from the Anglo-Irish by using the term *Saxanaibh* for the former while retaining the description *Ghalloibh* for those of longer standing in Ireland. The poets could be more extreme when it suited their purpose, and hostile descriptions such as *dubhghall* (black foreigners) or *faolchon allmhardha* (foreign wolves) were frequently applied to the new English. Again it is evident from the vocabulary that poets had no love for *an ghallsmacht* (foreign discipline) or *nós na nGallsa* (foreign custom). An occasional poet, such as Laoisioch Mac an Bháird, went so far as to disown an Irish lord, and possible patron, who had adopted the ways of the English and compared him unfavourable with his brother who had abandoned all rather than compromise with the intruders.[5]

The English themselves realized that hatred was mounting against them throughout Ireland, and English admissions of increased Gaelic Irish hostility are one index of its intensity. Lord Deputy Fitzwilliam, in 1572, spoke of 'the contemptuous demeanors in everie rascall almost of the Irisherie' and asserted that the names of 'England and Englisshe [were] waxing generally and toto apparantly hatefull' to the Irish. This hatred seems to have penetrated to the lowest level of society, since it was those employed as servants by the younger Thomas Smith, who stabbed him to death and 'caused Maister Smithe to be eaten up with dogges after he had been boiled'. The earl of Essex claimed also that the bodies of those English soldiers who had been killed in battle were afterwards mutilated by their enemies whose custom it was 'to cut off their privy parts, set up their heads and put them in their mouths'. These accounts may be exaggerated but they are acknowledgements by the English that their presence was resented by the Gaelic Irish who were not slow in emulating the example of such as Gilbert and Essex.[6] The Gaelic Irish, therefore, viewed the new English as interlopers upon their independence and reacted accordingly. The failure to present a united resistance to the onslaught is explained by the local nature of Irish society, as described in the first chapter, and this too enabled the English to use the device of divide and conquer to great effect. It was not until Hugh O'Neill injected himself into Gaelic Ulster that someone was able to exploit this intense hatred of the English.

The reaction of the Palesmen and the Anglo-Irish lords was

different in that they had hitherto been regarded, and had regarded themselves, as the representatives of the English interest in Ireland, and they resented being displaced by the new English administrators and adventurers. Their actions were guided, therefore, by a sense of epigoneship; they wanted to preserve rights and liberties that they had enjoyed for centuries. The Anglo-Irish of the Pale were, by the 1560s, well accustomed to defending their position against aggressive deputies, and when their efforts in Ireland failed them they were usually in a position to appeal to the crown to favour their cause. Their attempt to curb the power of Lord Deputy Sussex, which has been described in chapter 2, was typical of Anglo-Irish behaviour throughout the first half of the sixteenth century, and certainly since 1534. The earl of Kildare, as has been noted, supported them in their actions and identified himself more with the Palesmen than with the other feudal lords in Ireland.

The conquest, launched in the 1560s, threatened the position of the outlying lords as well as those in the Pale, and they – or at least the Butlers – reacted initially as the Palesmen had done. The parliament of 1569-71 witnessed a strident opposition in the Commons headed by Sir Edmund Butler – brother to Ormond – and the Palesman Sir Christopher Barnewall. This was the first indication that the landowners of the Pale and the feudal lords were joining forces against Sidney's programme, and there is some evidence that the early divisions broke on a regular basis with the Anglo-Irish landed interests voting together against the representatives of the towns and the deputy's placemen. This was so noticeable and consistent that Sidney claimed in later years that a conspiracy had been organized from Rome to defeat his purpose.[7] There is no evidence to support this contention, and the cohension of the opposition is explained by the Anglo-Irish landowners sensing themselves under attack from an authoritarian deputy and refusing to be a party to their own destruction. The financial bills, calling for the renewal of the subsidy of 13s 4d per plough-land for the defence of the Pale, and the bill to impose a duty on wine met with the expected opposition, but were eventually passed for ten years. It was the bills dealing with the realm of civility and legal administration that encountered the greatest opposition. Bills for the repair of churches and building of schools at the landowners' expense were rejected, as was that for establishing a university on the lands of the archbishopric of Dublin. The bill for suppressing Irish captainries, other than those authorized by the queen, met with opposition from the feudal element who saw it as a threat to their control over Gaelic areas. The bill declaring illegal the practice of coyne and livery met with stiff and persistent opposition and was eventually rejected.

It is obvious that all of these bills were intended to promote Sidney's programme of reform and were contrary to the interests of the landowners in parliament. The bill against coyne and livery is a case in point. There had been frequent legislation to control the practice, but the lord deputy now wished to abolish it completely, thus depriving the Anglo-Irish lords of their principal source of power. On these grounds alone the bill would have been opposed, but the lord deputy wished further to win a regular tax from the tenants who had formerly been subject to coyne and livery, thus diverting to the crown a form of rent and service that had previously been paid by the tenant to his lord. It is true to say, therefore, that the members complied with these bills which served their own purpose and those – such as the posthumous attainder of Shane O'Neill – which were aimed at reform of Gaelic areas. There was, however, a determined resistance by the landed interests to those bills which in any way reflected upon their own civility or threatened their position. The parliament witnessed a coalition between the landowners of the Pale and the Anglo-Irish feudal interests with both determined to curb the power of an authoritarian deputy who expected parliament to endorse his programme without criticism. Instead of the short parliament that the government had intended it stretched through eight sessions and two years, and the lord deputy had to admit defeat on certain important issues. Even then the passage of many of the bills can be explained by the withdrawal from parliament of some of those who had been the most bitter opponents of the lord deputy in the early sessions. Sir Edmund Butler was in armed rebellion against the government during the later sessions of parliament, which was a high price to pay for legislation.[8]

It cannot be said that the proceedings in parliament, of 1569-71, were the only cause of the feudal rebellions that broke out sporadically between 1569 and 1576. Their experience in parliament, however, convinced the Anglo-Irish of the futility of conventional opposition, since the lord deputy intended to continue with his programme of reform whether or not it was endorsed by parliament. Furthermore, the earl of Ormond had met with limited success in his efforts to dissuade the queen from pursuing the proposed course of action. Equally significant was the fact that those who were involved in colonization exploits, notably Sir Peter Carew, were seen to be the principal parliamentary advocates of the lord deputy's proposals. This too suggested that extraparliamentary resistance was the only way to frustrate the ambitions of the lord deputy and his greedy supporters. A study of the revolts is important, therefore, in highlighting the extent to which the Anglo-Irish had been alienated from the government, and the length to which they would go to preserve what they considered to be their corporate rights.

The rebellions were five in number: the one led by James Fitzmaurice Fitzgerald lasting from 1568 to 1573; the Butler rebellion of 1569 led by Sir Edmund Butler and his younger brothers Piers and Edward; the revolt of the earl of Thomond in 1570; and the two revolts by Ulick and John Burke, sons of the earl of Clanricard, in 1572 and 1576. Of these the most extreme was that of Fitzmaurice who wished to displace the earl of Desmond as head of the Fitzgerald house and availed himself of the opportunity to highlight the ineptitude of the earl and his brother, Sir John of Desmond, in opposing the government's actions in Munster. He succeeded in his purpose, and the Fitzgerald dependants, fearful of government activities and despairing of the release of the earl and his brother, accepted Fitzmaurice as their champion and 'furthwith, and as it had ben with one voyce, cried him to be their captain, and him they vowed to follow, and obey his comandment'. [9]

If we ignore this peculiarity of Fitzmaurice's insurrection, we can state that the five rebellions were by no means a total onslaught against the queen or her government in Dublin but were rather aimed specifically at ending local interference by the government. They were protests in arms when all constitutional methods of voicing dissent had failed. Rebellion was the last resort, and in some cases the only resort, open to provincial landowners who saw the government of Lord Deputy Sidney closing in on them from every side and threatening their power and property. To this extent they were extremely conservative movements led by men – with the possible exception of Fitzmaurice – who declared themselves loyal to the crown, but who considered that the agents of the queen were overstepping their authority. What they hoped to achieve, therefore, was to attract the crown's attention to their plight, in the hope that the queen would redress their grievances and re-establish them in their former positions.

The five rebellions had many common characteristics which illustrate their scope, purpose and progress. One striking feature was the leaders' discarding of English ways in favour of Gaelic practices. Fitzmaurice, and his ally the earl of Clancarr, turned their backs on English titles in favour of Irish ones; the latter was 'offended with any that calleth hym erle of Clancare' and aşsumed his old title of Mac Carthy Mór, while Fitzmaurice declared himself 'captayne of the Geraldines'. Sir Edmund Butler did not go quite so far, but John Hooker related in astonishment how he,

> little accounting that he was an Ireland man and descended of an honorable parentage, was entered into such a folly, or rather a phrensy, that he became not only a mere Irishman but also an Irish Kerne in apparel, behaviour and all other savage mannes of Irishry.[10]

The sons of Clanricard, or the 'Mac an Iarlas' as they were referred to, likewise symbolized their rebellion in 1572 by discarding their English attire, and again in 1576 when they escaped from prison in Dublin and returned to Connacht 'they were no sooner come over the Shannan in their flight but they cast awaie their English apparrel ... saying that those should be their pledge for their remaining by east Shenan'. The earl of Thomond, likewise, assumed the dress of a Gaelic chieftain and 'proclayed that all that ware Englysshe apparell should be stayed in his countrey'.[11]

It is difficult to assess the purpose behind this symbolic action, but one reason may have been to attract support from the dissatisfied Gaelic chieftains with whom they might make common cause. This may easily have been the intention of Fitzmaurice who attracted to his standard the Gaelic chieftains of south-west Munster who had been threatened by colonization, Mac Carthy Mór, McDonagh, O'Keeffe, O'Sullivan Mór and O'Sullivan Beare. The other rebels did not make common cause with any of Gaelic origin, but it is likely that they wished to make it known that they would have no option but to 'turn Irish every one' if the government did not desist from its actions.

Another trait that all the rebellions had in common was their reasserting claims to those traditional rights and immunities of which they had been deprived by the government. The first action of James Fitzmaurice Fitzgerald was to restore coyne and livery and the other military exactions that Sir John of Desmond had promised to forego. He also reimposed the Fitzgerald dominance over those of the lesser nobility who had been promised exemption from Desmond control. The earl of Clancarr also raised his traditional army and, in November 1568, resumed his trading with Spanish merchants, and is alleged to have imported '1,000 targets at the leaste and a far greater nomber of sworde blade, harquabuserie and other weapons'.[12] The Butlers also openly defied the government by extending the practice of coyne and livery beyond its normal limits.

They were presented with such an opportunity when the lord deputy requested the aid of Sir Edmund Butler against Fitzmaurice. Butler refused his support on the ground 'that he was able to do none' having had his military exactions curtailed. The invitation, however, presented Butler with a pretext to reassert his right to maintain a private army, and in the autumn of 1568 he mobilized a force of four hundred men and took 'in the county of Kilkenny and on the other borders therre, meate and drinke uppon those of the countrey without doing eny other great harmes'. The younger Edward Butler went to even greater extremes and raised a force in County Tipperary estimated as one thousand strong.[13] The earl of Thomond, likewise, raised an army in the traditional manner and laid claim to the castles of which he had been deprived by President Fitton. The young Burkes also raised an army both in 1572 and 1576 and invited large numbers of Scots mercenary soldiers to join them in their action.

The raising of troops was initially an act of defiance of the government, but when this evinced no response from London the armies were used, firstly to oust all new English presence from the provinces, and then to attack those who had favoured or who had benefited from the innovations. In June 1569 Fitzmaurice and McCarthý Mor, backed by a force estimated as large as two thousand, overthrew the St Leger settlement at Kerrycurrihy. The castle of Carrigaline and the abbey of Tracton, the two defensible buildings in the hands of the colonists, were taken by the rebels, all their moveable property was captured and the defenders were hanged. Both St Leger and Grenville were absent in England at the time, but their wives and followers found shelter in the fortified town of Cork. The rebels then surrounded Cork with an army and destroyed whatever property the townsmen left outside the walls, and they 'avowed never to departe untill they have the towne, onless the mayor will graunte to deliver owte of the towne my Ladie Sentleger and Mrs. Grenvill with the rest of the English men that be within the towne'. The townsmen refused to concede and were able to resist the besiegers until August 1569 when they were relieved by Lord Deputy Sidney.[14]

Having found the Corkmen intransigent, Fitzmaurice and his adherents next turned their attention to the lesser nobility of Munster who stood to benefit from a provincial presidency and who had, therefore, refused to join in the rebellion. Lord Roche had been molested consistently since 1568, Viscount Barry and Sir Dermot McCarthy of Muskerry were ousted from their lands, and 'divers landlords and freehoulders' were likewise deprived of their lands and castles.[15] There is evidence that Fitzmaurice and Sir Edmund Butler combined their efforts to persuade Sir Maurice Fitzgerald of the Decies to join them, and when persuasion failed they announced that 'Sir Edmond Butler and all the rest of the Butlers are become ffrends to the Geraldines and hath sworne to take the hedde of all such as shall confesse themselves to be trewe subjects unto the Queen's Majesty'. Towns in Munster fared particularly badly because the townsmen had welcomed government intervention in the province as a means of ending the forestalling practices of the lords. Kilmallock fared worst in that it was burned to the ground by the rebels, but they strove to reduce by famine all who refused to join them, and to 'torment her highnes' true subjects whome they understande to be furtherers of civilitie'.[16]

The aggressive stage of the Butler rebellion was almost a carbon copy of that of Fitzmaurice. The real issues were local, and the revolt bore the appearance of a vendetta between Sir Edmund Butler and Sir Peter Carew to such an extent that it was referred to by contemporaries both as 'Edmund Butler's warres' and 'Peter Carew his warres'.[17] Butler, unlike Fitzmaurice, enjoyed the support of most of the principal Ormond tenants, and Sidney averred that, with the exception of Sir Theobald Butler of Cahir and Lord Butler of Dunboyne who was a ward at court, 'all the Ormonists of what syrname soever they were . . . rebelled with him'.[18] Thus operating from a secure base the Butlers were able to concentrate their attention against the Carew settlement at Idrone, move outwards to attack the English presence in the neighbouring counties, and molest those who had favoured the innovations. Sir Edmund himself laid waste the Carew settlement in the same way that Fitzmaurice had destroyed the St Leger colony at Kerrycurrihy. As an example to other Englishmen who might intrude in Butler lands he took one of the principal tenants 'Robert Manneing an Englishe gent and leadeth him up and downe in a halter'.[19] Parts of Counties Carlow, Kildare and Dublin were laid waste by the Butlers, but Sir Edmund was most active in molesting the English colony in Leix-Offaly. Leix, as has been mentioned in the first chapter, had formerly been under Butler control, and the plantation there represented the first diminution of their power. This explains why it was a special target for Butler who invaded the county and killed

verey many of the inhabitants of the same, but most especially all the Englishmen, and for more despite to the action, he would cause English dead men's bodies to be stripped out of their English garments and their hose and dubletts (being stuffed and trussed) he would sett up as markes for his kerns to throw their darts at.[20]

Thus the Butlers manifested their hatred of the new English and their resentment of outside interference in their orbit of influence. Those within the earldom who had favoured the Sidney programme were harshly treated. One White, a recorder of the city of Waterford and probably a supporter of government policy, had his house at Knocktogher, County Kilkenny, destroyed by Sir Edmund Butler. Likewise Sir Piers Butler attacked the town of Callan and selected for special victimization one Fulke Comerford, 'a wealthy man of plate', probably a merchant who supported the government against the Butlers. Towns generally fared badly. Sir Edmund Butler joined forces with Fitzmaurice in laying siege, unsuccessfully, to Kilkenny, and in the most destructive act of the revolt Sir Edmund 'utterly spoyled' the annual fair at Enniscorthy and 'ravished killed or spoyled' the merchants and their families who had travelled from Wexford to attend there.[21]

The western revolts were more limited in scope but they displayed the same general characteristics. The earl of Thomond did not have to contend with the problem of a colony in his territory, but he resented the arrival of a provincial president, and gave as his reason for rebellion 'the feare he had of the lord president of Connaught, and the extorcion that the said lord president and his used upon the poore people and their oppression of the countrie'. Thomond withdrew and refused to negotiate with the president at Ennis but did not enter into open warfare with him. He did, however, arrest those who were sent by the president to parley with him, and he made it impossible for the president to linger in his territory by denying him food. Fitton reported that 'all the people . . . in the countrey were fledd away bothe man and beaste as thoughe we had beene ennemies', and they 'drowned . . . corne in the ryver rather than we should have yt'. Thus the president was compelled to withdraw from the lands of Thomond, and the earl was left to bring to heel the officers who had been appointed by the president, notably the sheriff, Tadgh Mac Morough O'Brien of Inchiquin, and William Martin, the provost-marshal. Likewise Donal O'Brien, the earl's principal rival, was now taken prisoner by Thomond, and raids were conducted on the lands of O'Shaughnessy.[22]

The Mac an Iarlas in their revolt resisted the presidency, and they attacked the towns that had favoured and supported the president, Galway, Athenry and Athlone. Galway was able to defend itself, but both Athenry and Athlone were burned, as were the lands east of the

River Shannon that were under the jurisdiction of the garrison at Athlone. Again, in 1576, when the two sons escaped to rekindle the rebellion they wreaked havoc on the towns of the province especially Athenry which was then being reconstructed after the earlier destruction. John Burke killed the workmen employed in fortifying the town and, once again, burned it to the ground 'rather than any English churle should enhabit or fortify there'.[23]

This was the extreme point of the rebellions and only James Fitzmaurice Fitzgerald presumed to carry it further. His main purpose, as has been noted, was to usurp the power of the earl of Desmond, and having done this his only hope of permanent success was to oust the English from the province. Thus from the beginning Fitzmaurice's rebellion assumed a wider dimension than any of the others as he identified with the Counter-Reformation against the heretic English. In his proclamation to the besieged townsmen of Cork, in July 1569, he stressed that the queen

> ys not contented to dispose all our worldly goods, our bodyes and our lyves as she lyst, butt must also compell us to forgoo the Catholyck faith by God unto his church given and by the see of Rome hitherto preserved to all Christen men.

It was the government's purpose, he claimed, to impose 'an other newly invented kind of religion', and he called on all

> that profess to be Christian men to abolish oute of that cittie that old heresy newly raised and invented, and namely Barnaby Daly and all therein that be Hugnettes booth men and women, and Greinvyles wife and children and to sett upp the service after in due forme and manner which ys used in Rome and throughout all Christendom.[24]

This outburst seems to have had little impact on the townsmen in 1569 – it was after all prior to *Regnans in Excelsis* – but Fitzmaurice by emphasizing the religious dimension of the English conquest was opening the way to establishing an alliance with Catholic Europe.

Few of the landowners in Munster were willing to go this far with Fitzmaurice, and few of the tenants in chief of the earldom identified with him, but in their efforts to accommodate both sides they 'remayned (or they semed) sound, yet their young and loose people went to him'.[25] When the lord deputy and Gilbert arrived with troops to quell the revolt few landowners were willing to join Fitzmaurice in attacking them, and his supporters fell away. In

February 1571 Fitzmaurice lost his staunchest ally MacCarthy Mór who submitted, claiming that he had been 'seduced' by Fitzmaurice into 'confederating with Sir Edmund Butler and the rest of the principall rebels'.[26] This left Fitzmaurice with only a small band, and he was eventually hunted down by Sir John Perrott who accepted an unconditional surrender from Fitzmaurice and his followers who were forced to 'yelde them selves in certeyne good townes with halters about their necks, and such lyke punnishment for terrors sake'. Fitzmaurice was thus brought to nothing and could expect only worse treatment from the earl of Desmond, so in the spring of 1575 he fled to the Continent to seek military support for his cause.[27]

The difference between the Munster revolt and that in the other provinces is explained by the fact that Fitzmaurice had little to lose and so could afford to go to extremes. The leaders of the other revolts were prominent landowners and earls – as in the cases of Mac Carthy Mór and Thomond – or close relatives of earls. All of these recognized that open conflict with government troops would result in inevitable defeat and confiscation of property, and they therefore sued for terms as soon as the lord deputy or his representative entered their territory backed by the royal army. Their action had shown the government the extremes to which they had been driven by the lord deputy's policy, and they also made it clear that the country was virtually ungovernable without their co-operation. In their negotiations they tried to bypass the Dublin government and sue directly with the queen in the hope that being suitably penitent they would obtain redress of their grievances. Thus their initial argument was that they had not been disloyal to the crown but, rather, had been forced to defend their property from those who had threatened their positions in the name of, but unknown to, the queen. Some went even further and claimed that their action was in defence of the queen from those who would usurp her authority in Ireland and England.

The Butlers, and more especially the earl of Ormond who had been absent from Ireland during the revolt but who feared for the lands and lives of his brothers, expounded the most complex causes for their rebellion. They stressed that they never intended to deny the queen's authority but had been driven to take the action they did because Sir Peter Carew and the lord deputy were conspiring to deprive them of their lands. Ormond portrayed his brother being attacked by Carew, and he made great play of the plunder taken by Carew's soldiers during the course of the revolt. The revolt, he claimed, had been deliberately fomented by Sidney and Carew to gain further land for plantation. Sir Edmund, he claimed, had been provoked by Carew who wished 'to come by the possessions of my brother's lands, and to make the better quarrell to his lyvinge my lord deputy proclaimed him rebell'.[28] The earl pointed also to the futility of constitutional methods since those on the Dublin council who criticized the government's action were, he claimed, branded as 'foolish, parsiall and affecsionate Ormandistes so that there mowthes be stopped'. No justice was to be had in Ireland, he claimed, and he requested that his brothers be tried in London rather than Dublin where the lord deputy 'seketh to intrap me'.[29]

The earl argued that the same held true of the other revolts since there were 'few in this land that do not think my lord deputy is determined to conquer and take there land from them by the sword'. The action of Carew, he stated, had convinced 'all of the lords and men of living dwelling owt of the Inglish Pale [that] there is a conquest ment to be made of all there countries', and 'serten foolish letters written in some fond sort by Mr. Warham St Leger or some other' had confirmed them in their fears.[30] The rebels, according to another witness, were convinced

> that her Majestie intended to ovveron them with a conquest . . . and therein they were greatly confyrmed when they considered howe earnestly her Majestie was bent for the establishing of presidents in sondry parts of the realm which semyd in theire opynions to import their present destrucon.[31]

Sir Edmund Butler himself confirmed these stories and claimed that he feared Sidney who had once threatened that 'he would sit on my skyrts ... and that he would make my harte strings ake'.[32] It was Sir Edmund who introduced the wider dimension by claiming that he considered himself to be defending the queen from her enemies. This was made possible by the fact that the Butler revolt coincided with the court intrigues of 1569 that culminated in the Northern Rebellion of 1569-70. The Butlers claimed to believe that Ormond had been a victim of the shift in power in England, and that 'the queen's Majesty and my lord of Ormond should be by treason put to deathe'. The perpetrator of such an act would of course have been the earl of Leicester, and this gives some plausibility to Sidney's account of Sir Edmund Butler's reason for revolt. Butler's fear, according to Sidney, was

> that the earl of Leycester, enemy to his brother and house should marie the Quene and be King of England, and that I[Sidney]

should be King of Ireland; their mortall foe and brother [in-law]
to the Earl of Leycester of whom I should hold Ireland.[33]

The earl of Thomond also linked his action with the simultaneous
disturbance in England and identified himself with the anti-
Leicester grouping when he proclaimed 'openly at his table that he
woulde do nothinge with the lord deputie nor lord president but as
the Duke of Norfolk would say'.[34]

Taken together, the rebellions of 1569-76 tell us a good deal about
the attitude of the Anglo-Irish feudal lords towards the changes that
were taking place. The centralizing policy of the government
obviously alienated the ruling elite in rural Ireland but while they
symbolized their estrangement by briefly adopting Irish dress or
titles they held back from making common cause with, and
providing leadership to, the Gaelic Irish. It is likely that this failure
to identify with the Gaelic Irish was largely explained by their sense
of superiority to the Irish whom they regarded as culturally inferior
to themselves. The knowledge that the lords, particularly Ormond,
had of political reality would certainly have made them hesitant to
enter into any organized conspiracy against the government, and it
is also likely that they still owed some residual loyalty to the English
crown. The revolts, therefore, bear a close resemblance to local
disturbances in sixteenth-century England in that the rebels were
satisfied that justice was on their side, and they were convinced that
the queen would rectify their grievance if only the truth was made
known to her. In other words, the rebels were defending group and
regional interests and privileges against the aggressive and
'unconstitutional' claims of the queen's representative in Ireland.
Thus, like most rebellions in the early modern period, the Irish
disturbances were conservative in nature and the only leader who
tried to break the mould – James Fitzmaurice Fitzgerald – quickly
lost his supporters.

The revolts are also significant in that they highlight the social
tension within Irish feudal society. In attempting to preserve their
positions the Irish lords were careful to suppress those within their
areas of jurisdiction who might have benefited from change, hence
the attacks on the towns. It is important to note that the leadership
came from the highest level of society, and in this respect the
rebellions were more restricted than contemporary revolts in
England or Continental Europe. In many early modern rebellions
those at the lower level of society were the first to respond to
government actions and pressurized their lords to participate with
them in revolt. Since Irish revolts were primarily in response to

colonization and administrative change, factors that most immediately concerned the large landholders, the nobles were the leaders and controlled the disturbances to suit their purposes.[35]

Because the rebellions were led by a social elite who had clearly defined conservative objectives it was consistent that they should identify themselves with the Howard faction who represented the interests of England's old aristocratic families against the ambitions of Leicester and his followers. Ormond, at court, had always supported the Howard grouping, and hoped through them to achieve a return to the pre-1534 situation in Ireland, with himself rather than Kildare acting as lord deputy. In the summer of 1569 it appeared that the Howards would prevail over the Dudleys at court, and thus there was more than a flickering hope in Ireland that Ormond would replace Sidney as lord deputy. The Northern Rebellion of 1569-70 ended the hopes of the Howard faction, and Leicester was undisputably supreme at court. This turn of events in England quenched the hopes that the Irish rebels had fostered of unseating the lord deputy, and the fact that they had looked to Norfolk as their champion meant that they now faced the danger of losing their lands.

The earl of Ormond who had intimate knowledge of events in England was the first to recognize the danger. On his return to Ireland, he sought to quell the revolts, and he pleaded for mercy for his brothers rather than Sidney's dismissal. The queen, in view of recent events in England, could not be expected to be lenient with rebels, and Ormond was desperate lest his brothers be indicted for treason. No longer did he denigrate Sidney but rather blamed his brother's actions on witchcraft:

> surely he was bewiched and so in a kynde of frensie (which held him longe) . . . this is the most true (yf I be a christen man) I will avow it to all the world.[36]

Instead of putting a brake on the government's programme or producing a return to the pre-1534 position, the rebellions placed the participants in a vulnerable position. The Leicester faction, now dominant at court, was unwilling to countenance any concessions to those who had opposed Sidney in Ireland and who had openly identified with the Norfolk faction during the recent disturbances in England. Lord Deputy Sidney wished to punish the malcontents and extend the scope of colonization beyond what he had originally intended. The queen was more lenient and pardoned the rebels on stern terms. The Butlers, for example, after they had paid recognizances were received to mercy on condition that they put their army at the government's disposal in quelling rebellion in Munster and Connacht.[37] Thomond was compelled to acknowledge the president's authority and surrendered most of his castles to the crown, while Clanricard was forced to concede £6,000 for the repair of Athenry, and his two sons had to remain in prison as an assurance of his future loyalty.[38]

We have little information on the attitude of the Anglo-Irish of the Pale towards the rebellions, but it seems that the principal landholders there sympathised with the rebels' cause. They, although less than the Anglo-Irish feudal lords, were being subjected to criticism by the new English, many of whom thought that the Anglo-Irish should be deprived of offices in the Dublin administration. Lord Chancellor William Gerrard, for example, said of the judges and officers of the courts that he found

> not eny so sownde in religion, so hable in knowledge and honest conversation . . . as I could wish. I see a show or a shadow of justice and the admynestracon of it, but farre from such dexteritie as is requisite.[39]

Such criticism added to the insecurity of the Palesmen, and they were driven to the point of rebellion in the late 1570s when Sidney insisted on their paying a regular tax to the government in lieu of purveyance which he wished to abolish. Were it not for the queen's intervention it is likely that they too would have risen in arms against the 'tyranny' of the lord deputy.

The years 1565-76 were therefore traumatic ones for the Anglo-Irish no less than for the Gaelic Irish. The feudal lords resisted the policy of the lord deputy by every possible means but were eventually driven to the point of deciding between outright rebellion against the queen or acceptance of the reform policy. Those who were guided by Ormond rejected rebellion and were quick to regulate their lives as the lord deputy required lest they be confused with the Gaelic Irish and treated accordingly. Ormond managed to retain a degree of immunity for his own territory, but he let it be seen that justice was administered fairly by his officers, and he himself supported successive lord deputies in the field whether or not he agreed with their policies. Both the earls of Thomond and Clanricard were advised by Ormond, and thus opened their territories to the full brunt of social reorganization. The majority of the landowners in the Pale likewise recognized that there was no longer any hope of a return to the pre-1534 situation and responded to the government's challenge by sending their sons in ever increasing numbers to be educated at the Inns of Court.[40] Those who had formerly identified with the Fitzgeralds were less willing to acknowledge defeat and watched their opportunity to confound the government's programme. It was suspected in 1575 that the earl of Kildare was plotting a revolt and one witness alleged that he had proclaimed:

> that if the callioght [*cailleach*, hag] of Englande (meaning the queen) were once dead, they in England wolde be with their horns one against another and that then the Erle of Kyldare and they his followers wolde kill all the Englisshe churles or dryve them to the sea; and that so the worlde be all theirs.[41]

The earl was arrested and brought to England on suspicion of treason, and that sharp reminder seems to have brought him to his senses. The Munster Fitzgeralds, however, never lost hope and joined with James Fitzmaurice Fitzgerald when he returned with a force from Catholic Europe. James Eustace, Viscount Baltinglass, was the only substantial Palesman to support the Desmond rebellion, and the fate of the insurgents made it clear that Ormond had chartered the correct course.

The fact that the majority of the Anglo-Irish complied with the wishes of the government does not mean that their resentment of the changes had evaporated. Their behaviour was motivated by fear rather than by love for reform, and it became increasingly obvious to them that no matter how anglicized they became they would be treated as aliens by the new English. Thus the factors that compelled them to modify their life styles forced the Anglo-Irish in upon each other so that their sense of corporate identity was strengthened rather than weakened. This may explain why so many of them were attracted towards Counter-Reformation Catholicism, a religion that gave them a new identity at a time when they were being shunned by those whom they had previously considered their supporters. Thus while the policy of the government might appear to have succeeded in compelling the Anglo-Irish to change their comportment, it really contributed to a breakdown in relations, since the Anglo-Irish now had a stronger sense of corporate identity than ever before and were, at the same time, more culturally removed from the Gaelic Irish than they had been previously.

8

Conclusion:

A pattern established, 1565–76

In 1565 Sir Nicholas Arnold, then lord justice in Ireland, petitioned Sir William Cecil for some guiding principle in governing the country. Cecil was able to offer little practical assistance, but he did caution Arnold 'to stir no sleeping dogs in Ireland untill a staff be provided to chastin them if they will byte. Many things in common weales are sufferd that are not liked'.[1] This remark was commonplace in 1565, and could be taken as a commentary on English policy in Ireland during the first half of the sixteenth century. Ten years later such a statement would have been unthinkable. By then the English had made their presence felt in every province, and not even the most remote lord could have been so dormant as to be unaware of the changes that were under way. There were no longer any 'sleeping dogs' in Ireland since the government, confident that they had the means at hand to chastise them, had aroused them to the necessity of adjusting their life styles to a new model of civility. Furthermore, there was no longer any tolerance of anomalies within the 'commonwealth'. Even the landowners of the Pale, who had hitherto been lauded for their exemplary living, were now found lacking and were accused of being tyrannical towards their tenants, contemptuous towards the government, and unfit to hold office at either local or central level.[2]

It is clear that between 1565 and 1576 the English government had changed its attitude towards Ireland and had resolved to assert its authority throughout the island. Fear of foreign intervention was certainly one factor behind this about turn, but of more immediate concern to the government was the fact that Ireland was a drain on crown revenue. The programme that Sir Henry Sidney presented in

1565 was attractive to the government, because it promised to reduce the country to civility without any appreciable expense in the short term, and with the long-term prospect that Ireland would be self-financing and, perhaps, yield a profit to the crown. The question facing the English Privy Council in 1565 was 'whether the Queenes Majestie be ... counselled to governe Ireland after the Irishe manner as it hath ben accustomed, or to reduce it as nere as maie be to the Englishe government'.[3] They chose the latter course and thus opened a new chapter in Anglo-Irish relations.

By 1576 it had become apparent that the new objective was more difficult to attain than had originally been projected. The English government had acquired much greater knowledge of, and influence in, Ireland than before 1565, but the cost of maintaining a presence in an extended area was great; the prospect of a balanced budget was more remote than ever. The figures for official expenditure on Ireland during the 1560s and 1570s show a sharp increase in receipts from England despite a slight improvement in the revenue from Ireland. The average annual expenditure during the 1560s was little short of £23,000, made up of £18,975 from England and £3,925 from crown revenue in Ireland. This figure had virtually doubled in the early 1570s (1569-73) when the average annual receipt from England was £36,182, and the revenue farmed in Ireland had increased to £6,841. An even more drastic escalation occurred between 1573 and 1575 when the expenses of Essex were added to the ordinary cost of government. When more normal conditions were restored, in the later 1570s, the gross receipts from England were still considerably higher than in the previous decades. The total expenditure between 1 October 1575 and 30 September 1579 was £163,283, which in terms of annual receipts represented an average figure of £31,847 from England, and £4,305 from Ireland. These were admittedly years of inflation but an annual increase from £18,975 to £31,847 over a decade was well ahead of any inflationary spiral.[4]

From the official viewpoint, therefore, the entire programme had proved a failure, and there was every reason why they should wish to revert to the pre-1565 situation. Sidney and his adherents in Ireland recognized this possibility, and did what they could to dissuade the government from any such action. There was no point in denying their inability to balance the budget, but they blamed their lack of success on the insufficiency of initial financial support from the crown, the ineptitude of Essex, the slim resources of the would-be colonizers, and the unwillingness of the Palesmen to put their resources at the government's disposal. Having cleared themselves on that score, they argued that it was now impossible for the government to withdraw from the provinces because the onslaught on the Irish lordships had produced a greater resistance than anticipated, and the Irish lords were conspiring with England's enemies on the Continent. It was argued that the Anglo-Irish resistence to Sidney's programme was 'made of purpose', and it was insinuated that the conspiracy had been hatched in Rome and constituted a threat to England's security. John Hooker, for example, represented the revolts as

a general conspiracy . . . to have prevented and withstanded the general reformation which was supposed should have been established throughout the whole land for the suppressing and reforming of the loose barbarous and most wicked life of that savage nation.[5]

Gilbert was more outspoken and asserted that Ireland was now a greater strategic threat to England than ever before. Withdrawal was out of the question, he claimed, because 'in times past the Irishmen never practised with any man owt of their own countrie', but of recent years had intrigued 'with all the papisticall princes of Christendom', and especially with Spain 'they accomptinge them selves to be naturally dissended from Spannyardes'. The Catholicism of the Anglo-Irish, which hitherto had received slight mention, now assumed great significance. Sidney, for instance, alleged that the opposition in the 1569-71 parliament had been directed from Rome, and in 1576 he thought it 'preposterous . . . to begin reformacion of the pollitique parte and to neglect the religious'; a sentiment very much at variance with his earlier views. He too stressed the strategic importance of Ireland and warned that 'if forren force invade it is lyke to fynd mutch freyndshyp as well for that the greatest sort are extreme papystes as wery thogh they wot not why of Inglysh government'.[6]

An analysis of the rebellions does not bear out these contentions, and it appears that James Fitzmaurice Fitzgerald was the only rebel who sought to identify with Catholic Europe. When the earl of Thomond fled the country in 1571 he ventured to France rather than Spain, and his purpose there was to meet with the English ambassador who might arrange for his meeting with the queen in England; a favour that had been denied him both by the lord president in Connacht and the lord deputy in Dublin. Again it appears that each rebellion in Ireland was a discrete event, and, apart from the brief liaison between Sir Edmund Butler and James

Fitzmaurice Fitzgerald, there was no effort at organizing a united front against the government. The allegations of Sidney and his adherents were obviously exaggerated, and may have been consciously attuned to the ears of the English privy councillors who were now terrified of Spain and ready to support any action designed to defeat the Counter-Reformation.

If such was their purpose they were remarkably successful. The death of Essex brought a temporary halt to colonization in Ireland, but this was not followed by the withdrawal of the English presence from the outlying areas. In 1575, when Sidney was appointed lord deputy for a second term, the army was maintained at its existing strength of 1,600 men, and the government sanctioned the reintroduction of presidents in Munster and Connacht to keep those provinces free from foreign influence.[7] Thus the ground gained by the English since 1565 was maintained, and the lord deputy was directed to make compacts with the outlying Gaelic chieftains and to compel them to redistribute their lands in certain estates among their followers. Sidney was none too optimistic of these arrangements, but he agreed to support the settlements militarily 'for a tyme' and keep 'the people . . . in obedience by violence and compulsion' in the hope that 'in one half an age come to passe' the Irish lords would not 'be of power to do any harme that may not easily be resisted'. Sidney was still convinced that the Essex scheme was 'the best and surest foundacion to buylde on', but since this had proved disastrous he was willing to mark time with moderate arrangements until circumstances favoured the more rigorous course of action.[8]

In 1576, therefore those who had been involved in Irish affairs during the previous hectic decade were able to take stock of the situation and look to the future. The picture seemed dismal at first, and there were moans of frustration from all sides. Those who had invested money in the colonization ventures were most embittered, as were the high government officials who had endorsed Sidney's programme in the vain hope that it would reduce the cost of Ireland to the crown. Sir Francis Walsingham voiced the general depression on the Privy Council when he spoke of 'the cursed distenye of that contrye being not ordeyned to receyve any good of any determynatyon agreed on for the reformatyon thereof'. Equally disappointed were those like Sidney and Fitzwilliam who had directed affairs in Ireland without any reward or recognition for their services. Fitzwilliam was assured that 'proffit here is none to be had for him that bearith either conscience towards God or duety towards her Majeste', and he thought of Ireland as 'a disease which grievously eateth inwardly . . . to the . . . waste of all the stuff applied unto the same'. Sidney too complained that he had received no reward for his efforts and despaired of 'the wretched calamitie of this barbarouse countrie'.[9]

Most observers were downcast rather than depressed, and after a short respite resumed the conquest of Ireland with renewed vigour. The first to recover were the soldiers and adventurers who were satisfied to remain in Ireland as long as they were assured of continued support from England. Many of these were less conscientious and dutiful than Fitzwilliam claimed to be, and they hoped to enrich themselves at the crown's expense if colonization were curtailed. Their continuance was also a novel feature, since previously the followers of a lord deputy returned to England with their patron, or were absorbed into the ranks of the Anglo-Irish through intermarriage. Not so with those who followed Sidney to Ireland and occupied posts in the army and administration, and involved themselves in colonization. Most of these were greedy, aggressive and self-assured adventurers who saw considerable prospects for their enrichment in Ireland, and who sought the overthrow of the existing elite in Ireland as the best means of advancing their fortunes. The majority, as has been mentioned, identified with the Dudley faction in England and as such had developed a strong corporate sense, and favoured the vigorous implementation of Sidney's programme with a view to their own enrichment. These were afraid lest the English government should lose its appetite for conquest, so they prompted their patrons to persist with the programme, and they played up the danger to England of having so much power in Ireland located in Catholic hands. The more prominent of the group sought their fortunes in the New World, but even these returned to Ireland when circumstances favoured them at the end of the Desmond rebellion.[10] The others retained their commissions in the army or posts in the administration, but many involved themselves in provincial government, particularly in Connacht where Nicholas Malby and Richard Bingham were coming to grips with the more Gaelicized parts of the province and making some land available for settlement. These individuals called persistently for a forward policy in Ireland, encouraged the seizure of property and justified the abridgement of due legal process that characterized Bingham's rule in Connacht.[11]

The continuous line of development of English policy in Ireland from 1565 onwards is also explained by a long succession of lord deputies who were guided in their actions by Sir Henry Sidney. Sidney's immediate successor in office, Sir William Drury, was promoted from being president in Munster; Lord Grey de Wilton who succeeded him was advised in everything by Sidney;[12] and the next two governors, Sir John Perrott and Sir William Fitzwilliam, had served their apprenticeship with Sidney. In consequence the lesser officers who had been first introduced into Ireland by Sidney were left undisturbed, and there was no great discontinuity as happened at the departure of Sussex from Ireland. All of this meant that there was a noticeable sense of purpose among successive governors in Ireland to the end of the sixteenth century; a fact that was noted by Sir John Davies in his speaker's address to the Irish House of Commons in 1613:

> How glad would Sir Henry Sidney have been to have seen this day: he that so much desired to reduce Ulster, but could never perfectly perform it: what honour would he have thought it unto himself if he might have held a parliament unto which that province should have sent so many worthy knights and burgesses as now it doth.[13]

Events in Ireland, 1565-76, have a significance in the general history of colonization that transcends English and Irish history. The involvement of men in Irish colonization who afterwards ventured to the New World suggests that their years in Ireland was a period of apprenticeship. Professor D. B. Quinn has established that the use of a propaganda campaign to muster support for a colony and the application of the joint stock principle to colonization were both novel techniques which were applied none too successfully in Ireland, but without which the English could hardly have pursued successful colonization in the New World. Essex, for instance, acknowledged that some financial arrangement was essential to successful colonization, since he found it 'impossible ... to be assured of thadventures stickinge to me but onlie by theare woords; for bonds they woulde come in none'. All were satisfied that the organization of a colony was a bigger undertaking than had originally been allowed for, and required devoted attention and support from the crown and Englishmen of substance. Sidney was convinced that 'such ... as are neadie and have no wealthe I think them not the fittest tenants here', and Davies, at the beginning of the next century, expounding on the 'foolishness' of leaving major projects to private individuals, cited the examples

in the time of Queen Elizabeth when Sir Thomas Smith undertook to recover the Ards, and Chatterton to reconquer the

Fues and Orier. The one lost his son, and the other himself and both their adventures came to nothing. [14]

An even more significant break with the past was the change in attitude towards the Gaelic Irish, and this too was to have consequences in the history of American colonization. It has been noted how Sidney and his adherents fitted the native Irish into their mental world picture. Certain traits of the Gaelic way of life, notably the practice of transhumance, were accepted as evidence that the Irish were barbarians, and the English thus satisfied themselves that they were dealing with a culturally inferior people who might be subdued by extralegal methods. Many of the English colonizers were at first unsure of themselves and looked to Roman practice for further justification for their actions. The Roman example seems to have been cited less frequently by the colonizers who ventured to North America since their concept of cultural evolution had been sharpened as a result of their Irish experience. Writers, such as Thomas Hariot, who had Irish as well as American experience frequently compared habits of the Gaelic Irish with those of the Amerindians. Again contemporary observers like Theodore De Bry claimed to see a resemblance between the ancient Britons and the Indians drawn by the artist John White, thus implying that they considered the Indians, like the Irish, to be at the same primitive level of development as the ancient Britons had been. [15] It appears therefore that the Irish experience confirmed and reinforced the English idea of barbarism, and those, such as Gilbert, Raleigh and Frobisher, who had experience in both spheres, had little difficulty in applying that notion to the indigenous population of the New World. [16]

We find the colonists in Virginia using the same pretexts for the extermination of the Amerindians as their counterparts had used in the 1560s and 1570s for the slaughter of segments of the native Irish population. Every adventurer claimed that his primary purpose was to reform the Irish, and in the words of Sir Thomas Smith, 'to reduce that countrey to civilitie and the maners of England'. It is evident, however, that no determined effort was ever made to reform the Irish, but rather, at the least pretext – generally resistance to the English – they were dismissed as a 'wicked and faythles peopoll' and put to the sword. [17] This formula was repeated in the treatment of the Indians in the New World. At first the English claimed their mission to be that of civilizing the native inhabitants, but they quickly despaired of this, particularly after 1607 when the first permanent settlement was established in Virginia. Thereafter relations between the English and the Indians were tense, more emphasis was given to the barbaric traits of the native population, and, after the Indian insurrection of 1622, the colonizers exulted in the fact that they are now absolved from all restraints in dealing with the 'barbarous' population. It may be significant that their principal spokesman on that occasion was Edward Waterhouse whose uncle and namesake had served as secretary to Essex in Ulster at the time of the massacre of the Clandeboye O'Neills.[18]

Again we find the same indictments being brought against the Indians, and afterwards the blacks, in the New World as had been brought against the Irish. It was argued that the Indians were an unsettled people who did not make proper use of their land and thus could be justly deprived of it by the more enterprising English. Both Indians and blacks, like the Irish, were accused of being idle, lazy, dirty and licentious, but again few serious efforts were made to draw any of them from their supposed state of degeneracy. In fact, the English brought with them to America the assumption that barbarians must first be civilized before being Christianized, as evidenced by the statement of the older Hakluyt that 'to plant Christian religion without conquest will be hard . . . in vain seemith our voyage, unless this nature may be altered, as by conquest and other good means it may be, but not on a sudden'.[19]

We have here a few of the lessons that the English gained from their Irish experience and later applied in the New World. Equally significant are the lessons that they failed to learn. The sixteenth-century colonizer was a proud disdainful person, but he was also insecure and needed to remind himself constantly of his own superiority by looking to the inferiority of others. Those who came to Ireland had a preconceived idea of a barbaric society, and they merely tailored the Irishman to fit this ideological strait jacket. There were of course many aspects of Gaelic life that did not so easily fit this model, but the English refused to make any adjustments, lest, perhaps, it disturb their own position at the top of the ladder of cultural development.

The most flagrant example of this blindness and obstinacy was their retaining the belief, contrary to all evidence, that barbaric societies were invariably divided into two neat categories – the barbarous tyrants or 'cruell cannibales' who held the meek labourers in utter bondage.[20] Edmund Tremayne's censures were reserved for the ruling caste in Ireland who, he claimed, had 'mor authoritie than any lord over bond-men'. Barnaby Rich agreed with this and thought England's role in Ireland should be to defend the poor tenants from the 'thraldome' to which they were being subjected by those 'helhounds' of lords whose only ethic was to 'defend me and spend me'. Even the earl of Essex claimed this to be his mission in Ireland, and Sir Thomas Smith idealized 'the churle of Ireland as a very simple and toylesome man desiring nothing but that he may not bee eaten out with' Irish exactions. [21] It was of course some of these 'simple and toylesome' men, whom the younger Smith had taken into his service, who murdered him, but not even this could disabuse the English. A contemporary of Spenser could still state emphatically that:

> there are two sortes of people in Ireland to be considered of . . . the one called the kerne, the other the chorle. The kerne bredd up in idlenesse and naturally inclined to mischiefs and wickednesse, the chorle willing to labour and take pains if he might peaceably enjoy the fruites thereof. [22]

This writer might have been speaking of the Amerindians because, as Professor Edmund Morgan has shown, the English in the New World used the same form of categorization and displayed the same reluctance to learn from experience. Morgan claims that this blindness to reality can be explained by wishful thinking by the English who expected to find a ready work force in America. There is certainly some truth to this as can be seen in Smith's desire, like that of the English in Virginia, to retain the supposed docile natives as 'fermors or copieholders' in his colony. The retention of such a myth in the face of adversity must, however, be taken as indicating the colonist's insecurity: he needed to think of himself as setting out on a crusade, bringing the 'gentle government' of the English to the oppressed. If he was to admit that the oppressed did not exist, or were not anxious to avail themselves of English justice, then the colonists *raison d'être* was called in question. [23]

It is thus evident that the experience gained by the Elizabethans in Ireland opened their minds to an understanding of process and development, thus enabling them to arrive at a concept of cultural evolution from which they drew practical conclusions in order to provide moral respectability for colonization in America as well as Ireland. The acceptance by the English of these new standards of civility had consequences for their domestic affairs as well. Many of the 'barbaric' traits that they condemned in the Irish, notably ignorance of religious doctrine, transhumance and partible inheritance, were prevalent in the upland regions of England and Wales with the result that there was now a growing demand for conformity with the accepted norm of civility. One member of parliament in 1628 remarked 'that there were some places in England which were scarce in Christendom where God was little better known than amongst the Indians', while another Englishman in 1652 stated 'we have Indians at home – Indians in Cornwall, Indians in Wales, Indians in Ireland'.[24] This growing awareness of civility is also likely to have heightened the distinction between the Lowland and Highland areas of Scotland and served to justify the stern measures used in bringing the latter to heel. Samuel Johnson said of Cromwell and the Scots that 'he civilized them by conquest, and introduced by violence the useful arts of peace', and in doing so was emulating the ancient Romans. Boswell too gave credit to the English for bringing manners and civilization to the Scots: 'we have taught you and we'll do the same in time to all barbarous nations . . . to the Cherokees'.[25]

Thus it appears that the events in Ireland from 1565 to 1576 are important not only in that they produced a pattern of conquest that was later employed in Ireland and the New World, but also because they sharpened the English concept of civility with the result that the English thereafter looked differently at others and at themselves.

Notes

1 *Irish Society at the accession of Queen Elizabeth I*

1. Davies to Salisbury, 24 August 1609 (H.M.C., *Salisbury MSS,* XXI, 121).
2. 'Sidney's Memoir', *U.J.A.,* 1st ser., III, 97.
3. Drury to Privy Council, 6 January 1579 (P.R.O., S.P.63/65/4).
4. For accounts of official journeys see the reports of the Athlone pursuivant (T.C.D., MS 581, E.3. 18), and 'Sidney's Memoir'.
5. See C. W. Russell, 'On the "Duties upon Irishmen" in the Kildare Rental Book', *Royal Irish Acad., Proc.,* XL sec. C, 1-18. I owe this information to Miss Katherine Simms.
6. L.M. Cullen, *An Economic History of Ireland since 1660* (London 1972), p. 8, where he ventures an estimate of one and a half millions for Ireland in 1641.
7. *Ulster Maps c.f. 1600;* Googe's map of Drogheda (P.R.O., S.P. 63/45/60, I); F. Moryson, *An Itinerary,* IV, 189; Edmund Campion, *A Historie of Ireland,* pp. 2-3.
8. D. M. Woodward, *The Trade of Elizabethan Chester,* esp. pp. 12-13; Ada Longfield, *Anglo-Irish Trade in the Sixteenth Century, passim.*
9. Sidney and council to Privy Council, 13 April 1566 (S.P. 63/17/8). Grey merchants were also employed by traders in the southern and eastern towns; see H. J. Hore and J. Graves, eds., *The Social State of the Southern and Eastern Counties of Ireland in the Sixteenth Century,* pp. 83, 102, 135.
10. *Ibid;* Baron Finglas, 'Breviat of Ireland', in *Hibernica,* ed. Walter Harris, I, 99.
11. T.C.D., MS T.4. 5, f. 22; also a safe-conduct granted by Henry mac Eoghain O'Neill in 1463 (T.C.D., MS T. 4. 6, ff. 164-7); for the sixteenth century see 'Notes on the decline of the English', undated (B.M., Cott. MSS, Titus B.XII, f. 120).
12. Clancar to Corbine, June 1568 (S.P. 63/27/57, I): Denton to Cecil, 16 January 1567 (S.P.63/20/11); Fitton to Smith, 12 August 1563

(S.P.63/42/5).

13. G. O. Sayles, 'The Rebellious First Earl of Desmond', in *Medieval Studies Presented to Aubrey Gwynn,* pp. 203-29; inquisition of Desmond's lands (Dublin, P.R.O.I., MS M. 5038).

14. Sidney to the queen, 20 April 1567 (S.P.63/20/66, f. 136, v); Clanricard to the queen, 15 February 1559 (S.P.63/1/16, 17); Waterhouse to Sidney, 15 September 1577 (Arthur Collins, *Letters and Memorials of State,* I, 225-6); see also Hore and Graves, *Southern and Eastern Counties,* pp. 83, 111, 246, 273.

15. *A.U.,* III, 108, 130; Wingfield to Sussex, 23 February 1561 (S.P.63/3/22); Sidney to Dudley, 1 March 1566 (S.P.63/16/35).

16. Sidney to the queen, 20 April 1567 (S.P. 63/20/66, f. 136, v); Tremayne, 'Notes for the reformation of Ireland', June 1571 (S.P.63/32/66); Campion, *Historie,* pp. 2-3. It is significant that an Englishman, Richard Lukar, was mayor of Waterford from 1567 to 1570.

17. Longfield, *Anglo-Irish Trade, passim.*

18. Report to Pelham, undated (B.M., Harleian MSS, 7004, no. 215); Sidney to the queen, 20 April 1567 (S.P.63/20/66, f. 138, v); Corbine to Cecil, 21 March 1569 (S.P.63/27/57).

19. Gearóid Mac Niocaill, *Na Burgéisí,* II, 518; John Smythe to Burghley, 18 July 1573 (S.P.63/41/86); same to Winchester, April 1569 (S.P.63/28/10).

20. Sidney et. al. to the queen, 12 November 1566 (S.P.63/19/43); Sidney and council to Privy Council, 13 April 1566 (S.P.63/17/8); Davies to Salisbury, 1606 (*Historical Tracts,* pp. 262-3); see also R. J. Hunter, 'Towns in the Ulster Plantation', *Studia Hibernica,* XI (1971), 40-79, esp. 68-73.

21. See *Irish Pat. Rolls of Jas. I, passim;* 'Sidney's Memoir', *U.J.A.,* III, 96.

22. *Cal. Pat. Rolls, 1467-77* [etc.] (London 1906-), pp. 161, 193, 583, 596; *1476-85,* pp. 20, 39, 160.

23. Fitzwilliam and Weston to the queen, 20 August 1568 (S.P.63/25/70); The earl of Ossory in 1537 was accused of monopolizing the timber trade, see Hore and Graves, *Southern and Eastern Counties,* p. 192.

24. Inquisition of Desmond's lands (P.R.O.I., MS M. 5037, 5038); 'Sidney's Memoir', *U.J.A.,* III, 96.

25. *Account Roll of the Priory of the Holy Trinity,* ed. J. Mills (Dublin 1891), pp. 57, 61; *Calendar of Justiciary Rolls,* II, ed. J. Mills (Dublin 1914), 13; P.R.O.I., R.C. 8/1/96, 103; for the sixteenth century see Challoner's notes, undated (B.M., Cott. MSS, Titus B.XII, f. 51). I am grateful to Miss Katherine Simms for the earlier references.

26. Mac Niocaill, *Na Burgéisí,* II, 397-8; 'Sidney's Memoir', *U.J.A.,* VI, 179; Fitzwilliam and Weston to Piers and Malby, 11 August 1568 (S.P.63/25/77, I); same to the queen, 20 August 1568 (S.P.63/25/70); Michael Dolley, 'Anglo-Irish Monetary Policies, 1172-1637', *Hist. Studies,* VII, 45-64; see also Essex to Privy Council, 8 October 1574 (S.P.63/48/3).

27. Luke Gernon, 'A discourse of Ireland, anno 1620', in C. L. Falkiner, *Illustrations of Irish History and Topography*, pp. 345-62, esp. 355; C. O'Danachair, 'Representations of Houses on some Irish Maps of c. 1600', in *Studies in Folk-life*, ed. G. Jenkins, pp. 91-103; Moryson, *Itinerary*, IV, 202.

28. Tremayne, 'Notes for the reformation of Ireland', June 1571 (S.P.63/32/66).

29. Report of Sussex, 1562 (*Cal. Carew MSS, 1515-74*, p. 343); Sidney to Walsingham, 20 March 1577 (S.P.63/57/41); report of Gerrard, 1581? (S.P.63/60/29); notes by Mr Challoner, undated (B.M., Cott. MSS, Titus B.XII, f. 51).

30. The substitution of Irish betaghs for tenants of English descent in the Anglo-Irish areas had been an on-going process, even within the Pale since the fourteenth century. The original Irish betagh class, whether the word derives from *bodagh*, the highest grade of the unfree, or *biatach*, the lowest grade of the free, was never bound to the soil, and it is a possibility that the status of the betagh class, in the eyes of Gaelic and Anglo-Irish alike, had been depressed by the sixteenth century because of their introduction to Anglo-Irish areas where they might not have been accorded the same free status. I am indebted to Miss Katherine Simms for the substance of this note. See also Gearóid Mac Niocaill, 'The Origin of the Betagh', *Ir. Jurist*, current ser. I, 292-8.

31. N. P. Canny, 'The Formation of the Old-English Elite in Ireland', pp. 1-12.

32. Sidney to Privy Council, 15 April 1566 (S.P.63/17/13).

33. Rowland White, 'Discourse touching Ireland, 1571' (S.P. 63/31/32); Sidney to privy council, 15 April 1566 (S.P.63/17/13); letter of Privy Council, 20 August 1603 (Dublin, P.R.O.I., Acta Regia Hibernica, R.C., 2/1/13); see N.P. Canny, 'Hugh O'Neill, and the Changing Face of Gaelic Ulster', *Studia Hibernica*, X, esp. 25-32.

34. Register of Archbishop John Prene (T.C.D., MS T/4/5, ff. 33-5); Canny, 'Hugh O'Neill', *Studia Hibernica*, X, 30.

35. Mac Niocaill, *Na Burgéisí*, II, 397-8; by the lord deputy and council, 7 November 1566 ('Acts Pr. Cl. Ire.', 1566-71', p. 20); Lord Roche to lords justices, 14 September 1568 (S.P.63/25/4, IX).

36. Canny, 'Hugh O'Neill', *Studia Hibernica*, X, 27; Essex to Privy Council, 10 March 1575 (S.P.63/50/4).

37. Moryson, *Itinerary*, III, 254; Sidney to the queen, 20 April 1567 (S.P.63/20/66, f. 141); *Irish Pat. Rolls of Jas. I*, p. 301; Gerrard to Burghley, 20 May 1577 (S.P. 63/58/31); 'Sidney's Memoir', *U.J.A.*, VI, 179.

38. Jean Graham, 'Rural Society in Connacht, 1600-40', in *Irish Geographical Studies*, ed. N. Stephens and R. E. Glasscock, pp. 192-208; Joan Thirsk, 'The Farming Regions of England and Wales', in *The Agrarian History of England and Wales*, IV.

39. *A.C.*, p. 580; it is evident that tradesmen were also imported into the Anglo-Irish areas and billeted on the inhabitants; see Hore and Graves,

Southern and Eastern Counties, pp. 89, 111, 131, 200, 217, 245.

40. S.P., 65/7, f. 31, d; f. 27, v; f. 30, v.

41. Moryson, *Itinerary,* IV, 194; Rowland White, 'Discourse', (S.P.63/31/32); Fitzwilliam and council to Privy Council, 28 June 1572 (S.P.63/36/48).

42. *Measgra Dánta,* ed. T. F. O'Rahilly, pp. 1-2.

43. T.C.D., MS 581, E.3. 18; Tremayne, 'Advice on Ireland', (B.M., Add. MSS, 48015).

44. White, 'Discourse' (S.P.63/32/31).

45. See a report of the responsibilities of William Peppard, sometime sheriff of County Meath (Dublin, P.R.O.I., Ferguson MSS, VI, f. 192); see also D. B. Quinn, 'Anglo-Irish Local Government, 1485-1534', *I.H.S.,* I, 354-81.

46. 'Cal Fiants Eliz.', fiants nos. 379, 380, 381; 'Gerrard's notes', *Analecta Hibernica,* no. 2, 114-15; Tremayne, 'Notes', (S.P.63/32/66); Tremayne, 'Causes' (S.P.63/32/65).

47. *Liber Munerum* (List of officers), ed. R. Lascelles; D. F. Cregan, 'Irish Catholic Admissions to the English Inns of Court, 1558-1625', *Ir. Jurist,* new ser., V, esp. 98-100· Tremayne, 'Notes', June 1571 (S.P.63/32/66).

48. *Ibid.*

49. Ormond to Fitzwilliam, 17 January 1575 (Oxford, Bodl. Lib., Carte MSS, vol. 55, no. 72).

50. 'Some Documents on Irish Law and Custom in the Sixteenth Century', ed. K. W. Nicholls, in *Analecta Hibernica,* no. 26, esp. pp. 107, 115-7; Mac Noicaill, *Na Burgéisí,* II, 399.

51. Kenneth Nicholls, *Gaelic and Gaelicised Ireland,* p. 38.

52. Nicholls, *Gaelic and Gaelicised Ireland,* pp. 31-7; Tremayne, 'Notes', (S.P.63/32/66); Sir John Davies, *Discovery,* pp. 295-6.

53. Quinn, 'Anglo-Irish Local Government', *I.H.S.,* I, 354-81; examination of Desmond, 17 February 1568 (S.P.63/23/42).

54. Sidney and council to Privy Council, 13 April 1566 (S.P. 63/17/8); Ormond to the queen, 16 July 1559 (S.P.63/1/45); same to Fitzwilliam, 6 August 1575 (Oxford, Carte MSS, vol. 55, no. 175); Ormond's claim (S.P.63/64/42).

55. Clanricard to the queen, 15 February 1559 (S.P.63/1/16, 17); Waterhouse to Sidney, 15 September 1577 (Collins, *Letters and Memorials of State,* I, 225-6).

56. Nicholls, *Gaelic and Gaelicised Ireland,* esp, pp. 8-12.

57. The list was provided by Hugh O'Neill in 1603 (P.R.O., C. 66, 1685, last item but two).

58. Canny, 'Hugh O'Neill', *Studia Hibernica,* X, 7-35; Nicholls, *Gaelic and Gaelicised Ireland, passim;* G. A. Hayes-McCoy, 'Gaelic Society in Ireland in the late Sixteenth Century', *Hist. Studies,* IV, 45-61; Davies to Salisbury, 24 August 1609 (H.M.C., *Salisbury MSS* XXI, 121); N. P. Canny, 'The Flight of the Earls, 1607', *I.H.S.,* XVII, 389-99.

59. *A.F.M.,* the year 1561, p. 1587; Clanricard to Fitzwilliam, 15 October 1565 (S.P.63/15/15, I).

60. *Cork Hist. and Arch. Soc. Journal*, XIX (1913), 166-7; *Louth Arch. Journ.*, IV, 248-54; *Irish Pat. Rolls of Jas. I*, pp. 378-9.
61. Lords justices to the queen, 10 December 1567 (S.P.63/22/36).
62. Davies, *Hist. Tracts*, pp. 262, 276-7; Mac Niocaill, 'The Contact of Irish and Common Law', *Northern Ireland Legal Quarterly*, XXIII, 16-23.

2 *An unwelcome inheritance: the English presence in Ireland at the accession of Queen Elizabeth*

1. Richard Bagwell, *Ireland under the Tudors*, II, 10-11.
2. *Ibid.*, II, 42-3, 82-9, 234-8.
3. Sussex's opinion of Ireland, 11 September 1560 (*Cal. Carew MSS, 1515-74*, p. 302).
4. Brandan Bradshaw, *The Dissolution of the Religious Orders in Ireland under Henry VIII*, esp. 233-47; 'The Opposition to the Ecclesiastical Legislation in the Irish Reformation Parliament', *I.H.S.*, XVI, 285-303; and 'George Browne, First Reformation Archbishop of Dublin, 1536-54', *Jr. Eccles. Hist.*, XXI, 301-26; R. Dudley Edwards, *Church and State in Tudor Ireland, passim*.
5. Sidney to Privy Council, 12 December 1566 (S.P.63/19/71, f. 140); a book on the pale, 1560, 1561 (S.P.63/5/51); letter of the gentlemen of the Pale, 21 March 1562 (S.P.63/5/54).
6. 'On the disorders of the Irishry' (S.P.63/1/72, 73).
7. Brendan Bradshaw, 'The Beginnings of Modern Ireland', in *The Irish Parliamentary Tradition*, ed. Brian Farrell, pp. 68-87, esp. 75-8; Canny, 'The Formation of the Old-English Elite' pp. 12-14.
8. D. G. White, 'The Reign of Edward VI in Ireland: some Political, Social, and Economic Aspects', *I.H.S.*, XIV, 197-211; D. B. Quinn, 'Edward Walshe's "Conjectures"', *I.H.S.*, V, 303-22, esp. the introduction pp. 308-14.
9. See 'Articles of commission for martial law', 8 November 1566 (Dublin, R.I.A., MS 24, F.17, ff. 258-62).
10. D. G. White, 'The Tudor Plantations in Ireland', esp. chap. IX, 'Sussex and his critics, 1557-8'.
11. Memo from Ireland, 20 November 1562 (S.P.63/7/45); Commission to Wingfield, 25 December 1561 (*Cal. Pat Rolls Ire.*, p. 445); Sidney and council to Privy Council, 15 April 1566 (S.P.63/17/8).
12. White, 'The Tudor Plantations', chap, XII and pp. 341-2, 386; list of those receiving lands in Leix-Offaly (S.P.63/7/62); Quinn, 'Edward Walshe's "Conjectures"', *I.H.S.*, V, 303-22.
13. Accusations against Heron, 17 January, 1565 (S.P.63/12/12); fiant no. 281, 'Cal. Fiants Irel. Eliz.'; *Cal. Pat. Rolls Ire.*, pp. 410, 416; Anonymous to the queen, June 1562 (S.P.63/6/37).
14. Averaged from the figures given for Fitzwilliam's first account in S.P.65, no. 10.
15. Sidney to Cecil, 17 April 1566 (S.P.63/17/14).
16. R. Dunlop, 'Sixteenth Century Schemes for the Plantation of Ulster'; *Scot. Hist. Rev.*, XXII, 50-60, 115-26, 197-212; Bagwell, *Tudors*, I, 297-8;

White, 'The Tudor Plantations', esp. chap. IX, 'Sussex and his Critics, 1557-8'.

17. Queen to Sussex, 16 July 1559 (S.P.63/1/59); revised instructions to Sussex, 16 July 1559 (S.P.63/1/60).
18. See the queen to Sussex, 15 August 1560 (S.P.63/2/30); same to same, 21 August 1560 (S.P.63/2/31).
19. Extracts from letters of Fitzwilliam (S.P.63/2/15); Cusack to Cecil, 12 February 1562 (S.P.63/5/33).
20. James Hogan, 'Shane O'Neill comes to the Court of Elizabeth', *Féilcribhinn Tórna*, ed. S. Pender, pp. 154-72.
21. Arnold to Cecil 23 September 1562 (S.P.63/7/17); Sussex and council to Privy Council, 26 October 1562 (S.P.63/7/34); proclamation by the queen, 15 March 1563 (S.P.63/8/19).
22. *D.N.B.* s.v. Arnold, Sir Nicholas; queen to Dublin council (S.P.63/8/66).
23. Arnold to Cecil, January 1565 (S.P.63/12/20).
24. Wallace MacCaffrey, *The Shaping of the Elizabethan Regime.*
25. *Ibid.*, pp. 106, 137, 140; Bagwell, *Tudors*, II, 46-7.
26. Order of the Privy Council, 1 July 1563 (*A.P.C., 1558-70,* 109); Queen to Wroth and Arnold, 20 October 1563 (S.P.63/9/45); instructions to Wroth and Arnold, 20 October 1563, (S.P.63/9/45); Wroth to Cecil, 16 April 1564 (S.P.63/10/50); Captains Radcliffe, Stanley and Delves to Privy Council, 10 January 1564 (S.P.63/12/8); by Sussex, the grieves of the captains, 29 January 1565 (S.P.63/12/19).
27. Gerrard to the barons of the Irish exchequer, 10 September 1565 (B.M., Add. MSS, 4,767, f. 128); Draycott to Cecil, 29 September 1563 (H.M.C., *Cal. Salisbury MSS*, pt. I, 322).
28. Cecil's draft of instructions for Ireland, 1565 (S.P.63/14/2).

3 *The new departure: a programme for the conquest of Ireland*

1. D. B. Quinn, 'Henry VIII and Ireland, 1509-34', *I.H.S.*, XII, 318-44; D. B. Quinn, 'Edward Walshe's "Conjectures" ' , *I.H.S.*, V, 303-14; D. G. White, 'The Reign of Edward VI in Ireland: some Political, Social, and Economic Aspects', *I.H.S.*, XIV, 197-211.
2. Essex to the queen, 8 October 1575 (Oxford Carte MSS, vol. 55, no. 239).
3. *D.N.B.*, s.v. Radcliffe, Thomas.
4. *D.N.B.*, s.v. Sidney, Sir Henry; Arthur Collins, *Letters and Memorials of State,* introduction; R. Howell, *Sir Philip Sidney, the Shepherd Knight*, p. 22.
5. Sidney to Sussex, March 1557 (B.M., Landsdowne MSS, vol. 159, fl. 101).
6. Penry Williams, *The Council in the Marches of Wales under Elizabeth I,* pp. 251-2; 'Sidney's Memoir', *U.J.A.,* 1st ser., III, 347; Sidney to Philip Sidney, 1566 (Collins, *Letters and Memorials of State*, I, 8-9).
7. Cecil to Smith, 16 October 1563 (B.M., Lansdowne MSS, vol. 102, no. 66); Cecil's memorial on Ireland based on letters from Croft, Sidney

and Sussex (S.P.63/3/18).

8. Sidney's opinion on Ireland, 20 May 1565 (S.P.63/13/46); Sidney to Cecil, 17 April 1566 (S.P.63/17/14); Sidney to Throgmorton, 7 July 1567 (S.P.63/21/51).

9. Sussex, 'On the state of Ireland, 1562' (*Cal. Carew MSS, 1515-74,* pp. 344-9).

10. Cecil to Sidney, 22 March 1566 (S.P.63/16/67).

11. Sidney on the Public affairs of Ireland, 20 May 1565 (S.P.63/13/4/6); memo for Ireland by Cecil, June 1565 (S.P.63/13/75).

12. Sidney on public affairs, 20 May 1565 (S.P.63/13/46); Privy Council to Arnold, 22 June 1565 (S.P.63/13/69); Penry Williams, *The Council in the Marches of Wales,* pp. 197-204.

13. Sidney's opinion on Cecil's instructions, 5 October 1565 (S.P.63/14/3).

14. Sidney on public affairs, as above; Sir Francis Knollys to Cecil, 29 May 1566 (S.P.63/17/67).

15. Cecil's draft of instructions to Sidney, undated (S.P.63/14/2).

16. Sidney's opinion of Cecil's instructions (S.P.63/14/3).

17. Privy Council to Sidney, 5 October 1565 (S.P.63/15/4); patent for Sidney's appointment, 13 October 1565 (*Cal. Pat. Rolls Ire.,* 493).

18. *D.N.B. supplement,* s.v. Bagnal, Sir Nicholas; Bagenall to Cecil, 23 April 1560 (S.P. 63/3/94); queen's instructions to Sidney, 5 October 1565 (S.P.63/15/6); appointment of Bagenall to the marshalship of Ireland, 4 February 1566 (*Cal. Fiants Ire. Eliz.,* no. 809); M. E. Finch, *The Wealth of Five Northamptonshire Families,* p. 105; Cecil to Sidney, 4 November 1565 (S.P.63/15/37).

19. Sidney to Privy Council, 15 April 1566 (S.P.63/17/13); Sidney and council to Privy Council, 13 April 1566 (S.P.63/17/8); Sussex to the queen, 23 March 1566 (S.P.63/16/65).

20. Sidney's directives to seneschals, 1566 (S.P.63/17/13, I).

21. Instructions by lord deputy and council for St Leger, 1 February 1566 (S.P.63/16/22); Penry Williams, 'The Council in Munster in the Late Sixteenth Century', *Bull. of Irish Comm. of Hist. Sciences,* no. 123.

22. Lord deputy and council to Privy Council, 13 April 1566 (S.P.63/17/8); Sidney to Privy Council, 15 April 1566 (S.P.63/17/13).

23. Richard Bagwell, *Ireland under the Tudors,* I, 126, 282-6; *D.N.B.* s.v. St. Leger, Sir Anthony and Sir Warham.

24. *Sidney State Papers,* ed. T. O'Laidhin, pp. 22-5, 27-8, 34-8.

25. Sidney to Privy Council, 11 July 1566 (S.P.63/18/54); Sidney to queen, 20 April 1567 (S.P.63/20/66); account of Sidney's journey by Athlone pursuivant (T.C.D., MS 581, E.3. 18, ff. 76-91).

26. Bagwell, *Tudors,* II, 94; Sidney to the queen, 20 April 1567 (S.P.63/20/66); 'Sidney's Memoir', *U.J.A.,* III, 39-41.

27. Sidney to Privy Council, 15 April 1566 (S.P.63/17/13); queen to Knollys, 18 April 1566 (S.P.63/17/20); Cecil to Sidney, 16 June 1566 (S.P.63/18/19).

28. Croft's remembrances on Ireland, 12 February 1561 (S.P.63/3/17); Winchester to Cecil, 20 March 1566 (S.P.63/16/62); same to Sidney, 4

April 1566 (S.P.63/20/61); Winchester's opinions on Ireland, 23 June 1567 (S.P.63/21/33, I); queen to Sidney, 10 November 1565 (S.P.63/15/40); Sidney to Leicester, 1 March 1566 (S.P.63/16/35).

29. Cecil to Sidney, 27 March 1566 (S.P.63/16/67); same to Smith, 26 March 1566 (B.M., Lansdowne MSS, vol. 102, no. 71); queen to Knollys, 18 April 1566 (S.P.63/17/20); Knollys's memo on Ireland, 30 May 1566 (S.P.63/17/70).

30. *Sidney Papers*, pp. 16-18; *A.P.C., 1558-70*, pp. 344-7; Cecil to Sidney, 11 July 1566 (S.P.63/18/47); instructions to Randolph, 8 July 1566 (S.P.63/18/41); lord deputy and council to the queen, 22 November 1566 (S.P.63/19/55); Sidney to Privy Council, 12 December 1566 (S.P.63/19/71).

31. *A.F.M.*, V. pp. 1611-21; 'Sidney's Memoir', *U.J.A.*,III, 91; G. A. Hayes-McCoy, *Irish Battles*.

32. *Sidney Papers*, p. 42; Cecil to Sidney, 10 June 1566 (S.P. 63/18/19); Sidney to Cecil, 4 March 1567 (S.P.63/20/41).

33. Privy council to the queen, 5 July 1567 (S.P.63/21/48); *Sidney Papers*, pp. 68, 84; 'Sidney's Memoir', *U.J.A.*, III, 92-3; lords justices and council to the queen, 30 October 1567 (Oxford, Carte MSS, vol. 58, no. 52).

34. 'Sidney's Memoir', *U.J.A.*, III, 94.

35. Sidney to Throgmorton, 7 July 1567 (S.P.63/21/51); 'Sidney's Memoir', *U.J.A.*, III, 94.

36. Petitions of Sidney, April 1568 (S.P.63/23/53); Sidney to Fitzwilliam, 17 May 1568 (Oxford, Carte MSS, 58/227).

37. Leicester to Cecil, 20 March 1566 (S.P.12/39/41);Winchester's opinions on Ireland, 28 June 1567 (S.P.63/21/33, I)

38. Memo by Cecil, 22 December 1567 (S.P.63/22/49); Cecil's advice to the queen, 2 January 1568 (S.P.63/23/1); J. H. Andrews, 'The Irish Surveys of Robert Lythe', *Imago Mundi*, XIX, 22-31; Robin Flower, 'Laurence Nowell and the Discovery of England in Tudor Times', *Brit. Acad., Proc.*, XXI, 47-73; Cecil's compilation of Irish pedigrees (P.R.O., 31/16/70).

39. Petitions of Sidney, April 1568 (S.P.63/23/53).

40. Queen to Sidney, 11 July 1568 (*Cal. Pat. Rolls Ire.*, p. 212); instructions to Sidney, 1 May 1568 (S.P.63/24/29); instructions to Sidney, July 1568 (S.P.63/25/50, 51).

41. Cecil to Sidney, 11 August 1568 (S.P.63/25/64); same to same, 13 August 1568 (B.M., Lansdowne MSS, vol. 102, no. 74).

42. 'Sidney's Memoir', *U.J.A.*, III, 94-6; *Cal. Pat. Rolls Ire.*, p. 512; Sidney to Cecil, 30 November 1568 (Collins, *Letters and Memorials of State*, I, 40-1); same to same, 12 November 1568 (S.P.63/26/18); Cecil to Sidney, 6 January 1569 (S.P.63/27/2).

4 *The programme in action – colonization*

1. The queen's instructions to Sussex, 16 July 1559 (S.P.63/1/59).

2. Theodore K. Rabb, *Enterprise and Empire*, p. 376; D. B. Quinn, 'Ireland and Sixteenth Century European Expansion', *Hist. Studies*, I, 26.
3. Victor Treadwell, 'The Irish Parliament of 1569-71', *Royal Irish Acad. Proc.*, LXV, sec. C (1966), 61; Gilbert's discourse on Ireland, 1 February 1574 (B.M., Add. MSS, 48, 017 ff. 136-43); J. J. Silke, *Kinsale*, pp. 9-24; For Sidney's view see S. P.63/20/66 f. 138.
4. 'Sidney's Memoir', *U.J.A.*, 1st ser., V, 306; abstract of Sidney's letters, 5 July 1567 (S.P.63/21/48); Sidney to Walsingham, March 1577 (Collins, *Letters and Memorials of State*, p. 161).
5. 'Sidney's Memoir', *U.J.A.*, V, 306: Treadwell, 'Parliament', pp. 82-3; memo by Lucas Dillon, 11 April 1570 (S.P.63/30/60); J. H. Andrews, 'Geography and Government in Elizabethan Ireland', in *Irish Geographical Studies*, eds. N. Stephens and R. E. Glasscock esp. p. 185; J. H. Andrews, 'The Irish Surveys of Robert Lythe', *Imago Mundi*, XIX, 22-31.
6. J. Hooker, alias Vowell, 'Life of Sir Peter Carew', printed in *Cal. Carew MSS, 1515-74*, pp. lxvii-cxviii; Memorandum book of John Hooker, alias Vowell, (Camb. Univ. Lib., MS Mm.1. 32).
7. Order on Idrone by the lord chancellor, 24 December 1568 (S.P.63/26/58); the queen to Sidney, 16 February 1569 (*Sidney Papers*, pp. 102-4); Carew to Cecil, 26 December 1568 (S.P.63/26/59); the queen to Sidney, 6 June 1569 (Dublin, P.R.O.I., Ferguson MSS, VI, 164-6); Carew to Burghley, 28 August 1571 (S.P.63/33/47); Carew to Cecil (S.P.63/27/33).
8. Sidney to Cecil, 4 March 1567 (S.P.63/20/41); Treadwell, 'Parliament', p. 63.
9. Wingfield to Cecil, 12 November 1568 (S.P.63/26/22); Privy Council to Fitzwilliam, 21 January 1573 (S.P.63/39/14).
10. Sidney to Cecil, 17 April 1566 (S.P.63/17/14).
11. Leicester to Fitzwilliam (Oxford, Carte MSS, 57/197).
12. *Churchyarde's Choise*, sig, d,3; 'Sidney's Memoir', *U.J.A.*, III, 38n; Cecil to Sidney, 12 September 1568 (S.P.63/25/85); Leicester's statement on Horsey (Carte MSS, 56/76); D. M. Loades, *Two Tudor Conspiracies*, pp. 144, 179, 193, 204-5; Cecil to Sidney, 23 December 1565 (S.P.63/15/69).
13. Loades, *Two Tudor Conspiracies*, pp. 50, 109, 153-4, 207-8, 15-16, 95-6, 47, 93. *Churchyarde's Choise*, sig. d,3.
14. Sidney's opinion on Ireland, 20 May 1565 (S.P.63/13/46).
15. 'The Ulster Project', undated (S.P.63/9/83).
16. Sir Francis Knollys to Cecil, 19 May 1566 (S.P.63/17/56); Cecil to Sidney, 14 May 1566 (S.P.63/17/52).
17. Payment of £40 expenses to William Piers for his visit to court, 9 March 1565 (*A.P.C., 1558-70*); M. B. Donald, *Elizabethen Copper*, p. 52. This line of reasoning was first pursued by D. G. White in his thesis and while I disagree with his conclusions on the membership of the corporation I am greatly indebted to his meticulous treatment of 'The Ulster Project' both in dating the manuscript and in tracing the connection with the

evacuation of Le Havre; see his thesis 'The Tudor Plantations in Ireland', II, 166-9.

18. Sidney et al. to the queen, 12 November 1566 (S.P.63/19/43); 'Sidney's Memoir', *U.J.A.*, III, 38n.
19. Queen to Sidney, 11 June 1567 (*Sidney Papers*, pp. 65-8); notes by Knollys, 7 July 1567 (S.P.63/21/56); Cecil to Sidney, 20 July 1567 (S.P.63/21/64).
20. Loades, *Two Tudor Conspiracies*, pp. 105-6; *Churchyarde's Choise*, sig. k,2; William Camden, *Britannica*, pp. 82, 137; A. L. Rowse, *Sir Richard Granville*, pp. 49-51, 60-3.
21. Sidney to Cecil, 18 November 1566 (S.P.63/19/51); memorial of matters communicated orally by Ralph Knight, 15 June 1567 (S.P.63/21/20).
22. Thomas Lancaster to Leicester, 5 March 1566 (S.P.63/16/45); John Denton to Cecil, 16 January 1567 (S.P.63/20/11, I).
23. 'Sidney's Memoir', *U.J.A.*, III, 92-3; memorial by Cecil, 22 December 1567 (S.P. 63/22/48).
24. Sidney to Cecil, 17 April 1566 (S.P.63/17/14).
25. Memo by Cecil, May 1566 (S.P.63/17/17); Sidney to Cecil, 12 November 1568 (S.P.63/26/18).
26. Sidney to Cecil, as above; Knolly's opinion, 7 July 1567 (S.P.63/21/56); memorial by Cecil, 22 December 1567 (S.P.63/22/48).
27. Rabb, *Enterprise and Empire*, p. 283; Donald, *Elizabethan Copper*, pp. 43-7.
28. Winchester to Cecil, 28 June 1567 (S.P.63/21/33).
29. Sidney to Privy Council, 24 June 1570 (S.P.63/30/56).
30. Memo by Cecil, November 1567 (S.P.63/22/34); lords justices to Privy Council, 8 February 1568 (S.P.63/23/33, 33, I); Sidney to Privy Council, 24 June 1570 (S.P.63/30/56); offer of Sir Thomas Gerrard, 15 March 1570 (S.P.63/30/32).
31. Sidney, matters to be resolved for Ireland, April 1570 (S.P.63/30/48).
32. Sidney, matters to be resolved for Ireland, April 1570 (S.P.63/30/48); Burghley's memo, 1571 (S.P.63/34/41); Malby to Burghley, 9 October 1571 (S.P.63/34/25); petition of Captains Browne and Borrow, 1571 (S.P.63/34/42); R. Dunlop, 'Sixteenth Century Schemes for the Plantation of Ulster', *Scot. Hist. Rev.*, XXII, 116-19.
33. 'Sidney's Memoir', *U.J.A.*, III, 99.
34. Note of Grenville's men (S.P.63/28/39); Richard Bagwell, *Tudors*, II, 155-6; *D.N.B.* s.v. Pollard, Sir John, and Tremayne, Edmund; Tremayne to Cecil, 12 April 1570 (S.P.63/30/42); Tremayne to Pollard (S.P.63/29, 12, II); Arthur Collins, *Letters and Memorials of State*, introduction.
35. *The Voyages and Colonising Enterprises of Sir Humphrey Gilbert*, ed. D. B. Quinn, I, 122-4; J. A. Froude, *History of England*, X, 488; P.R.O., court of requests proceedings, bundle 271/66 where Brett is mentioned as from Leeds, Kent.
36. Guérau de Spes to King Philip, 14 June 1569 (*Cal. S.P. Spanish, 1568-79*, 165); Castelyn to Burghley, 16 January 1574 (S.P.63/44/8); *Cal. Pat.*

Rolls, Eliz. I, 1566-9, nos. 332, 1589; Corbine to Cecil, 21 March 1569 (S.P.63/27/57); Rabb, *Enterprise and Empire,* sub Castelyn on computer print out.

37. Petition to Privy Council, March 1569 (*Voyages of Gilbert,* ed. Quinn, I, 493); Gilbert's discourse, 1 February 1574 (B.M., Add. MSS, 48,017, ff. 136-43); incorporation of Society of Mineral and Battery Works, *Cal. Pat. Rolls, Eliz. I, 1566-9,* no. 1589; John Denton to Cecil, 16 January 1567 (S.P. 63/20/11, I).
38. Unsigned letter to Burghley, April 1573 (S.P.63/40/20).
39. Brett to Cecil, 3 June 1569 (S.P.63/28/21).
40. Perrott to Smith, 6 July 1573 (S.P.63/41/71); an offer for Ireland, April 1573 (S.P.63/40/20).
41. See the petitions by Brett (S.P.63/28/2 and S.P.63/28/61).
42. *Ibid;* for claims of Carew see S.P.63/33/50 and 55, both petitions of August 1571; for their anxiety to provoke rebellion see Gilbert's discourse, 1 February 1574 (B.M. Add. MSS, 48,017, ff. 136-43).
43. Brett's petition (S.P.63/28/2); answers to objections (S.P.63/28/5).
44. Brett's petition (S.P.63/28/2) and Cecil's comments (S.P.63/28/3).
45. Anonymous document (S.P.63/23/26); I have taken it that the author of this document, like Englishmen generally at the time, assumed that a plough-land corresponded to one hundred and twenty acres of fertile land plus waste. On the subject of measurement generally see J. H. Andrews, 'Geography and Government in Elizabethan Ireland', in *Irish Geographical Studies,* pp. 178-91.
46. On the subject of social mobility in England see Peter Laslett, *The World we Have Lost* (London 1963); W. G. Hoskins, *The Midland Peasant: the Economic and Social History of a Leicestershire Village,* pp. 201, 215, 311-313 for the prospects of a typical English peasant.
47. A memorial on the gentlemen's offer (S.P.63/28/9).
48. St Leger to Cecil, 3 June 1569 (S.P.63/28/18); same to same, 6 June 1571 (S.P.63/32/54); anonymous undated project (S.P.63/23/26).
49. Cecil to Fitzwilliam, 15 December 1571 (Oxford, Carte MSS, 131/11); same to same, 25 June 1568 (Carte MSS, 58/287); Smith to Fitzwilliam, 18 May 1572 (*Cal. S.P., For. 1583 and Add.,* p.489); Leicester to Fitzwilliam, 24 August 1572 (Carte MSS 57/227); Irish sub-committee June 1571 (S.P.63/34/47).
50. The account of the Smith exploit is based largely on D. B. Quinn, 'Sir Thomas Smith and the Beginnings of English Colonial Theory', *Proc. of Amer. Phil. Soc.,* LXXXIX, 543-60, and on M. Dewar, *Sir Thomas Smith: A Tudor Intellectual in Office,* pp. 156-70.
51. *Cal. Pat Rolls, Eliz., 1569-71,* no. 2167; *Cal. S.P., For. 1583 and Add.,* p.490.
52. Petition of Smith and associates, undated (*De L'isle and Dudley MSS,* II, 12-15); broadsheet and pamphlet bound together entitled *A letter sent by I.B. gentleman unto his very frende mayster R.C. esquire, S.T.C.,* no. 1048. The initials I.B. may stand for Jerome Brett who frequently used initials only; the style and matter, however, suggest that Sir Thomas Smith was the author.

53. Smith to Leicester, Sussex and Croft, 16 April 1572 (*Cal. S.P., For. 1583 and Add.*, pp. 477-8; Leicester to Fitzwilliam, 5 December 1572 (Oxford, Carte MSS, 56/39); Perrott to Smith, 6 July 1573 (S.P.63/41/71).

54. Smith to Privy Council, 16 April 1572 (*Cal. S.P., For. 1583 and Add.*, pp. 475-6); Smith to Sir Valentine Browne, 15 April 1572 (*Cal. S.P. For., 1583 and Add.*, p. 475); on Edward Knollys see Wingfield to Burghley (S.P.63/37/61); Joan Thisk, 'Younger Sons in the Seventeenth Century', *History*, LIV, 358-77.

55. The above is based on Professor Quinn's article on the Smith venture, *Proc. of Amer. Phil. Soc.*, LXXXIX, 543-60.

56. Edward Mansell to Burghley, 11 June 1572 (S.P.63/36/37); *D.N.B.* s.v. Mansell, Sir Robert (son to Sir Edward).

57. Orders of Sir Thomas Smith, 1 December 1573 (Essex county record office, MS D/Dsh., 01/2)., Dewar, *Sir Thomas Smith,* pp. 166-9.

58. Indentures between Smith and the adventurers, (Essex county record office, MS, D/Dsh., 01/1-10); others who contributed significant amounts were Edmund Verney, William Blaytsid and Francis Bruynynge; Dewar, *Sir Thomas Smith,* p. 169.

59. For a complete list of those who joined Essex June 1573 see S.P.63/41/64; also *Churchyarde's Choise,* sig. f,1. Sons of the treasurer (Burghley) are mentioned among those who accompanied Essex but there is no evidence that Thomas Cecil arrived; he may have been on one of the ships diverted by storm. Burghley is mentioned (S.P.63/43/9) as 'one of the first furtherers of this honorable enterprise'; see *A.P.C., 1571-5,* p.352 where St Leger is mentioned as 'servant' to Essex; this may be Warham St Leger, nephew to the original Warham, who certainly served with Essex (S.P.65/9, f.21).

60. Lawrence Stone, *The Crisis of the Aristocracy,* pp. 424, 455; for the officers and ships captains who served under Essex see Fitton's account, 1 April 1573 – 30 September 1575 (S.P.65/8, ff.33-7).

61. For the land divisions see S.P.63/48/81; Essex to the treasurer, the chamberlain and Leicester, 8 March 1574 (S.P.63/45/7); Essex mortgaged land in Essex worth £1,200 on 24 February 1574 (S.P.63/44/58).

62 For a narrative account see R. C. Morton, 'The Enterprise of Ulster', *History Today,* XVII, 114-21.

63. The figure is given in S.P.65 no. 10, a book of all receipts by the Irish treasurer 1555-1581; for the Rathlin massacre see Essex to Privy Council, 31 July 1575 (S.P.63/52/78); Essex to the queen, 31 July 1575 (Walter Bouchier Devereux, *Lives and Letters of the Devereux Earls of Essex,* I, 113-17). The entire cost of the campaign was well in excess of £100,000, see H. A. Lloyd, 'The Essex Inheritance', *Welsh History Review,* VII, 13-59.

64. For the location of the proposed fortifications see S.P.63/48/81; Essex wanted each adventurer to 'build a small castle with a bawn of stone and intrench a town' (B.M., Add. MSS, 48,015, ff. 296-300).

65. Sidney to Privy Council, 15 November 1575 (Collins, *Letters and*

Memorials of State, I, 75-80).

66. Wotton to Throgmorton, 25 December 1561 (B.M., Add. MSS, 35,830, f. 230); see also *A letter from I.B.*

67. Proposition by Brett, 1573 (S.P.63/40/56); Fitzwilliam to Burghley, 26 October 1572 (S.P.63/38/24).

68. 'Sidney's Memoir', *U.J.A.*, III, 94, 96.

69. This theme is dealt with in chapter 6 and also in the author's, 'The Ideology of English Colonization: fron Ireland to America', *William and Mary Quarterly*, XXX, 575-98.

70. Smith to his son, 16 March 1572 (*Cal. S.P., For. and Add.*, p. 465; Joan Thirsk, 'Younger Sons in the Seventeenth Century', *History*, LIV, 358-77; Arthur Collins, *Letters and Memorials of State*, I, 70-71.

71. For gentry and merchant investment see Rabb, *Enterprise and Empire;* he sees 1575 as a starting point but does not attach any importance to the disengagement from Ireland that coincided with this spurt in investment.

5 *The programme in action – provincial presidencies*

1. D. B. Quinn, 'Henry VIII and Ireland, 1509-34', *I.H.S.*, XII, 330-1; D. B. Quinn, 'Edward Walshe's "Conjectures" ', *I.H.S.*, V, 305-6.

2. Penry Williams, *The Council in the Marches of Wales*, pp. 11-12.

3. *Ibid.*, pp. 15-24.

4. M. E. James, *Change and Continuity in the Tudor North;* see the map of the marches with locations of royal garrisons, pp. 26-7.

5. F. W. Brooks, *York and the Council of the North*, p. 4; Rachel Reid, *The King's Council in the North*, pp. 92-112.

6. Reid, *King's Council*, pp. 121-44.

7. *Ibid.*, pp. 147-65; James, *Change and Continuity*, pp. 26-9.

8. A. G. Dickens, *Robert Holgate: Archbishop of York and President of the King's Council in the North*, esp. pp. 7-9.

9. Joyce Youings, 'The Council in the West', *T.R.H.S.*, 5th ser., X, 41-9; G. R. Elton, *The Tudor Revolution in Government*, pp. 345-6.

10. G. Scott Thomson, *Lords Lieutenants in the Sixteenth Century.*

11. James, *Change and Continuity*, p. 29.

12. Reid, *King's Council*, pp. 201-3.

13. *Ibid.*, pp. 203-8; James, *Change and Continuity*, pp. 38-9; Claire Cross, *The Puritan Earl: the Life of Henry Hastings, Third Earl of Huntingdon, 1536-95*, pp. 159-95; Dr Cross shows that Huntingdon tried to create a new political stability in the north as well as to destroy the old aristocratic society, p. 170.

14. Articles agreed upon between Desmond and Queen Elizabeth, 28 June 1562 (P.R.O., SP.63/6/3).

15. George Wyse to Cecil 29 October 1569 (S.P.63/29/77); copy of letter of Cusack to Northumberland, 1552 (S.P.63/54/29); Quinn, 'Edward Walshe's "Conjectures" ', *I.H.S.*, V, 321, where a council for Munster is proposed but no particulars provided.

16. Cusack to Sussex, 6 August 1563 (S.P.63/8/46); Cusack's suggestions for Shane O'Neill, 7 August 1563 (S.P.63/8/47); notes touching the government of Ireland, September 1563 (S.P.63/9/31).
17. Queen's commission for Munster, 28 February 1565 (S.P.63/12/47).
18. Report of Sussex, 1562 (*Cal. Carew MSS, 1515-74*, pp. 330-44); see chapter 3 above for further details.
19. 'Sidney's Memoir', *U.J.A.*, 1st ser. VI, 91; *Cal. S.P. Ire., 1601-3*, p. 254.
20. Penry Williams, *The Council in the Marches of Wales*, pp. 23, 38-43, 181-204.
21. Sidney to Privy Council, 27 February 1576 (Collins, *Letters and Memorials of State*, I, 89-97).
22. Sidney to Leicester, 1 March 1566 (S.P.63/16/35); the estimate given (S.P.63/16/23) included the cost of maintaining the soldiers.
23. Sidney on the queen's instructions, 5 October 1565 (S.P.63/14/3).
24. Queen's instructions to Sidney, 5 October 1565 (S.P.63/15/4).
25. Instructions by lord deputy and council to St Leger, 1 February 1566 (S.P.63/16/22).
26. 'Sidney's Memoir', *U.J.A.*, III, 43; on Desmond's fears of a conspiracy between Ormond and the government see St. Leger to Sidney, 3 July 1566 (S.P.63/18/54, 1).
27. 'Sidney's Memoir', *U.J.A.*, III, 97; lord justice to the queen, 23 March 1568 (S.P.63/23/74).
28. In the directions drawn up, October 1568, for Sir John Pollard then nominated president of Munster, it was made clear that County Tipperary was exempt from his rule but not County Kerry which was to be treated 'as any other place within the jurisdiction of this commission' (S.P.63/26/9). On Fitzmaurice preparing for war see lord justice to the queen, 16 July 1568 (S.P.63/25/45).
29. Queen's resolution on Sidney's petitions, 27 June 1568 (S.P.63/25/11); the list supplied by Sidney read as follows: Sir John Pollard, Sir William Fitzwilliam, Sir Peter Carew, Humphrey Gilbert, Sir Hugh Cholemley, Sir Andrew Corbitt, Nicholas Beaumont of Choleorton (S.P.63/25/64); Cecil to Sidney, 3 September 1568 (S.P.63/25/75).
30. Sidney's allowances to the coronel of Munster, 3 September 1569 (Dublin, P.R.O.I., Lodge's MSS, patent rolls etc., Henry VIII – 12 Eliz., ff. 29-31).
31. Sidney to Cecil, 4 January 1570 (S.P.63/30/2).
32. Formula of instructions and orders, 14 December 1570 (Collins, *Letters and Memorials of State*, I, 48-59); demands of Perrott on going to Ireland, November 1570 (S.P.63/30/94); Perrott to lords justice, 14 August 1571 (S.P.63/34/4, I); James Dowdall to Fitzwilliam, 31 August 1571 (Oxford, Carte MSS, 57, ff. 82-5).
33. Perrott to Leicester, 20 May 1571 (B.M., Add. MSS, 32,091, f. 240); same to Burghley, 2 November 1572 (S.P.63/38/29); same to same, 18 June 1573 (S.P.63/41/43); same to Privy Council, 9 April 1573 (S.P.63/40/6).
34. On the changing personnel on the Munster council see the instructions

to St Leger, Pollard and Perrott mentioned above notes 25, 28,32. Laws and orders proclaimed by Perrott at Limerick, undated (*Cal. Carew MSS,1515-74,*pp.409-12); Perrott to Burghley, 18 June 1573 (S.P.63/41/43).

35. Perrott to the queen, 13 July 1573 (S.P.63/41/76, II); Richard Bagwell, *Tudors*, II, 251-3.
36. 'Sidney's Memoir', *U.J.A.*, III, 352; Sidney to Privy Council, 27 February 1576 (Collins, *Letters and Memorials of State*, 89-97); Sidney to Walsingham, 25 February 1576 (S.P.63/55/20).
37. Sidney to Privy Council, 28 April 1576 (Collins, *Letters and Memorials of State*, 102-10); same to same, 27 February 1576 (Collins, *Letters and Memorials of State*, 89-97).
38. *Ibid;* order by Sidney, 27 February 1576 (S.P.63/55/22).
39. Sidney to Privy Council, 15 December 1575 (*Cal. Carew MSS, 1575-88,* pp. 30-5); same to Burghley, 3 May 1576 (S.P.63/55/41); same to Privy Council, 27 February 1576 (Collins, *Letters and Memorials of State*, I, 89-97).
40. Drury to Privy Council, 24 March, 1578 (S.P.63/60/25); depositions of Ronan and Fleming at Cork and Clonmel sessions, 1576 (S.P.63/56/55, 56); Drury to Queen Elizabeth, 20 March 1577 (S.P.63/57/42); for an example of an agreement with a lesser lord see Richard Beacon, *Solon his Follie,* pp. 87-88.
41. Desmond to Queen Elizabeth, 13 December 1573 (S.P.63/43/15); Drury to Leicester, 8 July 1577 (*Cal. Carew MSS, 1575-88,* pp. 104-5); Drury to Walsingham, 27 January 1578 (S.P.63/60/6).
42. Drury to Privy Council, 24 April 1577 (S.P.63/58/4); same to same, 6 July 1577 (S.P.63/58/60); note of yearly revenue, 29 March, 1576 (S.P.63/60/28); annual charge of Munster in Drury's time (S.P.63/64/21); anticipated rental from monastic lands (S.P.63/57/13, I).
43. Depositions of Ronan and Fleming at Cork and Clonmel, 1576 (S.P.63/56/55, 56).
44. See *D.N.B.* s.v. Fitton, Sir Edward; Cecil to Sidney, 11 August 1568 (S.P.63/25/64); Reid, *The King's Council in the North*, pp. 210-11; *D.N.B.*, s.v. Rokeby, Ralph; knowledge of Irish was a pre-requisite for the post (Dublin, P.R.O.I., Lodge's MSS, pat. rolls etc., Henry VIII – 12 Eliz., 127).
45. Cusack to Cecil, 16 March 1569 (S.P.63/27/45).
46. Fitton to Cecil, 15 April 1570 (S.P.63/30/43); Rokeby to Cecil, 4 January 1570 (S.P.63/30/4); The glyb was a plaited hair style worn in front favoured in Gaelic Ireland.
47. Fitton to Cecil, 15 April 1570 (S.P.63/30/43).
48. Clanricard to the lord deputy, 13 February 1573 (S.P.63/39/29); Fitzwilliam's account, 1573 (S.P.65/7, f. 30).
49. Fitzwilliam to Burghley, 24 March 1571 (S.P.63/32/44).
50. Fitton to Cecil, 15 April 1570 (S.P.63/32/43); Rokeby to Cecil, 15 April 1570 (S.P.63/32/44).
51. Fitton to Privy Council, undated (Oxford Carte MSS, 57, f. 539); same

to same, 29 October 1571 (S.P.63/34/27); by the lord deputy and council, 21 July 1576 (Dublin, N.L.I., MS 8065).

52. See the three sets of instruction to lords president in Munster; for the queen's views on the language barrier (S.P.63/10/49). Rokeby to Cecil, 4 January 1570 (S.P.63/30/4).
53. Fitton to Burghley, 20 May 1571 (S.P.63/32/39); same to same, 27 March 1574 (S.P.63/45/35), I).
54. Agard to Walsingham, 15 June 1576 (S.P.63/55/60); Sidney to Privy Council, 16 June 1576 (Collins, *Letters and Memorials of State*, I, 114-18).
55. *Ibid*. Sidney to Privy Council, 28 April 1576 (Collins, *Letters and Memorials of State*, I, 102-10); same to same, 27 February 1576 (Collins, *Letters and Memorials of State*, I, 89-97).
56. Collins, *Letters and Memorials of State*, I, 89-97.
57. Agard to Walsingham, 11 September 1576 (S.P.63/56/26).
58. Abstract of rents due to the queen in Connacht, 1577 (S.P. 63/59/71); see Sidney's claim of £1,137 rent (S.P.63/60/42); survey of monastic land (S.P.63/55/37, I).
59. Grenville mentioned as sheriff (S.P.63/28/37, 38); Fitton to Burghley, 31 January 1572 (S.P.63/35/12).
60. Sussex to Fitzwilliam, date uncertain (Oxford, Carte MSS, 57/195); plot for governing Ireland, 12 November 1568 (S.P.63/63/25); Walsingham to Sidney, 27 February 1578 (Collins, *Letters and Memorials of State*, I, 240).
61. Tremayne to Sidney, 24 January 1576 (S.P.63/55/6); Privy Council to Sidney, 23 January 1576 (S.P.63/55/5).

6 *The breakdown: Elizabethan attitudes towards the Irish*

1. Richard Beacon, *Solon his Follie*, pp. 82-3; Thomas Lee, 'A brief declaration of the government of Ireland', *Desiderata Curiosa Hibernica*, ed. J. Lodge, I (Dublin 1772), p. 95.
2. See J. R. Lander, *Conflict and Stability in Fifteenth-Century England* (London 1969).
3. *Cal. Pat. Rolls, Eliz. I, 1569-71*, no. 2167; draft patent to Essex, May 1573 (*Cal. Carew MSS, 1515-74*, pp. 441-2).
4. Edmund Spenser, *A View of the Present State of Ireland*, p. 9; Gilbert's discourse, 1 Feb. 1574 (B.M., Add. MSS, 48,017, ff. 136-43).
5. Smith to Burghley, 10 April 1572 (S.P.70/146, f. 79); Davies to Salisbury, 8 November 1610 (*Historical Tracts*, pp. 281-3).
6. J. A. Watt, *The Church and the Two Nations in Medieval Ireland*, x, 200-15; N. P. Canny, 'Hugh O'Neill', *Studia Hibernica*, X, esp. pp. 25-7, and also chapter 1 above. See also J. F. Lydon, *The Lordship of Ireland in the Middle Ages*, esp. pp. 279-95.
7. Sir James Croft, 'A brief remembrance of certen things concernyng Ireland', 12 February 1561 (S.P.63/3/17).
8. Queen to Fitzwilliam, 17 July 1573 (Oxford, Carte MSS, 56/26).
9. Essex to Privy Council, 31 July 1575 (S.P.63/52/78); Essex to the queen

(*Devereux Lives*, I, 113-17).

10. Essex to Burghley, 20 July 1573 (*Devereux Lives*, I, 30-1); Essex to Privy Council, 29 September 1573 (*Devereux Lives*, I, 37-9); Edward Barkley to Burghley, 14 May 1574 (S.P.63/46/15); Smith to Burghley, 10 April 1572 (S.P.70/146, f. 79).

11. Richard Bagwell, *Tudors*, II, 288-9; queen to Essex, 13 July 1574 (*Devereux Lives*, I, 52-3).

12. Sidney and council to Privy Council, 26 October 1569 (S.P. 63/29/70).

13. Sidney to Cecil, 4 January 1570 (S.P.63/30/2).

14. Thomas Churchyard, *Churchyarde's Choise* (*S.T.C.* 5235), sigs. q, l-r, l.

15. Witness the wonder caused by the appearance of Shane O'Neill at Queen Elizabeth's court as reported in W. Camden, *Annales Rerum Anglecarum et Hibernicarum, Regnante Elizabeth* (London 1615), pp. 69-70.

16. J. Bossy, 'The Counter-Reformation and the People of Catholic Ireland', *Hist. Studies*, VIII, 155-69; J. Bossy, 'The Counter-Reformation and the People of Catholic Europe', *Past and Present*, XLVII, 51-70).

17. See C. H. Garrett, *The Marian Exiles*.

18. Watt, *The Church and the Two Nations*, pp. 183-97; 'On the disorders of the Irishry' (S.P.63/1/72, 73).

19. Tremayne, 'Notes on Ireland', June 1571 (S.P.63/32/66).

20. Sidney to queen, 20 April 1567 (S.P.63/20/66, f. 138, v); Spenser, *View*, p. 84.

21. Fynes Moryson, *An Itinerary*, II, 381, III, 208-9.

22. For the careers of many of those mentioned see *Churchyarde's choise*.

23. Johann Boemus, *The Fardel of Facions*, trans. W. Waterman, 1555 (*S.T.C.*, 3197); see Margaret T. Hodgen, *Early Anthropology in the Sixteenth and Seventeenth Centuries*, esp. chap. 3.

24. Sidney to Leicester, 1 March 1566 (S.P.63/16/35).

25. Thomas Hacket, *The New Found Worlde or Antarticke*, trans. from André Thevet, 1568 (*S.T.C.*, 23950).

26. Sidney to Leicester, 1 March 1566 (S.P.63/16/35); Sir John Davies, *A Discovery of the True Causes why Ireland was never entirely Subdued*, p. 291.

27. Johann Boemus, *The Manners, Laws and Customs of all Nations* (*S.T.C.*, 3198), 106.

28. *A letter sent to I.B.* (*S.T.C.*, no. 1048) sig. c.1; Spenser, *View*, pp. 49, 50, 54, 56; Moryson, *Itinerary*, IV, 201.

29. Tremayne, 'Notes on Ireland', June 1571 (S.P.63/32/66).

30. Hooker, 'Life of Sir Peter Carew' in *Cal. Carew MSS, 1515-74* p. civ; Barnaby Rich, *Allarme to England*, (*S.T.C.*, 20978) sig. d.2; Barnaby Rich, *A Short Survey of Ireland*, p. 2. See also Moryson, *Itinerary*, IV, 203, who remarks that 'these wild Irish are not much unlike the wild beasts'.

31. Rowland White, 'Discourse touching Ireland' (S.P.63/31/32).

32. Weston to Cecil, 3 April 1568 (S.P.63/24/2); Fitzwilliam to Burghley, 25 September 1572 (S.P.63/37/60).

33. *A letter sent to I.B.*, sig. c.6.

34. Smith to Fitzwilliam, 8 November 1572 (Oxford, Carte MSS, 57/236).

35. Sir Thomas Smith, *De Republica Anglorum*, ed. L. Aston, pp. 130-1.

36. Spenser, *View*, p. 11; Davies, *Discovery*, pp. 272-3.
37. Essex to Privy Council, undated (B.M., Add. MSS, 48,015, ff. 305-14).
38. Petition of Thomas Smith, Jr. (*De L'isle and Dudley MSS*, II, 12-15); Sir T. Smith to Fitzwilliam, 18 May 1572, (*Cal. S.P., For. 1583 and Add.*, pp. 49-50).
39. Essex to Burghley, 10 September 1573 (*Devereux Lives*, I, 34-6).
40. Gilbert's discourse, 1 February 1574 (B.M., Add. MSS, 48,017, ff. 136-43).
41. Davies to Salisbury, 1 July 1607 (*Cal. S.P. Ire., 1606-8*, p. 213).
42. See Arthur B. Ferguson, 'Circumstances and the Sense of History in Tudor England', in *Medieval and Renaissance Studies*, III, ed. J. M. Headley, pp. 170-205.
43. Spenser, *View*, pp. 10-11.
44. 'Gerrard's Notes', *Analecta Hibernica*, no. 2, pp. 95-6.
45. Fitzwilliam to queen, 25 September 1572 (S.P.63/37/59); Perrott to Smith, 28 January 1573 (S.P.63/39/16); Essex to Ashton, 1 June 1575 (S.P.63/52/5).
46. J. H. Elliott, *The Old World and the New*, pp. 39-51.
47. Richard Eden, *The Decades of the New World of West India*, trans. from Petrus Martyr Anglerius 1555 (*S.T.C.*, 645); Elliott, *The Old World and the New*, p. 91; D. B. Quinn, 'Ireland and Sixteenth Century European expansion', *Hist. Studies*, I, 20-32.
48. Smith to Fitzwilliam, 27 April 1573 (Oxford, Carte MSS, 56, f. 57); Essex to Privy Council (B.M., Add. MSS, 48,015, ff. 305-14).
49. Leicester to Fitzwilliam, 24 August 1572 (Oxford, Carte MSS, 57/227); Eden, *The Decades*, preface, f. 9.2; for further extreme statements by Leicester see Carte MSS, 56/39, f. 97.
50. Davies to Salisbury, 8 November 1610, (*Historical Tracts*, p. 283).
51. Leicester to Ashton, May 1575 (S.P.63/51/48).
52. Gerrard to Walsingham, 8 February 1577 (S.P.63/57/18); Beacon, *Solon his Follie*, pp. 16, 91; Moryson, *Itinerary*, II, 201; Davies; *Discovery*, p. 208.
53. C. Hill, 'Puritans and "the Dark Corners of the Land"', *T.R.H.S.*, XIII, 77-102 esp. 79.
54. 'Note on the government of Ireland' by William Gerrard, undated (S.P.63/60/29).

7 *The breakdown: Irish reactions to the Elizabethan conquest*

1. See James Hogan, 'Shane O'Neill Comes to the Court of Elizabeth', *Féilscribhinn Tórna*, ed. S. Pender, pp. 154-72.
2. *A.F.M.*, V, 1681; *A.L.C.*, the year 1568, pp. 402-3.
3. *Measgra Dánta* ed. T. F. O'Rahilly, no. 26, pp. 41-44; Osborn Bergin, *Irish Bardic Poetry*, no. 19, pp. 85-8; Anne O'Sullivan, 'Tadhg O'Daly and Sir George Carew', *Eigse*, XIV (1971), 27-38; Miss O'Sullivan's translation reads as follows, 'I am not foolish like many other of my fellow poets, o honourable form stout in battle, I never opposed you'.

4. Aodh de Blácam, *Gaelic Literature Surveyed,* pp. 125-7; for an example of stirring bardic poetry of the early seventeenth century see *Measgra Dánta,* no. 54 'Mo thruaighe mar táid Gaoidhil' by Fearflatha O Gnímh.

5. *A.L.C.* pp. 404-5 where mention is made of war between 'Ghalloibh ocus Ghaoidhealaibh, Albanchaibh ocus Saxanaibh'; for 'Dughghall' see *Duanta Eoghain Ruaidh Mhic an Bháird,* ed. Tomás O Raghallaigh, p. 276 the poem *Dún na nGall;* for the other terms see Bergin, *Irish Bardic Poetry,* pp. 130, 115, 85; Laoisioch Mac an Bháird, *a fhir ghlacas a ghalldacht,* Bergin, *Irish Bardic Poetry,* no. 9, pp. 49-50.

6. Fitzwilliam to Burghley, 21 October 1572 (S.P.63/38/20); Thomas Churchyard, *Churchyarde's Choise,* sig. f,3; proclamation by Essex justifying the arrest of Brian Mac Phelim (S.P.63/48/57, I).

7. John Hooker's memo of parliament (Cambridge Univ. Lib. MS Mm 1-32, f.3); Sidney's memoir touching parliament (B.M., Add. MSS, 4,797, f.135); Edmund Campion, *A Historie of Ireland,* (1571), pp. 131-8.

8. On this parliament see T. W. Moody, 'The Irish Parliament under Elizabeth and James I: a General Survey', *Royal Irish Acad., Proc.,* XLV sec. C (1939), 41-81, and the more detailed Victor Treadwell, 'The Irish Parliament of 1569-71', *Royal Irish Acad., Proc.,* LXV sec. C, (1966), 55-89, on which the above is largely based.

9. 'Sidney's Memoir', *U.J.A.,* 1st ser., III, 97.

10. Mayor of Waterford to Sidney, 9 July 1569 (S.P.63/29/5); Hooker, 'Life of Carew', in *Cal. Carew MSS,* p.c.

11. Fitton to Fitzwilliam, 16 July 1572 (S.P.63/37/11, I); 'Sidney's Memoir', *U.J.A.,* V, 313-14; Fitton to Burghley, 8 July 1576 (S.P.63/56/3); Fitton's account, 7 November 1570 (S.P.63/30/91).

12. 'Sidney's Memoir', *U.J.A.,* III, 97; *A.F.M..,*VI, 1625-9; lords justices to queen, 16 July 1568 (S.P.63/25/45); Sidney to Cecil, 17 November 1568 (Arthur Collins, *Letters and Memorials of State,* I, 39).

13. 'Sidney's Memoir', *U.J.A.,* III, 97; lords justices to queen, 4 September 1568 (S.P.63/25/77).

14. A. L. Rowse, *Sir Richard Grenville of the Revenge,* pp. 87-8; Lady St Leger to Sidney, 18 June 1569 (S.P.63/28/37); Jasper Horsey to Sidney, same date (S.P.63/28/36); mayor of Waterford to same (S.P.63/28/40).

15. Lord Roche to lords justices, 14 September 1568 (S.P.63/20/4 IX); Horsey to Sidney, 18 June 1569 (S.P.63/28/36).

16. Carew to Sidney, 12 July 1569 (S.P.63/29/10); 'Sidney's Memoir', *U.J.A.,* III, 350; mayor of Waterford to Sidney, 9 July 1569 (S.P.63/29/5).

17. Dowling reported that in 1569 'Lagenienses omnibus enormitibus dediti; quidam dixere Peter Carew his warres, alii dixere Edmund Butlers warres', *Dowling Annals,* p. 40.

18. 'Sidney's Memoir', *U.J.A.,* III, 98.

19. Malby to Cecil, 21 June 1569 (S.P.63/28/45).

20. 'Sidney's Memoir', *U.J.A.,* III, 97.

21. Mayor of Waterford to Sidney, 8 July 1569 (S.P.63/29/5); 'Sidney's

Memoir', *U.J.A.*, III, 98.

22. A note of the events with the circumstances between the lord president and council of Connacht and the earl of Thomond, 1569 (S.P.63/30/91, ff. 192-5); Sidney to queen, 22 December 1570 (*Halliday MSS*, p. 215); Fitton, Clanricard et al. to Sidney, 23 January 1570 (*Halliday MSS*, pp. 201-3).

23. Clanricard's articles delivered to the Dublin council, 16 May 1571 (S.P. 63/32/35); Fitton to Privy Council, undated ((Oxford, Carte MSS, 57, f. 539). *Halliday MSS*, p. 282; Fitton . to Fitzwilliam, 16 July 1572 (S.P.63/37/11, I); Fitton to Burghley, 8 July 1576 (S.P.63/56/3).

24. Copy of Fitzmaurice's proclamation, 12 July 1569 (S.P.63/29/8).

25. 'Sidney's Memoir', *U.J.A.*, III, 98.

26. Submission of Clancar, 14 February 1571 (*Cal. Pat. Rolls Ire.*, pp. 542-3).

27. Perrott to Privy Council, 3 March, 1573 (S.P.63/39/40); on the submission see Perrott's description 23 February 1573 (S.P.63/39/33).

28. Ormond to Cecil, 24 July 1569 (S.P.63/29/23); 'Sidney's Memoir'. *U.J.A.*, III, 347-8; *Churchyarde's Choise*, c, 5, e,4.

29. Ormond to Cecil, 7 September 1569 (S.P.63/29/60).

30. *Ibid;* Ormond to Cecil, 24 July 1569 (S.P.63/29/23).

31. George Wyse to Cecil, 29 October 1569 (S.P.63/29/76).

32. 'Sidney's Memoir', *U.J.A.*, III, 347; deposition of Viscount Baltinglass, 19 June 1569 (S.P.63/28/42).

33. E. Laughlin to Sidney, 22 June 1569 (S.P.63/28/48); 'Sidney's Memoir', *U.J.A.*, III, 347. On the Northern Rebellion see Wallace MacCaffrey, *The Shaping of the Elizabethan Regime*, pp. 220-46, and Anthony Fletcher, *Tudor Rebellions*, pp. 91-106.

34. Fitton to Sidney, 22 February 1570 (S.P.63/30/15).

35. See Fletcher, *Tudor Rebellions* and *Preconditions of Revolution in Early Modern Europe*, eds. R. Forster and Jack Greene.

36. Ormond to Cecil, 5 March 1570 (S.P.63/30/27).

37. B. M. Add. MS, 19,837; recognizances for the Butlers and Thomond, ff. 6, 10, 11.

38. Clanricard to Upper Ossory, 28 June 1576 (S.P.63/55/71).

39. Gerrard to Walsingham, 29 June 1576 (S.P.63/55/72).

40. D. F. Cregan, 'Irish Catholic Admissions to the English Inns of Court, 1558-1625', *Ir. Jurist*, V, 95-114.

41. Deposition of Hugh McThomas, 6 July 1575 (S.P.63/52/48, III).

8 *Conclusion: a pattern established, 1565-76*

1. Cecil to Arnold, 28 February 1565 (S.P.63/12/50).

2. See Gerrard to Walsingham, 8 February 1577 (S.P.63/57/16).

3. Commentary by Tremayne, undated (B.M., Add. MSS, 48,015).

4. A book of all receipts of the queen's treasurer in Ireland, May 1555–September 1581 (S.P.65 no. 10).

5. J. Hooker, 'Life of Sir Peter Carew', *Cal. Carew MSS, 1515-74*, p.c.

6. Gilbert's discourse, 1 February 1574 (B.M., Add. MSS, 48,017,

136-43); Sidney to Privy Council, 28 April 1576 (Arthur Collins, *Letters and Memorials of State*, I, 102-10); same to Walsingham, 20 June 1577 (S.P.63/58/80).

7. Queen's instructions to Sidney, 2 August 1575 (B.M., Cott. MSS, Titus B.XII, f. 155).

8. Sidney to Privy Council, 27 February 1576 (Collins, *Letters and Memorials of State*, I, 89-97; Sidney to Privy Council, 15 November 1575 (Collins, *Letters and Memorials of State*, I, 75-80.

9. Walsingham to Sidney, 28 January 1576 (Collins, *Letters and Memorials of State*, I, 85-6); Fitzwilliam to Privy Council, 7 January 1575 (S.P.63/49/14); Sidney to Walsingham, 14 December 1575 (S.P.63/54/18).

10. The lists compiled by T. K. Rabb show that many of those whom we encounter in Irish colonization later shifted their interests to adventures in North America and to speculative projects at home – see Theodore K. Rabb, *Enterprise and Empire*, s.v., Horsey, Leighton, Grenville, Gilbert, Henry Palmer, Thomas Chatterton, St. Leger, Wingfield, Talbot, Castelyn et al.

11. See Richard Beacon, *Solon his Follie*, where frequent references are made to Bingham's aggressive actions.

12. Sidney to Lord Grey, 17 September 1580 (Collins, *Letters and Memorials of State*, I, 279-83); see also Anthony Power's project for the reformation of Ireland (B.M., Cott MSS, Titus B.XII, f. 73) where Sidney is portrayed as the model lord deputy.

13. Sir John Davies, *Historical Tracts*, pp. 307-8.

14. D. B. Quinn, 'Sir Thomas Smith and the Beginnings of English Colonial Theory', *Proc. of Amer. Phil. Soc.*, LXXXIX, pp. 543-60; 'Ireland and Sixteenth Century European Expansion', *Hist. Studies*, I, 20-32; Essex to Burghley, 8 March 1574 (S.P. 63/45/7); Sidney to Walsingham, 28 April 1576 (Collins, *Letters and Memorials of State*, I, 110-11); Sir John Davies, *A Discovery of the True Causes why Ireland was never entirely Subdued*, p. 287.

15. For the citation of a Roman precedent to justify colonization in the New World see the preface to George Pekham, *A True Report of the Late Discoveries of the New-Found Lands* London (1583); Paul Hulton and D. B. Quinn, *The American Drawings of John White*, I, 10.

16. Howard Mumford Jones, *O Strange New World*, esp. chap. 5; Gary B. Nash, 'The Image of the Indian in the Southern Colonial Mind', *William and Mary Quarterly*, XXIX, 197-230.

17. Smith to Fitzwilliam, 8 November 1572 (S.P.63/39/30); Edward Barkley to Burghley, 14 May 1574 (S.P.63/46/15).

18. Nash, 'The Image of the Indian in the Southern Colonial Mind', *William and Mary Quarterly*, XXIX, 197-230; R. H. Pearce, *The Savages of America*, esp. chap. I; *D.N.B.*, s.v. Waterhouse, Edward.

19. *Ibid;* R. Hakluyt the elder, 'Reasons for Colonization, 1585', in *The Elizabethan's America*, ed. L. B. Wright (London 1965), pp. 26-36, esp. p. 31. For similar English attitudes towards blacks in Sierra Leone see P.

E. H. Hair, 'Protestants as Pirates, Slavers and Proto-Missionaires: Sierra Leone, 1568 and 1582', *Jrl. Eccles. Hist.*, XXI, 203-24, esp. 221-3.

20. The Decades of the *Newe Worlde of West India* trans. from Petrus Martyr Anglerius, a.2, dorso.

21. Tremayne 'Notes on the Reformation of the Irish', June 1571 (S.P.63/32/66); Barnaby Rich, *Allarme to England,* sig. e.1; Essex to Privy Council, (B.M., Add. MSS, 48,015, ff. 305-14); *A letter to I.B.*,sig. b.1.

22. Edmund Spenser, *A View of the Present State of Ireland*, p. 179.

23. Smith to Fitzwilliam, 8 November 1572 (Oxford, Carte MSS, 57, no. 236); Edmund Morgan, 'The Labor Problem at Jamestown, 1607-18', *A.H.R.*, LXXVI, 595-611.

24. Cited in Christopher Hill, 'Puritans and the "the Dark Corners of the Land" ', *T.R.H.S.*, XIII, 96-7; Keith Thomas, *Religion and the Decline of Magic,* esp. chap. 6, pp. 150-73.

25. Johnson, *Works,* III (1820), 234; Boswell, *Journey* (New York 1936), p. 210. I am grateful to Mr Stephen Blumm for both references.

Bibliography

A. MANUSCRIPT SOURCES

1. British Museum, London
Additional MSS:
4,763: Extracts from council books of St Leger, Bellingham, Croft, Sussex and Sidney – notes by Gilbert.
4,792: Tables of contents of council books, Dublin, 34 H-8-1605.
4,797: Sidney's notes on the parliament of 1569-71.
15,914: Sidney correspondence, 1558-1709.
17,520: Sidney papers, 1572-1626.
19,837: Recognizances in chancery of Ireland – Eliz.
32,091: Miscellaneous papers mostly addressed to Leicester.
35,830-2: Miscellaneous state papers including the correspondence of Sir Nicholas Throgmorton.
48,015 Yelverton papers, originally collected by Robert Beale
48,017 Clerk of Privy Council. Extensive source on
sixteenth-century
    Ireland.
Cotton MSS:
Titus B.X: Letter book of Lord Deputy Sidney 1575-8.
Titus B.XII: Miscellaneous papers on Ireland.
Harleian MSS:
4,943: Orders of Privy Council 1570-80.
7,004: Miscellaneous papers 1559-93.
Lansdowne MSS:
102: Miscellaneous papers by William Cecil.
111: Papers relating to Wales, Scotland, Ireland, Jersey and Guernsey.
159: Papers on Ireland chiefly 1556-1617.
Sloane MSS:
2,442: Instructions to Lord Deputies St Leger, Sidney and Fitzwilliam.

Stowe MSS:
162: Table of contents to Walsingham's papers on Ireland.

2. Cambridge University Library
MS. Mm. 1.32: The memorandum book of John Hooker, alias Vowell in 1568-9 while agent in Ireland to Sir Peter Carew.

3. Dublin, National Library of Ireland
MS. 8065: Proclamations by Lord Deputy Sidney.

4. Dublin, Public Record Office of Ireland
Frazer MSS: High sheriffs for Irish counties in office of arms (1302-1862).
Lodge's MSS: Articles with Irish chiefs, denizations, etc.
    Records of the rolls, vol. I, Henry VIII – 12 Eliz.
    Wardship, liveries and alienations.
Ferguson MSS vol. VII: Repertory to memoranda rolls, Ed. VI – Eliz.
MSS M. 5037-9: Survey of Desmond lands, pre-1586, after the Desmond rebellion.

5. Dublin, Royal Irish Academy
MS 24. F. 17: Dublin council book 1556-71.
MS 24. K. 20: Copies of letters by Sidney.

6. Dublin, Trinity College Library
MS 581, E.3. 18: Miscellaneous papers.
MS 581, E.4. 17: Dealing with sixteenth-century Ireland.
Caulfield MSS: Papers dealing with the Caulfield family of County Cork, but some refer to government administration in Munster.

7. Hatfield House
Salisbury MSS: Relevant items consulted on the microfilm in the B.M.

8. Essex County Record Office, Chelmsford
MS D/Dsh 01, nos. 1-10: Papers relating to Smith's effort to colonize the Ards in Ulster.

9. Lambeth Palace Library
Carew MSS: Relevant items consulted on the microfilm in the National Library of Ireland.

10. Oxford, Bodleian Library
Carte MSS, vols. 55, 56, 57, 58 and 131: Letters and papers relating to the career of Sir William Fitzwilliam in Ireland.

11. Public Record Office, London
State Paper Office
S.P.12: State Papers Domestic Series.
S.P.62: State Papers Ireland – Mary.
S.P.63: State Papers Ire., Eliz. to Geo. III, vols. 1-79, 1558-80.
S.P.65, No. 7: Account of Sir William Fitzwilliam, treasurer of Ireland 1573.
S.P.65, No. 8: Account of Sir Edward Fitton, treasurer of Ireland 1575.
S.P.65, No. 9: Account of the earl of Essex 1575.

S.P.65, No. 10: A book of all receipts by the Irish treasurer May 1555 – 30 September 1581.

S.P.70: State Papers Foreign Series.

Transcripts 31/16 no. 70: Transcripts of Burghley's notes on Irish pedigrees.

B. CALENDARS AND PRINTED
MANUSCRIPT SOURCES

Acts of the Privy Council of England 1542-7 [etc.] (London 1890 seq.). 'Acts of the Privy Council in Ireland, 1556-71', ed. J. T. Gilbert, in *H.M.C. rep. 15*, app. III (London 1897); known as *Halliday MSS*.

Annála Connacht, ed. A. Martin Freeman (Dublin 1944).

The Annals of Loch Cé, ed. W. M. Hennessy, 2 vols. (London 1871).

Annála Rioghachta Eireann: Annals of the Kingdom of Ireland by the Four Masters, ed and trans. John O'Donovan, 7 vols (Dublin 1851).

Annála Uladh, ed. W. M. Hennessy and B. MacCarthy, 4 vols. (Dublin 1887-1901).

Analecta Hibernica, including the reports of the Irish Manuscripts Commission (Dublin 1930-   ).

Archivium Hibernicum: or Irish Historical Records (Catholic Record Society of Ireland, Maynooth 1912-   )

Calendar of State Papers, Domestic Series, 1547-80 [etc.] (London 1856-   ).

Calendar of State Papers, Foreign Series, 1547-53 [etc.] (London 1861-   ).

Calendar of State Papers relating to Ireland, 1509-73 [etc.] 24 vols, (London 1860-   ).

Calendar of State Papers relating to English Affairs preserved principally at Rome, in the Vatican Archives and Library, 1558-71 [etc.] 2 vols (London 1916, 1926).

Calendar of State Papers relating to Scotland, 1547-63 [etc.] (Edinburgh 1898-   ).

Calendar of Letters, Despatches, and State Papers relating to the Negotiations between England and Spain, preserved at Simancas and elsewhere, 1458-1508 [etc.] (London 1862-   ).

'Calendar to Fiants of the reign of Queen Elizabeth' in *P.R.O.I., rep. D.K. 7-22* (Dublin 1875-   ).

Calendar of the Carew MSS, preserved at Lambeth, 1515-74 [etc.] 6 vols. (London 1867-73).

Calendar of Patent and Close Rolls of Chancery in Ireland, Elizabeth, ed. James Morrin (Dublin 1862).

'Calendar of the Irish Council Book, March 1581-July 1586', ed. D. B. Quinn, *Analecta Hibernica*, no. 24 (1967).

Calendar of Patent Rolls. Elizabeth I (London: Hist. MSS, Comm., 1966).

Calendar of Ormond Deeds, vol. 5 (1548-83), ed. E. Curtis (Dublin: Irish MSS Comm., 1943).

'Calendar of Fitzwilliam Papers (1558-94)', among the Carte MSS at the Bodleian Library, Oxford. Consulted in typescript with the kind permission of the editor Mr Brian Trainor of the Public Record Office of Northern Ireland.

Calendar of the MSS of the Marquis of Salisbury, part XIII (London– Hist. MSS Comm., 1915).

'Ceart Ui Neill', ed. Myles Dillon in *Studia Celtica*, I, no. 1 (1966), 1-18.

Collins, Arthur: *Letters and Memorials of State* – from the De L'isle and Dudley papers – 2 vols. (London 1746).

The Compossicion Booke of Conought, ed. A. M. Freeman (Dublin: Irish MSS Comm., 1936).

Curtis, E., and R. B. McDowell, *Irish Historical Documents, 1172-1922* (London 1936).

Davies, Sir John, *Historical Tracts* (Dublin 1787).

De L'isle and Dudley MSS vols. I and II (London: Hist. MSS Comm., 1925).

Devereux, Walter Bourchier, *Lives and Letters of the Devereux Earls of Essex in the Reigns of Elizabeth, James I and Charles I*, 2 vols. (London 1853).

Dowling Annals: the Annals of Ireland by Friar John Clyne and Thady Dowling, ed. R. Butler (Dublin 1849).

Fitzwilliam Accounts, 1560-5 (Annesley Collection), ed. A. K. Longfield (Dublin: Irish MSS Comm., 1960).

'Gerrard's Notes of his Report on Ireland, 1577-8', in *Analecta Hibernica*, no. 2 (1931), pp. 93-291.

'Guide to English Financial Records for Irish History, 1461-1558', ed. D. B. Quinn, *Analecta Hibernica*, no. 10 (1941), 3-69.

Haynes, S., *A Collection of State Papers . . . 1542 to 1570* (London 1740).

Halliday MSS – see 'Acts of the Privy Council in Ireland'.

Harris, Walter, ed., *Hibernica: or some Ancient Pieces referring to Ireland*, 2 vols. (Dublin 1747).

Hore, H. J. and J. Graves, eds. *The Social State of the Southern and Eastern Counties of Ireland in the Sixteenth Century* (Dublin 1870).

Irish Patent Rolls of James I: facsimile of the Irish Record Commissioners' Calendar Prepared prior to 1830 with forward by M. C. Griffith (Dublin 1966).

Liber Munerum publicorum Hiberniae, ed. R. Lascelles, 2 vols. (London 1852).

Maxwell, C., *Irish History from Contemporary Sources, 1509-1610* (London 1923).

'Minute Book of the Corporation of Dublin, known as the "Friday Book" 1567-1611', ed. H. F. Berry, *Royal Irish Acad., Proc.*, XXX, sec. C (1913), 477-514.

Murdin, W., *A Collection of State Papers . . . 1571-96'* – from Salisbury MSS (London 1759).

Patentee Officers in Ireland, 1173-1876, ed. J. L. J. Hughes (Dublin: Irish MSS Comm. 1960).

Short title Catalogue of Books Printed in England . . . 1475-1640, eds. A. W. Pollard and G. R. Redgrave (London 1926).

Sidney State Papers, 1565-70, ed. T. O'Laidhin (Dublin, Irish MSS Comm., 1962) 'Additional Sidney State Papers, 1566-70',ed. B. Quinn, *Analecta Hibernica*, no. 26 (1970), 89-102.

'Sidney's Memoir or Narrative addressed to Sir Francis Walsingham, 1583', *Ulster Journal of Archaeology* 1st ser., III (1855), 37-44; 91-99; 346-353; V (1857), 305-15; VI (1858), 179-195.

'Some Documents on Irish Law and Custom in the Sixteenth Century', ed.

K. W. Nicholls, *Analecta Hibernica*, no. 26 (1970), pp. 105-29.

State Papers Concerning the Irish Church in the Time of Queen Elizabeth, ed. W. M. Brady (London 1868).

Ulster and other Irish Maps, c. 1600, ed. G. A. Hayes-McCoy (Dublin: Irish MSS Comm., 1964).

The Voyages and Colonising Enterprises of Sir Humphrey Gilbert, ed. D. B. Quinn, 2 vols. (London 1940).

The Walsingham Letter-book, or Register of Ireland, eds. J. Hogan and N. McNeill O'Farrell (Dublin: Irish MSS Comm., 1959).

C. CONTEMPORARY PAMPHLETS AND LITERARY SOURCES

A funerall sermon . . . 26 . . . November . . . 1576 . . . by Richard . . . bishoppe of Saint Davys, at the buriall of the Right Honourable Walter, Erle Marshall of Irelande (London 1577).

A letter sent by I. B. gentleman unto . . . mayster R. C. esquire, wherein is contained a large discourse of the peopling and inhabiting the cuntries called the Ardes (London 1571, *S.T.C.*, 1048).

Bagenal, Marshal, 'The Description and Present State of Ulster, 20 Dec. 1586', *Ulster Journal of Archaeology*, II (1854), 137-60.

Beacon, Richard, *Solon his Follie* (Oxford 1594).

Bergin, Osborn, *Irish Bardic Poetry*, texts and translations compiled and edited by David Greene and Fergus Kelly (Dublin 1970).

Boemus, Johan, *The Manners, Laws and Customs of all Nations*, with a preface by Edward Aston (*S.T.C.*, 3198).

Boemus, Johan, *The Fardel of Facions* (London 1555, *S.T.C.*, 3197).

Boorde, Andrew, *The Fyrst Boke of the Introduction of Knowledge*, ed. F. J. Furnivall for the *Early English Text Society*, extra ser., X (1870).

Camden, William, *Britannica, Newly Translated into English* (London 1695).

The history of Queen Elizabeth (London 1688).

Campion, Edmund, *A Historie of Ireland* (1571), edited with introduction by R. G. Gottfried (New York 1940).

Churchyard, Thomas, *Churchyarde's Choise, a General Rehersall of Warres* (London 1579, *S.T.C.*, 5235).

A Discourse of the Queenes Majesties Entertainment . . . whereunto is adjoined a Commendation of Sir Humphrey Gilbert's Vertuous Journe (London 1578).

The Miserie of Flaunders, Calamitie of Fraunce, Misfortune of Portugall, Unquietnes of Irelande, Troubles of Scotlande and the Blessed State of England (London 1579).

The Most True Reporte of J. Fitz. Morrice Death (London 1579).

A Prayse and Report of Maister Martyne Frobiosher's Voyage (London 1578).

A Scourge for Rebels (London 1584).

Cox, Richard, *Hibernia Anglicana or the History of Ireland from the Conquest thereof by the English to this Present Time* (London 1689).

Davies, Sir John, *A Discovery of the True Causes why Ireland was never entirely*

Subdued (London 1612), printed in H. Morley, ed., *Ireland under Elizabeth and James I* (London 1890).

Duanta Eoghain Ruaidh Mhic an Bháird, ed. Tomás O Raghallaigh (Gaillimh 1930).

Derricke, J., *The Image of Ireland* (London 1581).

Dymmok, John, 'A Treatise of Ireland c.1600', in *Tracts Relating to Ireland* (Dublin 1842).

Eden, Richard, *The Decades of the Newe Worlde of West India*, trans. from Petrus Martyr Anglerius (London 1555, *S.T.C.*, 645-8).

The History of Travayle in the West and East Indies, trans. from Peter Martyr, ed. R. Willes (London 1577, *S.T.C.*, 649).

Gernon, Luke, 'A Discourse on Ireland, anno 1620', in C. L. Falkiner, *Illustrations of Irish History and Topography* (London 1904), pp. 345-62.

Hacket, Thomas, *The New Found Worlde or Antarticke*, trans. from André Thevet (London 1568, *S.T.C.*, 23950).

Harington, Sir John, *A Short View of the State of Ireland in 1605* (Oxford 1879).

Holinshed's Chronicles of England, Scotland and Ireland, vol. VI, *Ireland* (London 1808).

Hooker, John, alias Vowell, 'Life of Sir Peter Carew', in *Cal. Carew MSS, 1515-74*, pp. lxvii-cxviii.

Le Challeux, Nicholas, *A True and Perfect Description of the Last Voyage of Navigation . . . into Terra Florida* (London 1566).

Leicester's Commonwealth, the Copie of a Letter Wryten by a Master of Arte of Cambridge . . . Anno 1584, suppressed by proclamation 1585 and republished London 1641.

Markham, Gervase, *The Newe Metamorphosis* (1600), B.M., Add. MSS, 14,824.

Measgra Dánta: Miscellaneous Irish Poems, ed. T. F. O'Rahilly (Cork 1927).

Moryson, Fynes, *An Intinerary* (London 1617), 4 vols. (Glasgow 1907-8).

'The Manners and Customs of Ireland', in C. L. Falkiner, *Illustrations of Irish History and Topography* (London 1904), pp. 211-325.

'On the Commonwealth of Ireland', in *Shakespeare's Europe*, ed. C. Hughes (New York 1967), pp. 185-260.

Perrott, Sir James, *The Chronicle of Ireland, 1584-1608*, ed. H. Wood (Dublin: Irish MSS Comm., 1933).

Plomer, H. R. and T. P. Cross, eds., *The Life and Correspondence of Lodowick Bryskett* (Chicago 1927).

Ribaut, Jean, *The Whole and True Discoverye of Terra Florida* (London 1563).

Rich, Barnaby, *Allarme to England* (London 1578).

A New Description of Ireland (London 1610).

A Short Survey of Ireland (London 1609).

Smith, Sir Thomas, *De Republica Anglorum: a Discourse on the Commonwealth of England*, ed. L. Alston (Cambridge 1906).

Spenser, Edmund, *The Shepherd's Calendar and Other Poems*, ed. Philip Henderson (London 1932).

A View of the Present State of Ireland . . . in 1596, ed. W. L. Renwick (Oxford 1970).

Stanihursti, Richardi, *De Rebus in Hibernia Gestis* (Antwerp 1584).

The Famous History of the Life and Death of Captain Thomas Stukeley (London 1605), in *The School of Shakespeare*, vol. I, ed. Richard Simpson (1878).

The Bardic Poems of Tadhg Dall O hUiginn, ed. Eleanor Knott for *Irish Texts Society*, nos. 22-3 (Dublin 1920).

V[enner] R[ichard], *England's Joy* (*S.T.C.*, 21358).

D. SECONDARY SOURCES

Andrews, J. H., 'Geography and Government in Elizabethan Ireland', in *Irish Geographical Studies*, eds. N. Stephens and R. E. Glasscock (Belfast 1970), pp. 178-91. 'The Irish Survey of Robert Lythe', *Imago Mundi*, XIX (1965), 22-31. 'Robert Lythe's Visit to Ireland', *Analecta Hibernica*, no. 24 (1967), pp.232-42

Andrews, K. R., *Drake's Voyages: a Re-assessment of their Place in Elizabethan Maritime Expansion* (London 1967).

Bagwell, Richard, *Ireland under the Tudors*, 3 vols. (London 1885-90).

Binchy, D. A., *Críth Gablach* (Dublin 1941).

'The Linguistic and Historical Value of the Irish Law Tracts', *British Academy, Proceedings*, XXXIX (1943), 195-227.

Bindoff, S. T., et al., eds. *Elizabethan Government and Society: Essays Presented to Sir John Neale* (London 1966).

Bonn, M. J., *Die Englische Kolonisation in Ireland*, 2 vols. (Stuttgart and Berlin, 1906).

Bossy, J., 'The Counter-Reformation and the People of Catholic Europe', *Past and Present*, XLVII (1970), 51-70.

'The Counter-Reformation and the People of Catholic Ireland, 1596-1641', *Historical Studies*, VIII (1971), 155-69.

Bottigheimer, K. S., *English Money and Irish Land* (Oxford 1971).

Bradshaw, Brendan, 'The Beginnings of Modern Ireland', *The Irish Parliamentary Tradition*, ed. Brian Farrell (Dublin 1973), pp. 68-87.

The Dissolution of the Religious Orders in Ireland under Henry VIII (Cambridge, 1974).

'George Browne, First Reformation Archbishop of Dublin, 1536-54', *Jr. Eccles. Hist.*, XXI (1970), 301-26.

'The Opposition to the Ecclesiastical Legislation in the Irish Reformation Parliament', *Irish Historical Studies*, XVI (1969), 285-303.

Brooks, F. W., *York and the Council of the North* (London 1954).

Butler, W. F. T., *Gleanings from Irish History* (London 1925).

Byrne, F. J., *The Rise of the Ui Neill and the High-Kingship of Ireland* (Dublin: National University of Ireland, published lecture 1969).

Cam, Helen M., *Liberties and Communities in Medieval England* (Cambridge 1944).

Canny, N. P., 'Changing Views on Gaelic Ireland', *Topic: 24: Themes in Irish Culture* (Washington, Pa. 1972),pp. 19-28

'The Flight of the Earls, 1607', *Irish Hist. Studies*, XVII (1971), 380-99.

'Hugh O'Neill, Earl of Tyrone, and the Changing Face of Gaelic

Ulster', *Studia Hibernica*, X (1970), 7-35.

'The Formation of the Old English Elite in Ireland', National University of Ireland, O'Donnell Lecture (1975).

'The Ideology of English Colonization: from Ireland to America', *William and Mary Quarterly*, XXX (1973) 575-98.

Chaunu, Pierre, Conquête et Exploitation des Nouveaux Mondes (Paris 1969).

Clarke, Aidan, *The Old English in Ireland, 1625-42* (London 1966).

Cregan, D. F., 'Irish Catholic Admissions to the English Inns of Court, 1558-1625', *Irish Jurist*, new ser., V (1970), 95-114.

Cross, Claire, *The Puritan Earl: the Life of Henry Hastings, Third Earl of Huntingdon, 1536-95* (London 1966).

Davis, David B., *The Problem of Slavery in Western Culture* (New York 1966).

de Blácam, Aodh, *Gaelic Literature Surveyed* (Dublin 1933).

Delany, V. T. H. 'The Palatinate Court of the Liberty of Tipperary', *Amer. Jrl. of Legal Hist.*, V (1961), 96-117.

Dewar, M., *Sir Thomas Smith: a Tudor Intellectual in Office* (London 1964).

Dickens, A. G., *Robert Holgate: Archbishop of York and President of the King's Council in the North* (London 1955).

Dictionary of National Biography, ed. Stephen and Lee, 2nd ed., 22 vols. (London 1908-9).

Dodds, M. H. & R., *The Pilgrimage of Grace and the Exeter Conspiracy*, 2 vols. (Cambridge 1915).

Dolley, Michael, 'Anglo-Irish Monetary Policies, 1172-1637', *Hist. Studies,* VII (1969), 45-64.

Donald, M. B., *Elizabethan Copper: the History of the Company of Mines Royal 1568-1605* (London 1955).

Elizabethan Monopolies: History of the Company of Mineral and Battery Works 1565-1604 (Edinburgh 1961).

Dunlop, Robert, 'Plantation of Leix and Offaly 1556-1622', *E.H.R.*, VI (1891), 61-96.

'Sixteenth century Maps of Ireland', *E.H.R.*, XX (1905), 331-5.

'Sixteenth Century Schemes for the Plantation of Ulster', *Scot. Hist. Rev.*, XXII (1924-5), 50-60, 115-26, 197-212.

'Some Aspects of Henry VIII's Irish Policy', in *Owens College Historical Essays*, eds. T. F. Tout and J. Tait (London 1902), pp. 279-305.

Edwards, R. Dudley, *Church and State in Tudor Ireland* (London 1935).

'Ireland, Elizabeth I and the Counter-Reformation', in S. T. Bindoff, *Elizabethan Government and Society*, pp. 315-39.

Edwards, R. D. and Moody, T. W., 'History of Poynings's Law 1494-1615', *Irish Historical Studies*, II, (1941) 241-5, 415-24.

Elliott, J. H., *The Old World and the New 1492-1650* (Cambridge 1970).

'The Mental World of Hernan Cortes', *T.R.H.S.*, XVII (1967), 41-58.

Elton, G. R., *The Tudor Constitution* (Cambridge 1968).

The Tudor Revolution in Government, paperback edition (Cambridge 1969).

Esler, Anthony, *The Aspiring Mind of the Elizabethan Younger Generation*

(Durham, N.C. 1966).

Falls, C., *Elizabeth's Irish Wars* (London 1950).

Ferguson, Arthur B., *The Articulate Citizen and the English Renaissance* (Durham, N.C. 1965).

    'Circumstances and the Sense of History in Tudor England: the Coming of the Historical Revolution', in *Medieval and Renaissance Studies*, III, ed. J. M. Headley (Chapel Hill, N.C.1967).

Finch, M. E., *The Wealth of Five Northamptonshire Families* (Oxford 1956).

Fletcher, Anthony, *Tudor Rebellions* (London 1968).

Flower, Robin, 'Laurence Nowell and the Discovery of England in Tudor Times', *British Academy, Proceedings*, XXI (1935), 47-73.

Froude, J. A., *History of England, from the Fall of Wolsey to the Defeat of the Spanish Armada*, 2nd ed. (London 1870).

Fussner, F. Smith, *The Historical Revolution, 1580-1640* (London 1962).

Garrett, C. H., *The Marian Exiles: a Study in the Origins of Elizabethan Puritanism*, 2nd ed. (Cambridge 1966).

Gottfried, R. B., 'The Early Development of the Section on Ireland in Camden's "Britannia" ', *Jrl. English Lit. Hist.*, X (1943), 17-30.

Graham, Jean, 'Rural Society in Connacht, 1600-40', *Irish Geographical Studies*, eds. N. Stephens and R. E. Glasscock (Belfast 1970), pp. 192-208.

Hair, P. E. H. 'Protestants as Pirates, Slavers and Proto-Missionaries: Sierra Leone, 1568 and 1582', *Jrl. Eccles. Hist.*, XXI (1970), 203-24.

Hale, J. R., 'Sixteenth Century Explanations of War and Violence', *Past and Present*, LI (1971), 3-26.

Hammerstein, Helga, 'Aspects of the Continental Education of Irish Students in the Reign of Queen Elizabeth I', *Hist. Studies*, VIII (1971), 137-53.

Hayes-McCoy, G. A., 'Gaelic Society in Ireland in the late Sixteenth Century', *Hist. Studies*, IV (1963), 45-61.

    Scots Mercenary Forces in Ireland, 1565-1603 (Dublin 1937).

    Irish Battles (London 1969).

Hill, Christopher, *Puritanism and Revolution* (London 1968).

    'Puritans and "the Dark Corners of the Land" ', *T.R.H.S.*, XII (1962), 77-102.

Hinton, E. M., *Ireland through Tudor Eyes* (Philadelphia 1935).

Hodgen, Margaret T., *Early Anthropology in the Sixteenth and Seventeenth Centuries* (Philadelphia 1964).

Hogan, James, 'The Irish Law of Kingship with Special Reference to Aileach and Cenél Eoghain', *Royal Irish Acad., Proc.*, XL, sec. C (1932), 186-254.

    'Shane O'Neill comes to the Court of Elizabeth', *Féil-Scribhinn Tórna*, ed. S. Pender (Cork 1947), pp. 154-72.

Hoskins, W. G., *The Midland Peasant: the Economic and Social History of a Leicestershire Village* (London 1957).

Howell, R., *Sir Philip Sidney, the Shepherd Knight* (London 1968).

Hughes, J. 'Sir Edmund Butler', *Jrl. of the Royal Hist. and Arch. Assoc. of Ire.*, 4th ser., I (1870), 153-92, 211-31.

Hulton, Paul and Quinn D. B., *The American Drawings of John White, 1577-90*, 2 vols. (London 1964).

Hurstfield, Joel, *The Queen's Wards: Wardship and Marriage under Elizabeth I* (London 1958).

Irish Geographical Studies in Honour of E. Estyn Evans, eds. N. Stephens and R. E. Glasscock (Belfast 1970).

Jackson, Donald, *Intermarriage in Ireland, 1550-1650* (Montreal 1970).

James, M. E. *Change and Continuity in the Tudor North: the Rise of Thomas, First Lord Wharton* (York 1965).

'Obedience and Dissent in Hernician England', *Past and Present*, XLVIII (1970), 1-78.

Jones, Howard Mumford, *O Strange New World: American Culture, the Formative Years* (New York 1964).

'The Origins of the Colonial Idea in England', *Amer. Phil. Soc. Proc.*, LXXXIX (1945), 448-65.

Jordan, Winthrop D., *White over Black, American Attitudes toward the Negro, 1550-1812* (Baltimore, Md. 1969).

Keene, B., *Life and Labor in Ancient Mexico* (New Brunswick, N. J. 1963).

Kelley, Donald R., *Foundations of Modern Historical Scholarship: Language, Law and History in the French Renaissance* (New York 1970).

Lehmberg, S. W., *Sir Walter Mildmay and Tudor Government* (Austin 1964).

Levy, F. J., *Tudor Historical Thought* (San Marino 1967).

Lloyd, H. A. 'The Essex Inheritance', *Welsh History Review*, VII (1974), 13-59.

Loades, D. M., *Two Tudor Conspiracies* (Cambridge 1965).

Longfield, Ada K., *Anglo-Irish Trade in the Sixteenth Century* (London 1929).

Lydon, James F., *The Lordship of Ireland in the Middle Ages* (Dublin 1972).

MacCaffrey, Wallace, *The Shaping of the Elizabethan Regime: Elizabethan Politics, 1558-72* (London 1969).

MacCurtain, Margaret, *Tudor and Stuart Ireland* (Dublin 1972).

Mac Niocaill, Gearóid, 'The Contact of Irish and Common Law', *Northern Ireland Legal Quarterly*, XXIII (1972), 16-23.

Na Burgéisí, 2 vols. (Dublin 1956).

'The Origin of the Betagh', *Irish Jurist*, current ser., I (1966), 292-8.

McCracken, E., 'The Woodlands of Ireland', *Irish Hist. Studies*, XI (1959), 271-96.

Martin, F. X. *Friar Nugent, 1569-1635: an Agent for the Counter Reformation* (Rome 1962).

'Ireland, the Renaissance and the Counter Reformation', *Topic: 13 Studies in Irish Hist.*, pp. 23-33.

Medieval Studies Presented to Aubrey Gwynn, eds. J. A. Watt, J. B. Morrall and F. X. Martin (Dublin 1961).

Moody, T. W., 'The Irish Parliament under Elizabeth and James I: a General Survey', in *Royal Irish Acad., Proc.*, XLV, sec. C (1939), 41-81.

The Londonderry Plantation, 1609-41 (Belfast 1939).

Morgan, Edmund, 'The Labor Problem at Jamestown, 1607-18', *Amer. Hist. Rev.*, LXXVI (1970), 595-611.

'Slavery and Freedom: the American Paradox', *Jour. of Amer. Hist.*, LIX 1972), 5-29.

Morton, R. C., 'The Enterprise of Ulster', *History Today*, XVII (1967), 114-21.

Nash, Gary B., 'The Image of the Indian in the Southern Colonial Mind', *William and Mary Quarterly*, XXIX (1972), 197-230.

Neale, J. E., *The Elizabethan House of Commons*, revised ed. (London 1963).
    Elizabeth I and her Parliaments, 2 vols., paperback ed. (London 1965).

Nicholls, Kenneth, *Gaelic and Gaelicised Ireland in the Middle Ages* (Dublin 1972).

O'Danachair, C., 'Representations of Houses on some Irish Maps of c. 1600', in *Studies in Folk-Life: Essays in Honour of I. C. Peate*, ed. G. Jenkins (London 1969).

O Laidhin, T., 'Sir Henry Sidney's first Lord Deputyship, *Bulletin of Irish Comm. of Hist. Sciences*, no. 80 (1957).

Otway-Ruthven, A. J., *A History of Medieval Ireland* (London 1968).

Parker, John, *Books to build an Empire: a Bibliographical History of English Overseas Interests to 1620* (Amsterdam, N. Israel 1965).

Pearce, R. H., *The Savages of America: a Study of the Indian and the Idea of Civilization*, 2nd ed. (Baltimore, Md. 1965).

Preconditions of Revolution in Early Modern Europe, eds. R. Forster and Jack Greene (Baltimore, Md. 1970).

Pulman, M. B., *The Elizabethan Privy Council in the Fifteen-Seventies* (Berkeley 1971).

Quinn, D. B., 'A Discourse on Ireland (circa 1599): a Sidelight of English colonial Policy', *Royal Irish Acad., Proc.*, XLVII, sec. C (1942), 151-66.
    'Agenda for Irish History, 1461-1603', *Irish Hist. Studies*, IV (1945), 258-69.
    'Anglo-Irish Local Government, 1485-1534', *Irish Hist. Studies*, I (1939), 354-81.
    'Anglo-Irish Ulster in the Early Sixteenth Century', *Belfast Nat. Hist. and Philosophical Soc. Report and Proc.* (1935), pp. 56-78.
    'Edward Walshe's "Conjectures" Concerning the State of Ireland [1552] ', *Irish Hist. Studies*, V (1947), 303-22.
    The Elizabethans and the Irish (Ithaca 1966).
    'Government Printing and Publication', *Royal Irish Acad., Proc.* XLIX, sec. C (1942), 45-129.
    'Henry VIII and Ireland, 1509-34', *Irish Hist. Studies*, XII (1961) 318-44.
    'Ireland and Sixteenth Century European Expansion', *Hist. Studies*, I (1958), 20-32.
    'The Irish Parliamentary Subsidy in the 15th and 16th Centuries', *Royal Irish Acad., Proc.*, XLII, sec. C (1935), 219-46.
    'The Munster Plantation: Problems and Opportunities', *Jrl. of Cork Hist. and Arch. Soc.*, LXXI (1966), 19-41.
    'Parliaments and Great Councils in Ireland 1461-1586', *Irish Hist. Studies*, III (1943), 60-77.

Raleigh and the British Empire, 2nd ed. (London 1962).

'Sir Thomas Smith and the Beginnings of English Colonial Theory', *Proc. of Amer. Phil. Soc.,* LXXXIX (1945), 543-60.

Rabb, Theodore K., *Enterprise and Empire: Merchant and Gentry Investment in the Expansion of England, 1575-1630* (Cambridge, Mass. 1967).

Rae, T. I., *The Administration of the Scottish Frontier 1513-1603* (Edinburgh 1966).

Read, Conyers, *Lord Burghley and Queen Elizabeth,* paperback ed. (London 1965).

Mr. Secretary Cecil and Queen Elizabeth, paperback ed. (London 1965).

Reid, Rachel, *The King's Council in the North* (London 1921).

Rowe, J. H. 'Ethnography and Ethnology in the Sixteenth Century', *Kroeber Anthropological Society Papers,* no. 30 (1964), pp. 1-19.

Rowse, A. L., *Sir Richard Grenville of the Revenge* (Boston and New York 1937).

Scarisbrick, J. J., *Henry VIII* (Berkeley 1968).

Seven Centuries of Irish learning, ed. B. O. Cuiv (Cork 1961).

Silke, J. J., *Kinsale: the Spanish Intervention in Ireland at the End of the Elizabethan Wars* (New York 1970).

Simms, Katherine, 'Appendix to "ordinances of the White Earl", on Irish exactions', consulted in typescript with the kind permission of the author.

Stone, Lawrence, *The Crisis of the Aristocracy* (Oxford 1965).

'Elizabethan Overseas Trade', *Econ. Hist. Rev.,* current ser., II (1949-50), 30-58.

Thirsk, Joan, 'Younger Sons in the Seventeenth Century', *History,* LIV (1969), 358-77.

Thirsk, Joan, ed., *The Agrarian History of England and Wales,* IV (1500-1640) (Cambridge 1967).

Thomas, Keith, *Religion and the Decline of Magic* (London 1971).

Thomson, G. Scott, *Lords Lieutenants in the Sixteenth Century* (London 1923).

Treadwell, Victor, 'The Irish Parliament of 1569-71', *Royal Irish Acad., Proc.,* LXV, sec. C (1966), 55-89.

Vaughan, Alden T., 'Blacks in Virginia: a Note on the First Decade', *William and Mary Quarterly,* XXIX (1972), 469-78.

Verlinden, Charles, *The Beginnings of Modern Colonization* (New York 1970).

Les Origines de la Civilisation Atlantique (Paris 1966).

Warren, W. L., 'The Interpretation of Twelfth-Century Irish History', *Hist. Studies,* VII (1969), 1-19.

Washburn, Wilcomb E., *Redman's Land, White Man's Law: A Study of the Past and Present Status of the American Indian* (New York 1971).

Watt, J. A. *The Church and the Two Nations in Medieval Ireland* (Cambridge 1970).

White, D. G., 'The Reign of Edward VI in Ireland: some Political, Social, and Economic Aspects', *Irish Hist. Studies,* XIV (1965), 197-211.

'The Tudor Plantations in Ireland, pre. 1571', 2 vols. (Dublin University thesis, 1969).

Williams, Neville, *Thomas Howard, Fourth Duke of Norfolk* (London 1964).

Williams, Penry, *The Council in the Marches of Wales under Elizabeth I* (Cardiff

1958).

'The Council in Munster in the Late Sixteenth Century', *Bulletin of the Irish Comm. of Historical sciences*, no. 123.

Wilson, Philip, *The Beginnings of Modern Ireland* (Dublin 1912).

Woodward, D. M., *The Trade of Elizabethan Chester* (Hull 1970).

Youings, Joyce, 'The Council in the West', *Trans. of the Royal Hist. Soc.*, 5th ser., X (1960), 41-59.

Index

Agard, Francis, 54, 80
agriculture, 13-16
Alford, Lancelot, 114
Amerindians, 133, 160-3
Anglo-Irish attitudes, 18-20, 93,
  120, 123-5, 127-8, 129, 135-6,
  139-40, 150, 152-3
Antrim, 62, 90
Any, 22
Ardee, 4
Ardglass, 7
Ards peninsula, 77, 85-8
aristocratic delegation, 31, 32
Armagh, 5, 7, 24, 25, 63, 64, 96;
  archbishop of, 5, 52
Arnold, Sir Nicholas, 41, 47, 53, 154
Asseroe, 7
Athboy, 4
Athenry, 2, 4, 6, 15, 111, 113, 146,
  152
Athlone, 2, 5, 35, 59, 69, 108, 112,
  146

Bacon, Lord Keeper, 84
Bagenall, Sir Nicholas, 52, 53, 76,
  85
Baltinglass, Baron, 19, 153
Bardic poetry, 138
Barkeley, Edward, 89, 121
Barkeley, John, 88

Barnewall, Sir Christopher, 140
Barry, Viscount, 57, 106, 107, 144
Beacon Richard, 135
Bellingham, Sir Edward, 34, 35
Bermingham, 112
betaghs, see peasants
Bingham, Richard, ix, 135, 158
black rent, 3, 6, 27
boat building, 6, 15
Bodkin, Gregory, mason, 15
Boemus, Johann, 126, 127
Bole, John, archbishop, 5
Borrow, Thomas, 77
Boswell, James, 163
Brett, Jerome, 79, 80, 81, 86, 88
Bristol, 6, 7, 9, 73
Browne, Thomas, 77
Browne, Sir Valentine, 73, 86
Bry, Theodore de, 160
Budockshide, Philip, 72
Burgh, Lord Deputy, 14
Burghley, Lord, see Cecil
Burkes of Clanricard, 6, 112; John
  and Ulick, (Mac an Iarlas), 110,
  113-14, 142-7; McWilliam, 112
Butler, Sir Edmund, 1, 68, 106, 140,
  141, 142-6; Edward, 142-7; Lord,
  of Dunboyne, 145; Piers, 142-7;
  Sir Theobald, 145
butter-making, 16

Byrne family, 34, 36; country, 54

Callan, 146
Campion, Edmund, 6
cannibalism, 126
Carew, Sir George, 138
Carew, Sir Peter, 68, 72, 76, 78, 82, 89, 118, 123, 127, 141, 145, 148-9
Carlow, County, 36, 53, 54, 145
Carrickfergus, 7, 8-9, 64, 70
Cary, Francis, 88
Cary, John, 89; Michael, 89
Cashel, 6;archbishop of, 96
Castelyn, Edward, 79-80
Cateau-Cambrésis, Treaty of, 38, 41
Cavan, 7, 8, 9, 27
Cecil, Sir William (later Lord Burghley), 41, 43, 48, 49, 51-2, 58, 60, 62-3, 65, 69, 73, 75, 76, 80, 81, 84, 86, 87, 91, 100, 108, 110, 154; Thomas, his son, 80, 81
Champernoun, Sir Arthur, 71, 89, 133; John, 72
Chatterton Thomas, 77, 85, 89, 159
Cheevers, Sir Christopher, 68
Chester, 9, 97
Chester, Dominick, 7
church land, 31, 63, 69, 78, 107, 114, 140
Churchyard, Thomas, 122
civility, concept of, 28, 33, 55, 62, 64, 67, 103, 124, 125, 128, 129, 135, 140-1, 162-3
Clancar, earl of (McCarthy Mór), 5, 13, 57, 82, 142, 143, 148
Clandeboy, 88-9, 119, 130
Clanricard, earl of, 6, 15, 22-3, 34, 49, 52, 96, 108-16, 152
Clare, county of, 20
Clifford family, 94
Clogher, 13
Clonmel, 6
Cloyne, 25
cóisir, 12
colonization in Ireland, 38, 51, 62-92, 118-36
colonization in the New World, 66,

86, 133, 159-63, 184 n.10
Comerford, Fulke, 146
commissions, 43, 100
Connacht, ix, 2, 9, 14, 15, 22, 23, 25, 47-58, 63, 64, 69, 97, 101, 104, 108-16, 118, 138, 152, 157, 158
Corbet, Sir Andrew, 108
Corbine, John,5, 79
Cork, 2, 4, 6, 22, 55, 69, 102, 104-5, 106, 115, 144; bishop of, 55; county, 78
Cosby, Francis, 54
coshery, *see cóisir*
Counter-Reformation, 147, 153
Coursey, Lord, 57
Cowley, Henry, 54
coyne and livery, 18, 21, 25, 56, 99, 103, 106, 109, 117, 140-1, 143-4
craftsmen, 15, 67
Croft, Sir James, 35, 58, 76, 84, 86, 120, 134
Cromwell, Thomas, 31, 94, 95, 97
cuddy, *see cuid oíche*
cuid oíche, 12, 21
cultural process, concept of, 129-36, 162-3
Cusack family, 19
Cusack, Robert, 54
Cusack Thomas, Lord Chancellor, 20, 39, 93, 96, 109

Dacre family, 94
Damporte, Robert, 113
Davies, Sir John, 1, 8, 21, 24, 119, 126, 129-30, 131, 134, 135, 159-60
Delvin, Baron, 18, 27
Denton, John, 5, 73, 80
Derry, 7, 58, 59
Desmond, earls of, 1, 5-6, 9, 13, 21, 22, 23, 29, 49-50, 52, 55-8, 69, 78, 96, 99-142; Sir John of, 56, 61, 81, 99-100, 142
Dillon family, 19
Dillon, Robert, 108-9
Dingle, 7
Dokray, James, 8
Docwra, Sir Henry, 4

Donegal, 7
Down, county, 73, 77
Downpatrick, 7
Drake, Francis, 89, 90
Drogheda, 4. 5, 8
Drury, Sir William, 104, 106-8, 158-9
Dublin, 1-9 *passim*, 20, 28, 29, 59, 145
Duckett, Lionel, 73, 75
Dudley supporters, 42, 46, 53, 70, 72-3, 78, 92, 158,
Dundalk, 4, 6

Eden, Richard, 85, 133, 134
education, 3, 64, 127-8
Elizabeth I, 38-44, 55-65, *passim*, 66, 76, 80, 89, 91, 99, 100, 118, 120, 121, 142, 148-50, 151-2
English attitudes, 29-44, 66-92 *passim*, 98, 117-33, 139-40, 154-63
Enniscorthy, 9, 146
Errigalkeerogue, erenagh of, 13
Essex, earl of, 14, 81, 85, 88-92, 113-14, 119, 120-1, 122, 123, 130-1, 133-4, 137-8, 155, 159, 162
Evenfeld, Mr. 79
extortion, 11, 21, 25-6, 107

fairs, 8-10
Fearsat Mór battle of, 59
Fermanagh, 15, 24-5, 27
Fethard, 6
filí, see Bardic poetry
fishing, 6-7, 16, 73
Fitton, Sir Edward, 101, 108-12, 115, 138, 144, 146
Fitzgerald, James, 67-8, 82
Fitzgerald, James Fitzmaurice, known as Fitzmaurice, 100-2, 105, 108, 115, 142-8, 150, 153, 156-7
Fitzgerald, Sir Maurice, 57, 145
Fitzgeralds of Munster, 153
Fitzmaurice, Lord, 57
Fitzmaurice, Patrick, 61
see also Fitzgerald, James Fitz-

maurice
Fitzpatrick, Sir Barnaby, baron of Upperossory, 57, 106
Fitzwilliam, Sir William ix, 35, 36, 53, 61, 87, 91, 104, 115, 128, 132, 139, 157-8, 159
Fitzwilliams, Thomas, 54
Fleming, Thomas, 27
Flemings of Meath, 27
forestalling, 5
freeholders, 105
Froude, J. A., 79
fur, 6

Gaelic society, 3-29 *passim*, 109, 119-20, 123-8, 131, 135-6, 142-3, 160-2
gallóglaigh, 21
Galway, 2, 4, 6, 9, 15, 20, 96, 106, 109, 112, 113, 146
Gernon, Luke, 10
Gerrard, Gilbert, 43, 52
Gerrard, Sir Thomas, 76
Gerrard, Sir William (Lord Chancellor), 11, 14, 132, 135, 152
Gilbert, Sir Humphrey, 59, 60, 67, 72, 79, 101-2, 115, 119, 121, 127, 131, 147, 156, 160
Gormanston, Viscount, 18
Governors of Ireland, 1, 2, 31-46, *passim*, 52-164 *passim*
Grenville, Sir Richard, 72, 78, 101-2, 115, 144
grey merchants, 4-5, 8, 164n. 9

Hacket, Thomas, 126
Hakluyt, R., 161
Hariot, Thomas, 160
Henry VIII, 31-3, 45
Heron, Captain, Nicholas, 36, 54
Heron, Richard, 8
hides, 6-7
Holgate, Robert, bishop of Llandaff and archbishop of York, 95
Hooker, John, 68, 156
Horsey, Edward, 58, 70
Howard faction, 42, 57, 95, 151

Howth, Baron, 18

Idrone, co, Carlow, 68, 118, 145
inquisitions, 113

Johnson, Samuel, 163
joint-stock organization of finance,
    86-7

Kavanagh family, 34, 36, 54, 68
Kells, 4
Kerry, 1. 22, 23, 29, 55, 99, 177 n. 28
Kerrycurrihy, 77-8, 80, 81, 144
Kilconnell, 111
Kildare, county of, 11, 54; earls of,
    3, 11, 18, 23, 31, 36, 38-42, 75, 96,
    115-16, 140, 145, 151, 153
Kilkenny, 4, 17, 20, 30, 53, 61, 144,
    146
Kilkenny, Statutes of (1366), 26,
    120, 132
Kilmallock, 4, 6, 145
Kinsale, 2, 4, 6, 29
Knocktogher, 146
Knollys, Edward, 86
Knollys, Sir Francis, 58, 62, 71, 72,
    76, 84
Knollys Henry, 89

Lancaster, Thomas, 73, 88
language, 20, 135
law, 17-18, 29; English common, 33,
    48, 50, 52, 54, 60, 61, 98, 102,
    117-20, 132; Gaelic or Brehon, 22,
    54, 103, 109, 117, 123-4, see mar-
    tial law.
Lecale, 75
Lee, Bishop Rowland, 94, 95, 97
Lee, Captain Thomas, 118
Leicester, earl of 42-4, 45, 53, 57-8,
    62, 70, 76, 80, 84-8, 134, 149-50
Leicester faction, 42, 151
Leighton, Thomas, 70, 75, 79
Leinster, 3, 9, 14, 20, 22, 33, 34, 36,
    48, 53-4, 59, 61, 68
Leith, Robert, 63, 67
Leix, county, 53, 61, 145

Leix-Offaly plantation, 2, 35-44, 49,
    70, 75, 145
Limerick, 2, 4, 6, 9, 10, 22, 55, 69,
    96, 106; bishop of, 55
Linen making, 16
Localism, 1-44 *passim*
Lodge, Sir Thomas, 75
London merchants, 4-10, 73, 75, 79
Lord deputyship of Ireland, *see*
    governor of Ireland
Lord-Lieutenant of Ireland, *see*
    governor of Ireland
lordships, 1, 5-7, 10-13; Anglo-
    Irish, 20-8, 29, 49-52, 95-7, 103,
    107, 115-16, 117, 131, 139-53,
    156; feudal, *see* Anglo-Irish;
    Gaelic, 20-8, 29, 33, 107
Loughfoyle, 59, 71
Lough Foyle, 72, 73
Louth, Baron, 18
Lynch, Dominick, 15

Mac an Bháird, Laoisioch, 139
Mac an Iarlas, *see* Burke
MacBruaideadha, Maoilín Og, 138
McCartan country, 76, 85
McCarthy, Sir Cormac Mac Teigh,
    106
McCarthy, Sir Dermot of Muskerry,
    57, 144
McCarthy, Sir Donagh of Carberry,
    57
McCarthy Mór, *see* earl of Clancar
McDermott, 112
MacDiarmada, Ruaidhri, 138
Mac Donnell, Sorley Boy, 38
Mac Donnells of Antrim, 40, 59
McDonoughs 82, 143
McGeoghegan, Ross, 61
Mac Mahon, Gilpatrick, 9
Mahons, 59, 112
Mac Murrough, 3, 36
McNamaras, 112
MacNéill Oig, Eoghan, 6
McSwynes, 82
Maguire, 59
Mahoneys, 82

Malby, John, 89
Malby, Sir Nicholas, 70, 76, 85, 89, 114, 158
Mansell, Sir Edward, 87
manufacturing, 6
martial law, 18, 34, 54, 82, 99, 101, 108, 110, 111, 117-18, 122, 130
Martin, William, 146
Mary, Queen, 34, 36, 45, 53, 66, 94
Maryborough, 35, 55
massacres, 89, 121, 161; of Rathlin Island, 90, 120
Maston, co Meath, 68
Mayo, county, 113
Meath, 11, 53; bishop of 52
merchants in Ireland, 1, 4-10, 36, 66, 73, 75, 79
Mildmaye, Walter, 84
Monaghan, ix
Moryson, Fynes, 4, 10, 12, 16, 127, 135
Mountjoy, Lord deputy, 125
Mullingar, 4
Munster, 2, 5, 6, 7, 16, 20, 23, 30, 47-58, 60, 61, 63, 64, 66, 68, 77-84, 96, 97, 99-108, 118, 121-2, 132, 145, 152, 157; Plantation, 21, 81

Navan, 4
Neville family, 94
New Ross, 4
Newry, 85
nomadism, 15, 126
Norfolk, duke of, 95; faction, *see* Howard faction
Norman conquest of Ireland, 118-19, 122-3
Norris, John, 89, 90; William 89
North America, *see* colonization in the New World
Northern Rebellion, 1569, 95, 149-50, 151
Northumberland, earl of, 84

O'Briens, 112
O'Brien, Sir Daniel, 105

O'Brien, Donal, 138, 146
O'Brien, Tadgh, 110, 146
O'Cahan country, 14
O'Callivans, 82
O'Carroll, lord of Ely O'Carroll, 57, 61, 106
O'Connors, 5, 59
O'Connor Don, 112
O'Connor Roe, 112
O'Connor Sligo, 61, 112
O'Dálaigh, Lochlann Og, 138
O'Dálaigh, Tadgh, 138
O'Donnells, 25, 40, 58, 59, 137
O'Donnell Calough, 2, 59, 71
O'Donnell, Niall Garbh, 13
O'Donnell, Rory, 13
O'Driscolls, 82
Offaly, county, 53, 61
O'Flaherty, 112
O'Hanlon, 59; country, 77, 85
O'Keeffes, 143
O'Kelly, 112
Olderfleet, 64
O'Loughlin, 112
O'Malleys, 15, 112
O'Moores, 5
O'Neills, of Ulster, 8, 24-7, 62, 64
O'Neill of the Fews, 5
O'Neill, Sir Brian McPhelim, 87, 89, 120-1, 137, 161
O'Neill, Henry Mac Eoghain, 13
O'Neill, Hugh, 13, 24, 61, 131, 139
O'Neill, Shane, 6, 12-13, 25-7, 33-4, 37-44, 50-1, 53, 58-9, 61, 70, 71, 96, 126, 134, 137, 141
O'Neill, Toirdelbach Ruadh, 13
O'Neill, Turlough Luineach, 2, 24, 64, 77, 89
O'Reilly, John, 61
O'Reilly, 8, 59
Ormond, earl of, 1, 3, 6, 21, 22, 23, 29, 49-50, 55-8, 60 61, 96, 99, 100, 105-6, 115-6, 141, 145, 148, 151, 152-3; earldom of , 2
Ormond-Desmond feud, 1, 21, 23, 29-30, 41, 56, 99
O'Rourke, 112

O'Shaugnessy, Sir Roger, 14, 113, 146
O'Sullivans, 82, 143
O'Toole family, 34, 36
oyer and terminer, 93, 99

palatinate jurisdictions, 22, 29, 49-50, 55, 98, 117
Pale society, 3, 4, 6, 9, 10-14, 16, 17, 18-27, 31-44, 93, 120, 135-6, 139
Palmer, Henry, 76
Parker, Archbishop, 135
parliament, Irish, 3, 32-3, 52, 64, 140-2
pastoralism 14
peasants, 10-18, 21-7, 166 n. 30
Percy family, 94, 95
Perrott, Sir John, 81, 86, 101-4, 133, 148, 159
Philipstown, 35, 55
Piers, William, 70-1
Pilgrimage of Grace, 94
Pipho, Robert, 54
Plunkett family, 19
Pollard, Sir John, 78, 101, 177,n. 28
population 3-4, 164 n. 6
primogeniture, 20, 33-4, 62
private armies, 1, 11-12, 17, 21, 31, 39, 50, 94, 107,
profiteering, 5
protection, 1, 3, 5, 6, 7
Provincial Councils in Ireland, *see* Provincial Presidencies
Provincial Council in North of England, 47, 93, 94-5, 114-15
Provincial Council in Wales, 47, 93-4, 97-8, 114-15, 117
Provincial Presidencies in Ireland, 47-65, 93, 95-116, 117
purveyance, 5, 12, 18, 32, 152

Radcliffe, Sir Henry, 35, 36, 54
Randolph, Captain, Edward, 59, 70
Rathkeale, 6
Rathlin Island massacre, 90, 120
rebellions of 1569-71, 141-53, 156
religious affairs, 16, 31, 111, 123-7,
147, 153, 156
Rich, Barnaby, 127, 161
Rich, Lord, 89
Richmond, duke of, 94
Roche, Lord, 13, 57, 107, 144
Rokeby, Ralph, 108-9, 110
Roman precedents, 88, 125, 128-30, 135, 160, 163
Roscommon, 109, 112, 113
Russell, Edward, 88

St Leger, Sir Anthony, 33, 35, 45, 55
St Leger, Sir Warham, 52, 53, 54-6, 77-84, 89, 99, 100, 101-2, 115, 119, 123, 132, 133, 144, 149
St Loe, Edward, 70, 79
salt, 6-7
Scotland, 163
Scots (of Ulster) 9, 15, 62-3, 66-74, 77,89, 90, 120, 133, 144
seneschal scheme, 33-44. 48, 54, 61, 118
sheriffs, 17-18, 50, 67, 104, 105, 107, 113, 118
Sidney, SirHenry, 2, 6, 8, 9, 11, 13, 14, 35, 44, 46-75, 90-2, 93, 97-116, 123, 124, 131, 132, 133, 137-8, 140-53, 154-60; Philip, his son, 66
silk, 6
Slane, Baron 19
Sligo, 7, 59, 113
Smith, Sir Thomas, 85-8, 120, 121, 126, 128-9. 133, 159, 162; George his brother, 88; Thomas, his son, 85-8, 123, 139
Smyth, John, 7-8
Spanish *conquistadores*, 66
Spanish precedents, 66, 126, 133-4
Spenser, Edmund, 124-5, 126, 129, 132
spinning, 16
Stanley, Sir George, 35, 36, 53
Stukeley, Thomas, 54, 78, 133
surrender and regrant, policy of, 2, 33-4, 49, 50, 62-3, 105, 113
Sussex, earl of 2, 11, 30, 35-44, 45-8, 57-8, 60, 61, 86, 95, 96-8, 115, 140

Sussex faction, 35-44, 46, 57-8
Swords, co. Dublin, 67

Talbot Gilbert, 79
Thomond, earl of, 6, 10, 20, 22-3,
  34, 49, 52, 105, 106, 107, 138,
  142-7, 148, 152, 156; territory of,
  108-16
Thynne, Sir John, 87
timber, 6, 9, 73, 82, 165 n. 23
Tipperary, 22, 23, 29, 99, 102, 106,
  177 n. 28
towns, 3-10, 23, 146-7, 150
Tracton, 78
Tralee, 9, 22, 107
transhumance, 14-15, 126, 160
travel conditions in Ireland, 1-3
Tremayne, Edmund, 6, 18, 19, 21,
  72, 78, 124, 161
Trim, 4
Trimleston Viscount, 18
tyranny, 55, 129; *see also* lordships
Tyrconnell, 27
Tyrone, 14, 24, 77; earl of, *see*
  O'Neill, Hugh

Ulster, 1, 2, 5, 7-9, 10, 14, 15, 17, 20,
  23, 40, 41, 47-53, 58-65, 69, 71-7,
  85-92, 96, 97, 118, 120-1, 125,
  132, 137
Ulster Project, 71-6, 134

Vaughan, Edward, 71
Virginia, ix, 1, 92, 160, 162

Wales, 6, 162-3; provincial councils,
  in 47, 93-4, 97-8, 114-5, 117
Warwick, Ambrose Dudley, earl of,
  70
Walsingham, Sir Francis, 157
Waterford, 1. 2, 4, 6, 16, 17, 20-1,
  22, 30, 55, 56, 165 n. 16; bishop
  of, 55
Waterhouse, Edward, 161
weaving, 6, 16
Westchester, 7, 73
West Country, the, 72-6, 83, 95
Westmeath, 11, 35
Weston, Dr. Richard, 60, 61
Weston, Robert, 128
Wexford, 9, 17, 23, 53
Wharton, Sir Thomas, 95
White, John, 160
White, Nicholas, 54
White, Rowland, 16, 127-8
White, recorder of Waterford, 146
Wicklow, 9, 20, 22, 23, 34, 36, 54
Wilton, Lord Grey de, 159
Winchester, marquis of 62, 76
wine, 2, 6-7, 8, 29, 140
Wingfield, Sir Jacques, 36, 69, 78,
  79
Winter, William 70, 71, 75
wool, 6-7, 16
  Wotton, Sir Nicholas, 90
women, 16

Youghal, 2, 4, 6, 29